Foundations Phonics

MASTERBOOKS® CURRICULUM

Author: Carrie Lindquist

Master Books Creative Team:

Editor: Laura Welch

Design: Jennifer Bauer

Cover Design: Diana Bogardus

Copy Editors:
Judy Lewis
Willow Meek

Curriculum Review:
Kristen Pratt
Laura Welch
Diana Bogardus

First printing: August 2016
Seventh printing: May 2020

Master Books®, P.O. Box 726, Green Forest, AR 72638

Master Books® is a division of the New Leaf Publishing Group, Inc.

ISBN: 978-0-89051-943-1
ISBN: 978-1-61458-554-1 (digital)

Unless otherwise noted, Scripture quotations are taken from the Holy Bible, New International Reader's Version®, NIrV® Copyright © 1995, 1996, 1998, 2014 by Biblica, Inc.™ Used by permission of Zondervan. All rights reserved worldwide. www.zondervan.com. The "NIrV" and "New International Reader's Version" are trademarks registered in the United States Patent and Trademark Office by Biblica, Inc.™

Printed in the United States of America

Please visit our website for other great titles:
www.masterbooks.com

Carrie Lindquist is a homeschool graduate, wife to Wayne, and momma to two energetic boys. She is a passionate advocate for homeschooling and loves helping new-to-homeschooling moms to realize that homeschooling through the early years isn't scary — it's really just an extension of all the fun things they are already doing with their children! When she isn't cleaning the endless little messes her boys create, you can find her encouraging moms to embrace the calling of everyday faithfulness.

Letter to the Parent

Your child is ready to learn to read — this can feel both incredibly exciting and a little scary as a parent! Before you delve right in, I want to take the time to remind you that teaching your child to read isn't big, scary, or complicated. In fact, it's really not that much different than all the playful learning activities you are already engaging your child in.

Chances are, you are already incorporating "school" into your days — reading books, pointing out colors, counting, completing projects, showing your child letters… The list goes on and on. This phonics and reading program is really just an extension of that.

This course has been designed to be a tool in your hands — remember, you are in control of it; it isn't in control of you. You know your child best. Use this program as a guide, and capitalize on his or her learning style, excitement level, interests, and talents. Don't feel pressured to complete the lessons in one sitting. If your student needs a break between lesson and worksheets, go with it. Enjoy the learning process with your child.

I also want to remind you that this program is full of suggested hands-on activities. But before you get overwhelmed, remember that they are suggested. If you complete one with your student after a lesson, that is awesome! If you complete them all, that is awesome! And if you don't get to any on a given day, your child will not suffer!

The vast majority of activities in this course utilize materials you most likely already have in your playroom or kitchen — things like flour, sugar, paint, play-dough, building blocks, etc. That means each lesson doesn't require you to spend time planning it out. If life is busy right now, you can literally pick up the guide, read the lesson with your student, and head to the kitchen for some letter fun without any planning! You will find a list of materials you may find helpful to have on hand on page number 11. These materials are by no means required to complete the program; they simply function as an enhancement to your child's learning. Most bonus activities are not lesson specific, so if your student absolutely loves a certain activity, re-use it in another lesson!

(Note: you may find it helpful to have a set of letter fridge magnets and/or letter cookie cutters, as these are used frequently in activities.)

If you picked up this program because your child is ready to read but isn't quite ready to write, your child is going to love this program! It is totally flexible to your needs: complete a hands-on activity in place of the worksheets and simply save the writing portion of the worksheets for when your student is ready for

writing. Capitalize on your child's interest and ability — and have fun in the process!

Learning at this stage is still very dependent on experience and play — and this course has been set up to meet that need. It's designed to be fun and engaging and provide plenty of opportunities for your student to continue learning through play. Ready to get started?

Table of Contents

Using This Teacher Guide

Features: The suggested weekly schedule enclosed has easy-to-manage lessons that guide the beginning reader with worksheets and all other assessments. The pages of this guide are perforated so materials are easy to tear out, hand out, grade, and store. Teachers are encouraged to adjust the schedule and materials needed in order to best work within their unique educational program.

Fun with Phonics! A great first course to develop important basic reading and writing skills! This colorful combination of phonics, listening skills, the alphabet along with letter recognition, sight words, and simple phrases help the student learn not only the sounds within words, but also what the words mean as your littlest learners begin to read. Complete with engaging activity sheets and scheduled reviews, students will enjoy coloring and other letter/word challenges. Bonus activities and the included teacher aids offer real world suggestions for extending helpful learning opportunities.

🕐	**Approximately 20 to 30 minutes per lesson, three to five days a week**
📋	**Includes materials list for activities**
✏️	**Worksheets for each section**
📄	**Designed for kindergarteners or first graders in a half-year course**

Course Description

This unique curriculum will take your student on a journey from the beginning of creation to the Resurrection of Christ as he or she learns each letter and corresponding sound. Designed to meet the needs of students who are ready to begin writing, as well as those who may not have mastered the hand-eye coordination skills yet that are needed for writing (see page 8). Throughout the course, the teacher reads the lessons and engages the student. The teacher then guides the student through the corresponding lesson worksheets and/or engages the student in suggested hands-on activities. Lessons take approximately 20–30 minutes to complete. This program has been designed to be completed over the first half of the school year. In our suggested schedule, the main lessons take place three times a week on Monday, Wednesday, and Friday. On Tuesdays and Thursdays, time is provided for reading to students, practicing sight words, completing bonus activities, or pointing out letters and sounds in the student's play, speech, and everyday activities. However, this program has been designed to be flexible to meet the needs of your student: it is a tool in your hands — you control it; it doesn't control you.

Course Objectives

Students completing this course will:

- ✔ Discover the basic foundations of letters and sounds to help students begin reading
- ✔ Learn to recognize letters and how simple combinations of letters create words
- ✔ Review words learned, while building a larger vocabulary each week
- ✔ Identify the shapes of letters, learning to write them out
- ✔ Explore various activities to make reading fun
- ✔ Develop a foundational understanding of Biblical history and salvation.

You will find teacher instructions and tips are italicized throughout the lesson text. Take time to pause and ask questions — engage your student and have fun! This program has been designed to create an excitement for the student; so as you read each lesson, be sure to convey the excitement of the lesson and the joy of discovery.

Each lesson covers an individual letter and sound or concept. We recommend emphasizing the letter sound covered in each individual lesson as you read. You'll find the letter or blend in bold throughout the text as a reminder.

Course Components

Throughout this course you will find the following components:

1. Introductory text for teachers to introduce the lesson of the day. Text for teachers throughout this teacher guide is in **_bold italics_** to distinguish it from the text that is read aloud for student instruction.

2. Letters and their sounds being emphasized will be found in **bold** on the teacher pages during portions with a special focus. Example emphasis letter/sound **Aa**: **A**lligators **a**nd **a**nts **a**te **a**pples. This is so the teacher can carefully sound out these words to help the student note the sound.

3. Review of sight words (from page 9) that correspond with different weeks of study, and can be made into index cards to make learning easier.

4. Materials List for optional bonus activities (page 11).

5. Suggested Daily Schedule (starting on page 13) that helps a teacher keep track of each day's lesson.

6. A Progress Chart (page 17) to help a student celebrate his or her learning.

7. Little Learner Activity Sheets that can be easily removed for the students to work on.

8. Weekly lessons that show the focus letter/sound that corresponds with the Little Learner Activity Sheets for the student. Regular text is read aloud to the student for direct instruction.

9. The Teacher Aids section contains helpful information including: how to hold a pencil, an assessment chart, book reading list, a recommended book list for reading practice, sight words, a basic phonics review, phonics learned throughout this course, additional reading practice, letter phrases students learn each week, bonus activities, and copywork practice.

Note: This course provides important foundational skills that prepare your student for any next-level language arts course, including _Language Lessons for a Living Education Level 1_, also available from Master Books. If used in combination with _Simply K_, it is recommended to complete Lessons 1-23 in _Simply K_, then add _Foundations Phonics_ alongside until _Simply K_ is complete. Then, you would complete the remaining lessons in _Foundations Phonics_.

Getting Started

This program has been designed to meet the needs of students who are ready to begin writing, as well as those who may not have mastered the hand-eye coordination skills that they'll need for writing. After a lesson, there are corresponding worksheets to help your child master the letter and sound, practice writing, and reading, and improve problem-solving skills.

- ✔ If your student is ready to begin writing, guide him or her through the worksheets and select a bonus activity from the lesson plan for some added fun!

- ✔ If your student isn't yet ready to begin writing, complete the coloring section, read the words together, and select a bonus activity or two after the lesson!

You will find that the words in the reading section begin with a mixture of uppercase and lowercase letters. This was done to help your student remember both letters, rather than get used to seeing just the lowercase. If your student forgets a letter's sound, simply remind him or her and continue sounding out the word.

Finally, if you find your student is struggling, becomes frustrated, or simply begins to "shut down" after a few lessons, it just may be that he or she isn't quite ready to learn to read — and that is okay! Take some time to research the skills a student must master before he or she can begin to read. If your student isn't yet ready, enjoy the process of getting there. Work to develop those skills through play and have fun together! Play memory games, read stories, point out letters and sounds. It won't be long before you find your student ready and excited to learn.

You'll find symbols above the vowel sounds in this course as your student learns to read. These are designed to help your student decode new words as they're learning. Depending on your accent, you may find that your family pronounces some words slightly different — and that's ok! You're welcome to adjust any symbols in the course. This can also be a fun way to discuss different accents around the world with your child!

Foundations: It's Not Just about Phonics

Just as learning to read is foundational for a child's education and far beyond, so the Truth given to us in the Bible becomes the foundation for a child's life—and eternity.

"Visit many good books, but live in the Bible." –Charles Spurgeon

This course is more than just a phonics program—it was written to help your child develop a firm Biblical foundation while he or she learns to read. As your child works through this program, he or she will learn about the creation of the world and how we are all designed by God. Your child will learn about God's commands, and man's choice to disobey. Your child will learn about how God in His mercy had a plan to save us, and he or she will watch His plan unfold throughout the pages of the Old Testament. Finally, your child will learn about Christ and how He ultimately defeated sin and death.

By the conclusion of this program, your child will have learned to read and will also have learned all about the Bible and God's plan for Salvation, about why it was so important Jesus came to save us, and what that means for him or her individually.

As I've written this program, I've prayed for you and your child. It is my prayer that as you both work through this course, you both will create some fun memories, share a lot of laughter, and that your child develops both a lifelong love for reading and a solid foundation of faith in the Lord Jesus Christ.

5 Indications your child is ready to start reading

1. Motivation – Sometimes, this is simply the biggest piece of the puzzle. If your child is unmotivated or seems to be in a constant state of frustration while reading, he/she just might not be ready yet—and that's okay! Focus instead on building his/her curiosity and excitement for reading through play and discovery. If your child is excited, curious, and wants to learn to read, the process will be much more enjoyable for you both.

2. Awareness – Your child recognizes that letters and words on a page have meanings and are related to words he or she hears and says.

3. Recognition – Your child can recognize letter shapes, names, and sounds.

4. Identification – Your child can listen to what is said and relate to it. He or she can relate a story back in his or her own words or find an application for his or her own life.

5. Discernment - Your child can hear a word and discern individual sounds in that word (e.g., the "c" sound at the beginning of the word "car" or the "g" sound at the end of "dog").

4 Indications your child is ready to start writing

1. Motivation – Here again, motivation and desire can be the biggest piece of the puzzle. It is motivation that gives your child the desire to continue working even when it's not easy.

2. Correct Grip – Your child can hold the pencil correctly and maintain the correct hold while writing, drawing, or tracing.

3. Ability– Your child can trace and copy lines, zig-zags, circles, and other basic shapes.

4. Connection – Your child understands there is a connection between speaking, reading, and writing.

Writing Readiness Assessment

Ask your student to trace or copy the lines below. Perfection isn't the goal. Watch to be sure your student maintains a proper grasp of the pencil throughout the whole worksheet. If your student can trace and copy the lines and shapes on this page while maintaining a proper pencil grasp, he or she should be ready to begin the writing portions of the lessons.

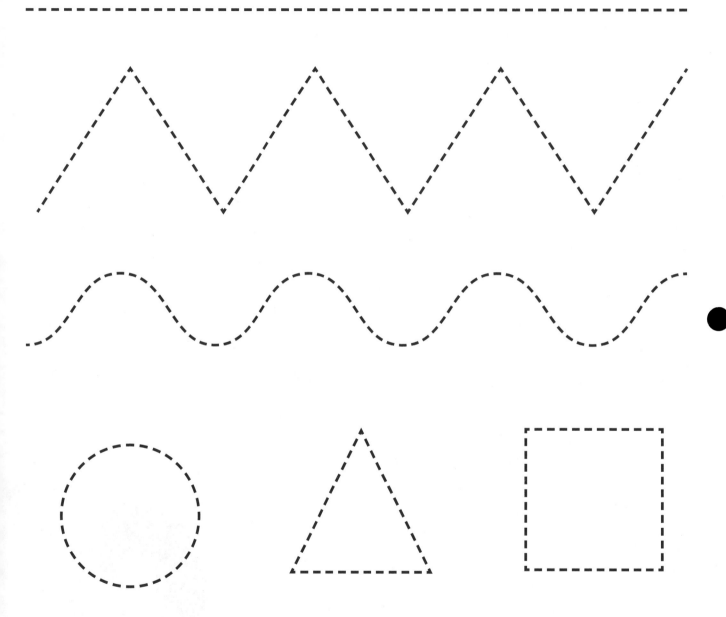

If your child is not yet able to maintain a proper pencil grasp or trace/copy the lines and shapes on the writing assessment, don't worry! Each child is different, and your child will be ready to begin writing at the perfect age for him or her. In the meantime, help your student practice proper pencil grasp while coloring or doodling. During lessons, begin teaching him or her how to write letter shapes by using his or her fingers to trace in sand, shaving cream, or by wetting his or her finger to "write" letters on pavement. Once your child is ready to begin writing, you can simple begin working through the writing portion of the lessons you've already completed.

Sight Words

These are words your child will encounter frequently in text. Learning these words by sight, rather than sounding them out each time, will help to increase your child's reading confidence and speed. You can write these sight words on the back of index cards, or purchase sight word flashcards online. Introduce each word to the student in the week specified and practice sight words with your student either after lessons or on the days between lessons.

It is important to note that mastery of these sight words will come over time — your child is not expected to have these words memorized in any particular amount of time. Enjoy the process and have fun practicing together! If your student is active, make it fun by letting him or her jump, clap, or dance after reading each word.

Week 2: and, an

Week 3: as, at, in

Week 4: is, it, if, did

Week 5: of, on, not

Week 6: a, I

Week 7: be, see

Week 8: all, but

Week 9: to, for, from, or, so, no, are, your

Week 10: he, was, his, how, can, we, had, will, has

Week 11: get

Week 12: the, that, this, than

Week 13: when, what, who, then, them

Week 14: they, out

Week 15: she

Week 17: have

Week 18: you, by, my, belong

Helpful Hints for Using this Course

1. Review the reading and writing indicators on page 7 to assess your child.

2. Prepare for the course by reading the materials list on page 11 and 12 and gathering any needed items. These items are not necessary, but will enhance your student's learning experience.

3. Be sure to have a small selection of books that would interest your child. Leave the books in a place he or she can access when he or she wants to look at them or read them.

4. Remember, the activities included are designed to enhance the learning process and add some extra fun to the lesson. But as always, you are in control of what activities you choose to do. Make sure they fit within your child's areas of interest as well as your own preferred education program. You may also incorporate activities your child already enjoys or ideas you find online!

5. We have included a Progress Chart for your child on page 17—we encourage you to place the chart where your child can see it (their room or on the refrigerator) and place stars or other stickers on the chart to show his or her mastery of the concepts in the course.

6. Remember, learning to read and write are important skills that need to be worked on daily. While the course materials cover 3 days a week, activities and other ideas are offered that you can incorporate into your daily schedule to help facilitate additional learning.

7. You know your child best—feel free to work through this program at a faster or slower pace. Your child learning to read is the most important thing, not sticking to the suggested schedule.

8. If you feel your child has not mastered a letter or topic, spend additional time working through or reviewing that lesson. Take time to practice those particular words with your student a couple times during the day. There is no need to rush through the program.

9. Throughout this program, Scripture is quoted from the New International Reader's Version (NIRV) and New King James Version (NKJV). If your family prefers a different translation, simply read these passages from the Bible of your choice as you work through lessons.

10. At the end of the course, students will have earned their Certificate of Completion found on page 293. If desired, you could incorporate this into a special family celebration once your child has learned to read!

Materials List

This is a list of items you may find helpful to have on hand for each week's bonus activities. It is recommended to save letters written on paper to save time in future activities and lessons.

Week 1

☐ flashlight
☐ loose letters (magnet, foam, game-piece, or something similar)
☐ toys
☐ child's book or magazine
☐ paper
☐ crayons
☐ washi or painter's tape

Week 2

☐ loose letters
☐ a child's book
☐ paintbrush, or similar object
☐ paper
☐ crayons
☐ marker*
☐ cake pan or similar container
☐ flour, uncooked rice, or sugar
☐ baking sheet

Week 3

☐ paper
☐ finger paint*
☐ washi or painter's tape
☐ sticky tabs
☐ paper or plastic cups
☐ permanent marker*
☐ small, soft ball
☐ scissors
☐ blue construction paper*

Week 4

☐ paper
☐ playdough
☐ plastic butter knife (or something similar for carving)
☐ letter blocks
☐ fridge magnets

Week 5

☐ sugar cookie recipe and ingredients
☐ letter cookie cutters (optional)
☐ washi or painter's tape
☐ finger paint*
☐ paper
☐ pool noodle (save for future lessons)
☐ permanent marker*
☐ building blocks with letters

Week 6

☐ sticky tabs
☐ world map or globe
☐ popsicle sticks

Week 7

☐ construction paper
☐ large container or paper bag
☐ scissors
☐ cookie sheet
☐ shaving cream

Week 8

☐ loose letters
☐ uncooked rice or sugar
☐ building blocks or Easter eggs
☐ permanent marker*
☐ paintbrush or similar object
☐ sticky tabs

Week 9

☐ popsicle sticks
☐ construction paper
☐ beanbag
☐ playdough
☐ cotton balls
☐ glue
☐ straw
☐ pom-pom ball

Week 10

☐ construction paper
☐ tape
☐ scissors
☐ paper
☐ crayons

Week 11

☐ small round candies (for example Smarties®, M&M®, or Mini's®)
☐ alphabet stamps and ink*
☐ toothpicks
☐ marshmallows
☐ paper
☐ page protectors
☐ dry erase marker
☐ toy car
☐ finger paint*

* **NOTE:** Be careful when using paints, ink, and permanent markers — and always supervise the child's use of them. They can stain clothing, carpets, and furniture.

Week 12

- [ ] fish dinner (lesson 35)
- [ ] paper
- [ ] crayons

Week 13

- [ ] baking sheet
- [ ] flour or sugar
- [ ] old magazine
- [ ] scissors
- [ ] glue
- [ ] construction paper

Week 14

- [ ] paper
- [ ] crayons

Week 15

- [ ] crayons
- [ ] paper
- [ ] finger paints*
- [ ] shaving cream
- [ ] baking sheet
- [ ] small round candies

Week 16

- [ ] paper
- [ ] crayons
- [ ] loose letters
- [ ] colored sand
- [ ] baking sheet

Week 17

- [ ] paper
- [ ] pipe cleaners
- [ ] alphabet stamps and ink*
- [ ] finger paint*
- [ ] q-tips
- [ ] tissue paper
- [ ] glue

Week 18

- [ ] paper
- [ ] crayons
- [ ] pencil
- [ ] scissors
- [ ] playdough
- [ ] markers*

Activity Tips

1. Organize your materials for each week in a basket or storage container.

2. Don't do the activities for the sake of just doing them. Make sure you have clear learning concept or goal in mind. Verbalize the concept before, during, and after the lesson.

3. Little learners love to help organize and pick up, so let them be part of both!

4. The activities can be modified as you feel it is needed, this includes changing included supplies to utilize materials you may already have on hand.

5. Use caution when using items like the small, round candies (such as the suggested Smarties®, M&M®, or Mini's®), they can be a choking hazard for younger children. So if you are doing the activities as a family, be sure to keep any small items that might be choking hazards away from them or modify the activity so they are not needed (big marshmallows instead of small candies, etc.).

* **NOTE:** Be careful when using paints, ink, and permanent markers – and always supervise the child's use of them. They can stain clothing, carpets, and furniture.

First Semester Suggested Daily Schedule

Date	Day	Assignment	Due Date	✓	Grade
		First Semester-First Quarter			
Week 1	Day 1	Read pages 19–20. Complete Little Learner Activity Sheet "Nn" pages 21–22.			
	Day 2	Take time for reading and/or bonus activities.			
	Day 3	Read pages 23–24. Complete Little Learner Activity Sheet "Dd" pages 25–26.			
	Day 4	Take time for reading and/or bonus activities.			
	Day 5	Read pages 27–28. Complete Little Learner Activity Sheet "Ăă" pages 29–30.			
Week 2	Day 6	Read pages 31–32. Complete Little Learner Activity Sheet "and" pages 33–34.			
	Day 7	Take time for reading and/or bonus activities.			
	Day 8	Read pages 35–37. Complete Little Learner Activity Sheet "Tt" pages 39–40.			
	Day 9	Take time for reading and/or bonus activities. Begin developing or using flash cards for sight words.			
	Day 10	Read pages 41–43. Complete Little Learner Activity Sheet "Ss" pages 45–46.			
Week 3	Day 11	Read pages 47–49. Complete Little Learner Activity Sheet "Pp" pages 51–52.			
	Day 12	Take time for reading and/or bonus activities.			
	Day 13	Read pages 53–55. Complete Little Learner Activity Sheet "Ĭĭ" pages 57–58.			
	Day 14	Take time for reading and/or bonus activities.			
	Day 15	Read pages 59–61. Complete Little Learner Activity Sheet "Ff" pages 63–64.			
Week 4	Day 16	Read pages 65–67. Complete Little Learner Activity Sheet "Ŏŏ" pages 69–70.			
	Day 17	Take time for reading and/or bonus activities.			
	Day 18	Read pages 71–73. Complete Little Learner Activity Sheet "Bb" pages 75–76.			
	Day 19	Take time for reading and/or bonus activities. Continue developing or using flash cards for sight words.			
	Day 20	Read pages 77–78. Complete Little Learner Activity Sheet "Review" pages 79–80.			
Week 5	Day 21	Read pages 81–83. Complete Little Learner Activity Sheet "Āā" pages 85–86.			
	Day 22	Take time for reading and/or bonus activities.			
	Day 23	Read pages 87–88. Complete Little Learner Activity Sheet "Īī" pages 89–90.			
	Day 24	Take time for reading and/or bonus activities. Review flash cards.			
	Day 25	Read pages 91–92. Complete Little Learner Activity Sheet "Åå" pages 93–94.			

Date	Day	Assignment	Due Date	✓	Grade
Week 6	Day 26	Read pages 95–97. Complete Little Learner Activity Sheet "Jj" pages 99–100.			
	Day 27	Take time for reading and/or bonus activities.			
	Day 28	Read pages 101–103. Complete Little Learner Activity Sheet "Ēē" pages 105–106.			
	Day 29	Take time for reading and/or bonus activities. Review flash cards.			
	Day 30	Read pages 107–108. Complete Little Learner Activity Sheet pages 109–110.			
Week 7	Day 31	Read pages 111–113. Complete Little Learner Activity Sheet "Mm" pages 115–116.			
	Day 32	Take time for reading and/or bonus activities.			
	Day 33	Read pages 117–119. Complete Little Learner Activity Sheet "Ll" pages 121–122.			
	Day 34	Take time for reading and/or bonus activities. Review flash cards.			
	Day 35	Read pages 123–125. Complete Little Learner Activity Sheet "Ŭŭ" pages 127–128.			
Week 8	Day 36	Read pages 129–131. Complete Little Learner Activity Sheet "Ōō" pages 133–134.			
	Day 37	Take time for reading and/or bonus activities.			
	Day 38	Read pages 135–137. Complete Little Learner Activity Sheet "Rr" pages 139–140.			
	Day 39	Take time for reading and/or bonus activities. Review flash cards.			
	Day 40	Read pages 141–142. Complete Little Learner Activity Sheet "Review" page 143–144.			
Week 9	Day 41	Read pages 145–147. Complete Little Learner Activity Sheet "Cc" pages 149–150.			
	Day 42	Take time for reading and/or bonus activities.			
	Day 43	Read pages 151–153. Complete Little Learner Activity Sheet "Ww" pages 155–156.			
	Day 44	Take time for reading and/or bonus activities. Review flash cards.			
	Day 45	Read pages 157–158. Complete Little Learner Activity Sheet "Hh" pages 159–160.			
First Semester-Second Quarter					
Week 1	Day 46	Read pages 161–163. Complete Little Learner Activity Sheet "Gg" pages 165–166.			
	Day 47	Take time for reading and/or bonus activities.			
	Day 48	Read pages 167–168. Complete Little Learner Activity Sheet "Kk" pages 169–170.			
	Day 49	Take time for reading and/or bonus activities. Review flash cards.			
	Day 50	Read page 171–172. Complete Little Learner Activity Sheet "Review" pages 173–174.			

Date	Day	Assignment	Due Date	✓	Grade
Week 2	Day 51	Read pages 175–177. Complete Little Learner Activity Sheet "th" pages 179–180.			
	Day 52	Take time for reading and/or bonus activities.			
	Day 53	Read pages 181–184. Complete Little Learner Activity Sheet "sp" pages 185–186.			
	Day 54	Take time for reading and/or bonus activities. Review flash cards.			
	Day 55	Read pages 187–188. Complete Little Learner Activity Sheet "ck" page 189–190.			
Week 3	Day 56	Read pages 191–193. Complete Little Learner Activity Sheet "Ĕĕ" pages 195–196.			
	Day 57	Take time for reading and/or bonus activities.			
	Day 58	Read pages 197–199. Complete Little Learner Activity Sheet "wh" pages 201–202.			
	Day 59	Take time for reading and/or bonus activities. Review flash cards.			
	Day 60	Read page 203–204. Complete Little Learner Activity Sheet "Review" page 205–206.			
Week 4	Day 61	Read pages 207–209. Complete Little Learner Activity Sheet "Ou" pages 211–212.			
	Day 62	Take time for reading and/or bonus activities.			
	Day 63	Read pages 213–215. Complete Little Learner Activity Sheet "Ch" pages 217–218.			
	Day 64	Take time for reading and/or bonus activities. Review flash cards.			
	Day 65	Read pages 219–220. Complete Little Learner Activity Sheet "Yy" pages 221–222.			
Week 5	Day 66	Read pages 223–224. Complete Little Learner Activity Sheet "Cc" pages 225–226.			
	Day 67	Take time for reading and/or bonus activities.			
	Day 68	Read pages 227–229. Complete Little Learner Activity Sheet "Sh" pages 231–232.			
	Day 69	Take time for reading and/or bonus activities. Review flash cards.			
	Day 70	Read page 233–234. Complete Little Learner Activity Sheet "Review" page 235–236.			
Week 6	Day 71	Read pages 237–238. Complete Little Learner Activity Sheet "Qq" pages 239–240.			
	Day 72	Take time for reading and/or bonus activities.			
	Day 73	Read pages 241–242. Complete Little Learner Activity Sheet "Gg" pages 243–244.			
	Day 74	Take time for reading and/or bonus activities. Review flash cards.			
	Day 75	Read pages 245–246. Complete Little Learner Activity Sheet "Ou" page 247–248.			
Week 7	Day 76	Read pages 249–251. Complete Little Learner Activity Sheet "Vv" pages 253–254.			
	Day 77	Take time for reading and/or bonus activities.			
	Day 78	Read pages 255–256. Complete Little Learner Activity Sheet "Ea" pages 257–258.			
	Day 79	Take time for reading and/or bonus activities. Review flash cards.			
	Day 80	Read pages 259–260. Complete Little Learner Activity Sheet pages 261–262.			

Date	Day	Assignment	Due Date	✓	Grade
Week 8	Day 81	Read pages 263–264. Complete Little Learner Activity Sheet "Yy" pages 265–266.			
	Day 82	Take time for reading and/or bonus activities.			
	Day 83	Read pages 267–269. Complete Little Learner Activity Sheet "Ūū" pages 271–272.			
	Day 84	Take time for reading and/or bonus activities. Review flash cards.			
	Day 85	Read pages 273–274. Complete Little Learner Activity Sheet "Xx" pages 275–276.			
Week 9	Day 86	Read pages 277–279. Complete Little Learner Activity Sheet "Ng" page 281–282.			
	Day 87	Take time for reading and/or bonus activities.			
	Day 88	Read pages 283–286. Complete Little Learner Activity Sheet "Zz" pages 287–288.			
	Day 89	Take time for reading and/or bonus activities. Review flash cards.			
	Day 90	Read page 289. Bonus activity on page 290. Complete Little Learner Activity Sheet "Review" page 291–292.			
		Final Grade			

Progress Chart

Lesson 1 Nn		Lesson 15 Åå		Lesson 29 Kk		Lesson 43 Qq	
Lesson 2 Dd		Lesson 16 Jj		Lesson 30 Review		Lesson 44 Gg	
Lesson 3 Ăă		Lesson 17 Ēē		Lesson 31 Th		Lesson 45 Ou	
Lesson 4 Blending		Lesson 18 Review		Lesson 32 Sp		Lesson 46 Vv	
Lesson 5 Tt		Lesson 19 Mm		Lesson 33 Ck		Lesson 47 Ea	
Lesson 6 Ss		Lesson 20 Ll		Lesson 34 Ěě		Lesson 48 Review	
Lesson 7 Pp		Lesson 21 Ŭŭ		Lesson 35 Wh		Lesson 49 Yy	
Lesson 8 Ĭĭ		Lesson 22 Ōō		Lesson 36 Review		Lesson 50 Ūū	
Lesson 9 Ff		Lesson 23 Rr		Lesson 37 Ou		Lesson 51 Xx	
Lesson 10 Ŏŏ		Lesson 24 Review		Lesson 38 Ch		Lesson 52 Ng	
Lesson 11 Bb		Lesson 25 Cc		Lesson 39 Yy		Lesson 53 Zz	
Lesson 12 Review		Lesson 26 Ww		Lesson 40 Cc		Lesson 54 Review	
Lesson 13 Āā		Lesson 27 Hh		Lesson 41 Sh			
Lesson 14 Īī		Lesson 28 Gg		Lesson 42 Review			

Review the alphabet with your child. Choose some letters as examples, and ask that the student point out the uppercase letter and/or the lowercase letter. As you do this phonics course, you can come back to this page and review the letters again on "off" days or even as a bonus activity as needed.

Aa Bb Cc Dd Ee

Ff Gg Hh Ii Jj

Kk Ll Mm Nn Oo

Pp Qq Rr Ss Tt Uu

Vv Ww Xx Yy Zz

N is for **n**othing, **n**one,
not eve**n** a bit!"

Detach and hand the student the
Little Learner Activity Sheet on page 21.

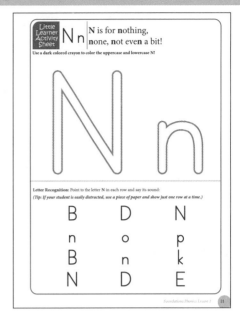

LESSON NARRATIVE

Intro to Program

You're learning to read, oh how exciting! Reading is fun. God made it that way! He gave us our language because He has something to say. God wants you to know that He loves you so much, and He wrote it all down in the very best book. The very best book — we call it the Bible — tells us the true story of all that there was, and ever will be. Through its words and its pages, we can learn and explore — learning to read it is a great big adventure!

> *This lesson covers the letter N. The sound of the letter N can be heard in the words nothing, none, and never. As you read through this lesson, place emphasis on the sound of this letter where it is found in bold throughout the text.*

Are you ready to start our great big adventure? Me too! Our adventure must start at the beginning. Can you guess what we'll find at the start of time?

Close your eyes! What do you see?

(Allow student time to answer, answer should be darkness, nothing, etc.)

Nothing and darkness, just like at the start. To begin our adventure, we'll read from the very best book — the Bible!

In the beginning, God created the heavens and the earth. The earth didn't have any shape. And it was empty. There was darkness over the surface of the waves. At that time, the Spirit of God was hovering over the waters (Genesis 1:1–2).

N is for **n**othing, **n**one, **n**ot even a bit! At the start of creation, the earth had **n**othing — **n**ot even a shape!

Today we will learn the letter **N**! The letter **N** makes the sound of **n**. Can you say it with me?

The N says **n**.

(Repeat if necessary to reinforce the sound to the student.)

Great job! The letter **N** looks like this:

Nn

(Ask the student to trace uppercase and lowercase N with finger on the Little Learner Activity Sheet.)

Each letter has two sizes, one big and one small. We call the big one the "uppercase" letter, and the small one the "lowercase" letter.

The uppercase **N** looks like this:

N

The lowercase **N** looks like this:

n

(Ask student to trace uppercase and lowercase N with finger on the Little Learner Activity Sheet. Make sure the student points to the correct one.)

I have a surprise for you on this adventure. God gave us a gift to make learning extra special! He gave us an imagination so that we can pretend. We can imagine the scenes and the stories taking place as we read — it's like watching a movie way up in your head! Can you tell me about a time you used your imagination?

(Allow student time to answer; remind student of a time if necessary.)

Your imagination can make reading so fun and exciting! Now close your eyes and imagine the darkness and nothing. Use your imagination as I read. God tells us what happened in the very next verse:

God said, "Let there be light." And there was light. God saw that the light was good. He separated the light from the darkness. God called the light "day." He called the darkness

"night." There was evening, and there was morning. It was day one (Genesis 1:3–5).

Now open your eyes. Can you imagine the bright light God made on that very first day? Show me one finger — on the first day God made day and **n**ight!

I heard a new **N** word, did you hear it too?

Tell me which word you hear the letter **N** in too:

Day   God   **Night**

That's right, it was **n**ight! On day **n**umber one God made day and **n**ight!

N is for **n**ight, which God created. Let's practice the letter **N** sound together. The **N** says **n**.

Now let's play a listening game! Do you hear the letter **N** in these words? Listen carefully to each one and tell me yes or no:

(Allow student time to answer yes or no after each):

Ned	Noah	Any
Tell	Cake	Take
Say	And	
Night	Dog	

Great job! Say it with me: **N** is for **n**othing, **n**one, **n**ot even a bit! But it wasn't for long, because God started creating! Are you enjoying our great big adventure?

You've learned the letter **N**, now it's time for some fun!

(Have the student complete the Little Learner Activity Sheet.)

BONUS ACTIVITIES

Don't feel like you need to get all—or any!—of the activities done in a single sitting. Choose one that interests your student and do it sometime during the day or spread several activities out during the course of the week. Be sure to read a story, draw a scene from today's lesson, or think of some N words with your student tomorrow!

- Gather a few of the student's favorite toys and create an uppercase and lowercase N shape.

- Scatter a few game piece letter tiles or similar loose letters on a table and ask student to find the N tile/s.

- Get a flashlight, turn off the lights, and help student use the flashlight to "draw" the letter N on the floor or ceiling using the beam. Remind student that there was darkness in the beginning, but God created light!

D is for **D**esign.
Throughout all of creation, Go**d** place**d** gran**d d**esign.

Detach and hand the student the
Little Learner Activity Sheet on page 25.

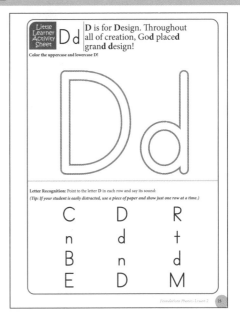

LESSON NARRATIVE

This lesson covers the letter D. The sound of the letter D can be heard in the words design, grand, and placed. As you read through this lesson, place emphasis on the sound of this letter where it is found in bold throughout the text.

Welcome back to our great big adventure! Do you remember the letter we learned about on our last adventure?

(Allow student time to answer N; remind student of letter and/or sound if necessary.)

That's right! We learned the letter N! N is for nothing, none, not even a bit! But it wasn't for long, because God started creating.

Now, close your eyes and start your imagination — I'm going to tell you what God created!

On day 1, God spoke and created day and night.

On day 2, God spoke and created the atmosphere.

On day 3, God spoke and created land, grass, flowers, and trees!

Are you still using your imagination? Let's keep going; it gets even more exciting!

On day 4, God spoke and created the sun, moon, and stars! Isn't that amazing?

On day 5, God spoke and created the birds and the fish.

On day 6, God spoke and created all the animals — can you tell me about your favorite animal?

(Allow student time to answer.)

But that wasn't all that God created on day 6, He also made someone very special — do you know who He created?

(Allow student time to answer. Answer should be man or Adam, but simply proceed if the student does not know.)

On day 6, God created man. He was a very special part of creation!

Now, on each of these days God said all He had made was very good. Through all of creation, Go**d** place**d** gran**d d**esign!

I heard a new sound; did you hear it too?

Yes, **D** is our new letter today!

The letter **D** makes the sound **d**. Can you say it with me?

The **D** says **d**.

(Repeat if necessary to reinforce the sound to the student.)

Great job! The letter **D** looks like this:

D d

(Ask student to trace uppercase and lowercase D with finger on the Little Learner Activity Sheet. Make sure the student points to the correct one.)

The uppercase **D** looks like this:

D

The lowercase **D** looks like this:

d

Through all of creation, Go**d** place**d** gran**d d**esign! **D** is for **d**esign.

Do you hear the **D** sound in "**d**esign"?

Repeat after me:

Throughout all of creation, Go**d** place**d** gran**d d**esign!

Yes, each creature is different in size, shape, noise, color, and pattern because God designed each one very special. And do you know what? God designed me, and He designed you! He made you different from me and gave you special gifts. Can you tell me how God designed you extra special?

(Allow student time to answer; guide as necessary.)

I'm gla**d** God **d**esigned you that way!

Now let's play our listening game! Do you hear the letter **D** in these words? Listen carefully to each one and tell me yes or no:

Day	Car	Map
Pen	**D**eer	Leaf
Brea**d**	Cup	
Duck	**D**og	

Awesome! Say it with me — throughout all of creation, Go**d** place**d** gran**d d**esign! Hasn't this adventure through creation been exciting? I can't wait to tell you what happens in our next lesson! But for now, you've learned the letter **D** and it's time for some fun!

(Have the student complete the Little Learner Activity Sheet.)

BONUS ACTIVITIES:

(Student has learned N and D so far.)

- Gather paper and crayons. Ask student to imagine and draw a new animal. Once the student is done, ask questions about their creation and point out the design. Remind student of God's grand designs in creation. Once finished, help the student draw a letter D on the top of the page to remind him/her of God's grand design.

- Help student find household objects that begin with or contain the letter D.

D d

D is for **D**esign. Throughout all of creation, Go**d** place**d** gran**d d**esign!

Color the uppercase and lowercase D!

Letter Recognition: Point to the letter **D** in each row and say its sound:

(Tip: If your student is easily distracted, use a piece of paper and show just one row at a time.)

C	D	R
n	d	t
B	n	d
E	D	M

Writing: Let's practice writing the letter **D**!

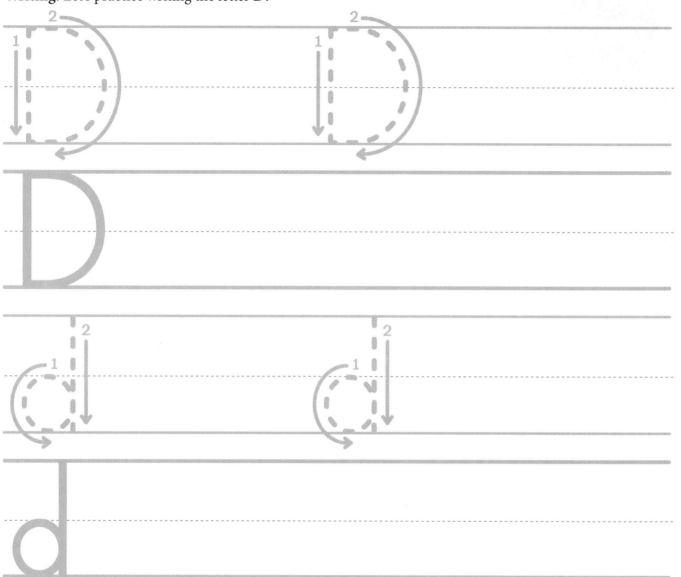

Activity: Color the pictures that start with D! (apple, dog, sock, dolphin, duck)

Ă is for Adam!

Detach and hand the student the
Little Learner Activity Sheet on page 29.

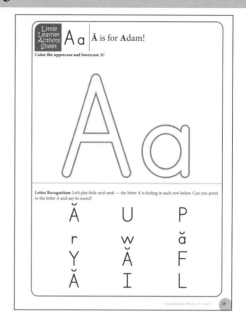

LESSON NARRATIVE

> *This lesson covers the short sound of the letter A. The short sound is designated within the lesson with the following symbol above the letters: Ăă. The short sound of the letter A can be heard in the words Ădam, ăpple, and săt. As you read through this lesson, place emphasis on the sound of this letter where it is found in bold throughout the text.*

Today I'm so very excited. We are going to learn an extra special letter in our adventure today! Are you ready to start? Well then, get your imagination in gear!

We've learned the letter N — do you remember the sound that it makes?

(Allow student time to answer; remind if necessary.)

Fantastic! The N says n.

And we've learned the letter D — can you tell me its sound?

(Allow student time to answer; remind if necessary.)

Great! The D says d.

In our last lesson, we learned what God created on each day — and we learned that through all of creation, God placed grand design! Get your imagination ready — here is the next part of our adventure!

God's grandest design was made on day 6. God shaped a man from the dirt and the Bible tells us that He breathed into man the breath of life — and man came alive! Oh, how exciting!

Now close your eyes and listen as I read from the very best book, the Bible!

> Then the LORD God formed a man. He made him out of the dust of the ground. God breathed the breath of life into him. And the man became a living person (Genesis 2:7).

God named the first man **A**dam.

Wait, I think I heard a new sound. Did you hear it too?

The letter **A** is for **A**dam.

The letter **A** looks like this:

Aa

The uppercase **A** looks like this:

The lowercase **A** looks like this:

(Ask student to trace uppercase and lowercase A with finger on the Little Learner Activity Sheet. Make sure the student points to the correct one.)

The letter **A** is extra special because it is called a "vowel." A vowel can make different sounds. Isn't that neat? The letter **A** can make three different sounds — wow!

Today we will learn just one sound of the letter **A**. Are you ready? Let's start!

A is for **A**dam. The **A** says **ă**.

When letters make different sounds, we use "symbols" on the top to tell you which sound they make while you learn. Today's symbol looks like a smiley-face above the letter **A**!

When you see a letter **A** that looks like this:

You can be sure that **A** says **ă** as is **A**dam!

(Ask student to point to letter on the Little Learner Activity Sheet and practice sound.)

You're doing so well! Hmm, but it seems I've forgotten some sounds! Can you point to each letter and tell me the sound?

What about these lowercase letters?

Thank you for helping me. I'm so glad you remember! Now let's go have some more fun with the letter **A**!

(Have the student complete the Little Learner Activity Sheet.)

BONUS ACTIVITIES:

(Student has learned N, D, and Ă so far.)

- Using washi or painter's tape, tape letters N, D, and A on the floor (spot test first to make sure the tape will not damage the floor). Instruct the student to jump from letter to letter and say its sound as you call its name.

- If the student has siblings, have everyone position themselves to make a big letter A on the ground. For students who do not have siblings, books or toys can be used to create the A letter.

- Get a book or a magazine and go on a letter A scavenger hunt! See how many times the letter A can be found.

 **A a** | **Ă is for Adam!**

Color the uppercase and lowercase A!

Letter Recognition: Let's play hide-and-seek — the letter A is hiding in each row below. Can you point to the letter A and say its sound?

Ă   U   P

r   W   ă

Y   Ă   F

Ă   I   L

Writing: Let's practice writing the letter **A**!

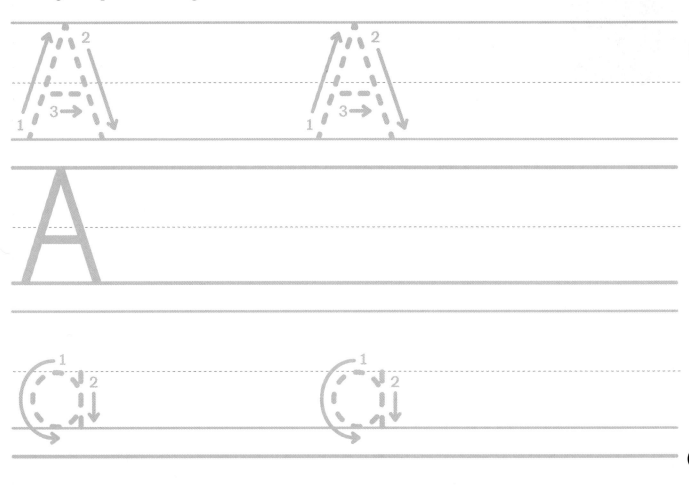

Activity: Draw a line from the uppercase letter to the lowercase letter!

N   d

D   a

A   n

Blending

Dăd

Detach and hand the student the
Little Learner Activity Sheet on page 33.

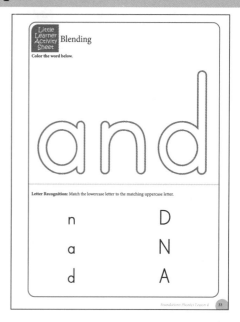

LESSON NARRATIVE

In this lesson, the student will begin blending sounds together to read words. Take a deep breath and relax—this is going to be fun! As students begin to blend, point to each individual letter and give them a chance to say the sound. If they get stuck, just remind them of the sound. After students have read each sound individually, move your finger across the word from left to right and help them say the sounds a little faster. Do this again faster and blend the sounds together to form the word. It may take students a few tries, or even a few lessons, to fully grasp blending and that is ok. Be patient and guide them along the process.

Are you ready to start our lesson today? Today will be great — do you want to know why?

(Allow student time to guess.)

You are going to start reading today!

We've learned three letters, and each of their sounds too.

Each letter makes a sound of its own, but letters don't really like to be alone. No, letters like friends, so they get together in groups!

When letters get together, they form words. Each letter says its sound and when we put all the sounds together, the sounds make a word.

Let's take a look:

Here is the letter D. Can you remember its sound?

D

(Allow student time to answer.)

That is right! **D** says **d** as in **d**esign.

When it is alone, the letter D just says d.

What about the letter A? Do you remember its sound?

(Allow student time to answer.)

Yes, that is right! A says ă as in Adam.

When it is alone, the A just says ă.

But when the letter D and the letter A sit side-by-side, they put their sounds together like this:

(Point to each letter and say the sound, then blend the letters together to sound out the word.)

Can you say the sounds with me?

(Point to each letter and say the sound, then blend the letters together to sound out the word.)

But wait! Our word isn't complete. We need to add another letter D! Let's add a D to the end and sound out the word!

(Point to each letter and say the sound, then blend the letters together with the student to sound out the word.)

Yay! You've read your very first word! I'm so proud, should we try another?

Let's start with the A, what sound does it say?

But now it's alone, so let's add an N!

(Point to each letter and say the sound, then blend the letters together to sound out the word.)

Wow! That is a word we use quite a lot when we talk. Here are some examples:

I saw **an** elephant at the zoo.

Don't step on **an** ant!

I'd like **an** apple, please!

Please get me **an** umbrella.

I think we'll be reading that word a lot! I know another word you can read, and this one we say even more than the first!

(Point to each letter and say the sound, then blend the letters together to sound out the word.)

Here are some ways we use that word:

I like peanut butter **and** jelly.

I saw a car **and** a bus.

Red **and** blue are my favorite colors.

I say please **and** thank you.

Hurray! You are reading. Are you excited?

So far on our great big adventure, we've learned N, D, and A! And now you have read your first three words, oh how exciting! In our next lesson, we will learn the letter T, but for now it's time for some more word fun!

(Have the student complete the Little Learner Activity Sheet.)

BONUS ACTIVITIES:

(Student has learned N, D, and Ă so far.)

- Gather A, N, and D fridge magnets, blocks, or similar loose letters and practice placing the letters together and combining their sounds.
- Ask student to draw a picture of his or her dad. Help him/her write "dăd" across the top.

- Read a book together and point out the words "and," "an," or "dad" if they appear in the text. Remind the student that the letters in the book are working together to form the words they hear — and the student will be reading all of those words very soon!

Color the word below.

Letter Recognition: Match the lowercase letter to the matching uppercase letter.

n   D

a   N

d   A

Writing: Let's practice writing the words we have learned.

dad

an

and

T is for **T**old.
God **t**old Adam **t**o obey.

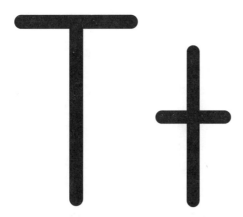

Detach and hand the student the
Little Learner Activity Sheet on page 39.

LESSON NARRATIVE

> *This lesson covers the letter T. The sound of the letter T can be heard in the words told, to, and teach. As you read through this lesson, place emphasis on the sound of this letter where it is found in bold throughout the text.*

It's time for another learning adventure today! Are you ready to go? Did you bring your imagination?

(Allow student time to answer.)

All right then, let's go! Do you remember what the letter A was for?

(Allow student time to answer. Answer should be A is for Adam.)

That's right! A is for Adam!

We learned that God created Adam on day 6 of creation. And on day 7, well, God blessed that day and rested!

Now, close your eyes and use your imagination as we read from the Bible!

> The LORD God had planted a garden in the east in Eden (Genesis 2:8).

> The LORD God put the man in the Garden of Eden. He put him there to farm its land and take care of it. The LORD God gave the

man a command. He said, "You may eat fruit from any tree in the garden. But you must not eat the fruit from the tree of the knowledge of good and evil. If you do, you will certainly die. (Genesis 2:15–17).

Can you imagine the beautiful garden that God made for Adam? What is the most beautiful thing that you've ever seen?

(Allow student time to answer.)

I am sure the garden of Eden was even more beautiful than that! Adam got to see God's creation — and it was perfect. There was no sadness, no sickness, no things that were bad.

God gave Adam special instructions. Do you remember what the Bible said they were?

(Allow student time to answer. Simply move on if student does not remember.)

> "... you must not eat the fruit from the tree of the knowledge of good and evil. If you do, you will certainly die" (Genesis 2:17).

God **t**old Adam **t**o obey.

Ooooh, I heard a new sound! Did you hear it too?

T is our letter today. **T** is for **t**old. The letter **T** says t. God **t**old Adam to obey.

The letter **T** looks like this:

(Ask student to trace uppercase and lowercase T with finger on the Little Learner Activity Sheet. Make sure the student points to the correct one.)

The uppercase **T** looks like this:

The lowercase **T** looks like this:

The **T** says **t**. Can you say it with me?

(Practice T sound with student.)

Repeat after me: God **t**old Adam **t**o obey.

Yes, God **t**old Adam **t**o obey because He loved Adam. Remember how sometimes I used to tell you not to touch something because it was hot and it would burn you?

(Allow student to answer.)

I **t**old you to obey because I love you and I didn't want you to get hurt. God is the same way. He tells us to obey because He knows the best way to go — and He doesn't want us to get hurt making the wrong choice.

God loved Adam, and **t**old him **t**o obey.

Now close your eyes. Start up your imagination while I read the next part of our adventure from the Bible!

The LORD God had formed all the wild animals and all the birds in the sky. He had made all of them out of the ground. He brought them to the man to see what names he would give them. And the name the man gave each living creature became its name. So the man gave names to all the livestock, all the birds in the sky, and all the wild animals" (Genesis 2:19–20).

Can you imagine all of the animals coming to Adam as he told them their names? It must have been quite a sight! What is your favorite animal?

(Allow student time to answer.)

What do you think you would have named it if you were Adam that day?

(Allow student time to answer.)

T is for **t**old. God **t**old Adam **t**o obey and Adam told the animals their names!

Let's play an animal game! I'm going to say the name of an animal. Can you tell me if you hear the **T** sound in its name? Tell me yes or no!

Tiger	Ant	Dog
Cat	Bird	Turtle
Elephan**t**	Toucan	

Great job! The **T** says **t**. God **t**old Adam **t**o obey. Hmm, do you think Adam will follow God's directions?

(Allow student time to answer.)

I guess we will find out in our next lesson! For now, we've learned the letter **T**, and it is time for some more **T** fun!

(Now begin the reading section. If your child needs to take a break from the lesson, let him or her begin the first page of the Little Learner Activity Sheet. Be sure to go back to the reading section of this lesson to complete it.)

I have some exciting news! Now that you've learned another letter, you can read some new words!

Here we go! Let's start with an A. Point to the A, what sound does it make?

But that A looks lonely. Should we add an n? Sound out the letters with me:

(Point to each letter and say the sound, then blend the letters together to sound out the word.)

Hey, we know that word! The more we practice, the more words you will start to recognize. We can add another letter onto the end to make a new word. Want to give it a try?

(Point to each letter and say the sound, then blend the letters together to sound out the word.)

Great job! Let's try one more word! Let's move the T from the end to the start and see what word we make! Can you sound it out with me?

(Point to each letter and say the sound, then blend the letters together to sound out the word.)

Fantastic! Tan is a color. Let's find something tan!

(Help student find an object that is tan.)

Isn't it neat? Each letter in a word works together, and the word tells us about something. When you read a new word, think about what it means. Now, let's practice writing the letter T!

(Have the student complete the Little Learner Activity Sheet.)

BONUS ACTIVITIES:

(Student has learned N, D, Ă, and T so far.)

- Using a cake pan, bury fridge magnet letters (or similar letters) in flour, uncooked rice, or sugar. Give student a brush and ask him/her to find and "excavate" the letter T.

- Help the student practice letter recognition by doing the activity on page 38.

- Help the student think of some more animal names that begin with T. See if you can find a book on one of those animals, and emphasize the T sound while you read!

One way to help your child blend sounds together is to compare blending to singing. Help your child "sing" the sounds together in a monotone way. Reminding your student to "sing" the sounds can help them begin to transition from reading each sound individually to reading them together.

Let's sing the alphabet song!

(Point to each letter with the student as you sing the song.)

Aa Bb Cc Dd Ee

Ff Gg Hh Ii Jj

Kk Ll Mm Nn Oo

Pp Qq Rr Ss Tt Uu

Vv Ww Xx Yy Zz

T t

T is for **Told**.
God **t**old Adam **t**o obey.

Color the uppercase and lowercase T!

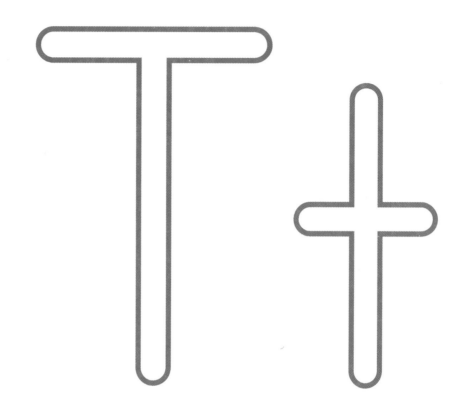

Activity: Say the name of each picture, and draw a line to the beginning letter in its name!

d

a

n

Writing: Let's practice writing the letter **T**!

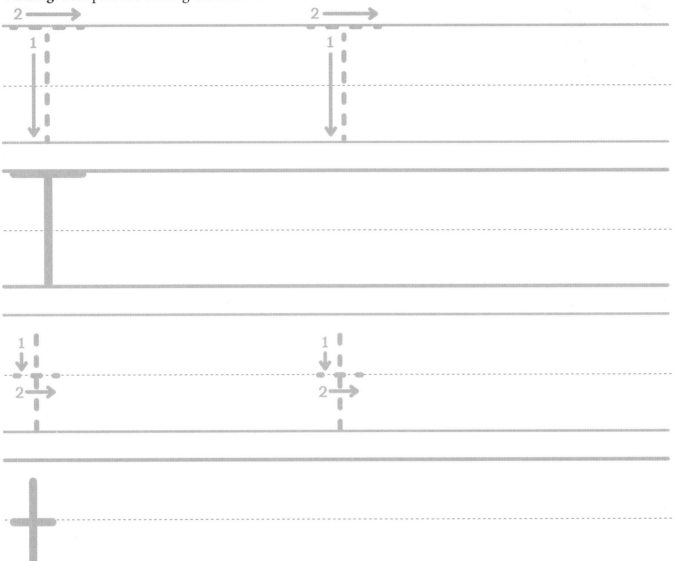

Activity: Color the ant brown.

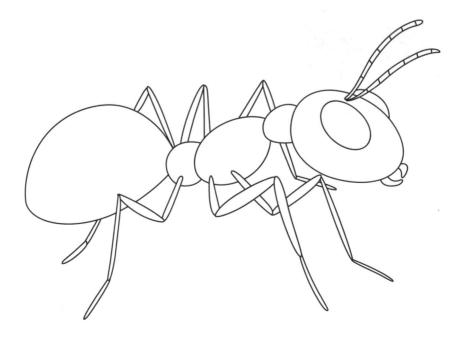

S is for **S**in.
Sin **s**eparate**s** u**s** from God, it's a very **s**ad thing.

Detach and hand the student the
Little Learner Activity Sheet on page 45.

LESSON NARRATIVE

This lesson covers the letter S. The sound of the letter S can be heard in the words sin, sad, and separate. As you read through this lesson, place emphasis on the sound of this letter where it is found in bold throughout the text.

Why hello there, are you ready for another Bible adventure? Before we get started, let's try to remember — can you tell me the letters we've learned so far?

(Allow student time to answer; guide as necessary. Student has learned N, D, A, and T.)

The N says n. Remember, N is for nothing, none, not even a bit. But it wasn't for long, because God started creating!

The D says d. Throughout all of creation, God placed grand design.

The A says ă. A is for Adam!

The T says t. God told Adam to obey.

On our adventure today, we'll find out if Adam obeyed God. So start your imagination and let's dive right in!

After Adam named all the animals, God noticed he was lonely. What do you think God did?

(Allow student time to answer.)

Close your eyes and imagine, I'll read from the Bible!

But Adam didn't find a helper that was just right for him. So the LORD God caused him to fall into a deep sleep. While the man was sleeping, the LORD God took out one of the man's ribs. Then the LORD God closed the opening in the man's side. Then the LORD God made a woman. He made her from the rib he had taken out of the man. And the LORD God brought her to the man (Genesis 2:20b–22).

Wow, how amazing! God made a woman just special for Adam. Her name was Eve.

Adam and Eve got to live in God's perfect garden — and they got to walk and talk with God. Can you imagine how amazing that would be?

The garden was perfect — no sin, sadness, or death. The days were all perfect, the food was delicious! But then, something terrible happened. Can you guess what it was?

(Allow student time to answer.)

Well, one day, the Bible tells us the serpent came to Eve in the garden. Let's read the next part of the story from the Bible:

The serpent was more clever than any of the wild animals the LORD God had made. The serpent said to the woman, "Did God really say, 'You must not eat fruit from any tree in the garden'?"

The woman said to the serpent, "We may eat fruit from the trees in the garden. But God did say, 'You must not eat the fruit from the tree in the middle of the garden. Do not even touch it. If you do, you will die.' "

"You will certainly not die," the serpent said to the woman. "God knows that when you eat fruit from that tree, you will know things you have never known before. Like God, you will be able to tell the difference between good and evil."

The woman saw that the tree's fruit was good to eat and pleasing to look at. She also saw that it would make a person wise. So she took some of the fruit and ate it. She also gave some to her husband, who was with her. And he ate it (Genesis 3:1–6).

Oh no, remember how God had told them to obey? Well, Adam and Eve decided not to — and they knew right away they had done something bad. They were ashamed and scared — feelings they had never felt before. Can you tell me about a time you were scared?

(Allow student time to answer.)

After Adam and Eve had eaten the fruit, they became scared of God and they hid. Do you know why?

(Allow student time to answer.)

When God tells us to obey and we decide not to, that is called **s**in.

S is our new letter for today, the **S** says **s**. **S**in **s**eparates u**s** from God, it i**s** a very **s**ad thing.

The letter **S** looks like this:

S s

(Ask student to trace uppercase and lowercase S with finger on the Little Learner Activity Sheet. Make sure the student points to the correct one.)

The uppercase **S** looks like this:

S

The lowercase **S** looks like this:

s

Now, say it with me, the **S** says **s**. Great job!

Sin **s**eparates u**s** from God, it's a very **s**ad thing. Because Adam and Eve chose not to obey like God had told them to, the world was no longer perfect. Suddenly, there was sadness, shame, sickness, and death. And saddest of all, because of their sin, Adam and Eve could no longer be close with God.

But all was not lost, because God still had a plan. And we'll learn all about it in the next lesson!

But for today, it's time to read some new words because we've learned a new letter today!

(Now begin the reading section. If your child needs to take a break from the lesson, let him or her begin the first page of the Little Learner Activity Sheet. Be sure to go back to the reading section of this lesson to complete it.)

Let's get started. We'll start with an **S**. What sound does the **S** make?

(Allow student time to answer.)

s

Great! Now, let's add an A. Let's make the sounds together. What do they say?

să

Let's add one more letter and finish the word. Sound it out with me to make it complete!

săd

Good job! **S**in **s**eparate**s** u**s** from God. It's a very **s**ad thing.

Sometimes, words have some of the same sounds. These are called "word families." Let's take a look at a word family. Here are two letters that we see at the end of words a lot. Can you read this ending sound for me?

ăd

How many words do you think we can make with that ending sound?

(Allow student time to guess.)

Let's take a look and read them together! We already know the ending sound in these words is "ăd", so we just need to say the starting sound and add the ending "ăd" Let's practice!

(Point to each letter and say the sound, then blend the letters together to sound out each word.)

săd

dăd

tăd

Those are just a few of the words we can make, but we have to learn more letters before we can make more! How neat! You've come so far in such a short time. You've traveled quite far on our great big adventure. Next week we'll learn all about God's great plan called Salvation. Now, it's time for some letter S fun!

(Have the student complete the Little Learner Activity Sheet.)

BONUS ACTIVITIES:

(Student has learned N, D, Ă, T, and S so far.)

- Give student a clean piece of paper. Explain how the paper is pure, clean, and perfect — just like God's creation was. Give student a marker and ask him/her to scribble on the paper. Ask the student if the paper is still clean and perfect. Allow time to answer, then say:

  "The paper was like God's creation, and the marker was like sin. God's creation was per-

  fect, but when Adam and Eve disobeyed God, it stained creation with sin. We can't take the marker off the paper, just like Adam and Eve couldn't take back their sin. But thankfully, God loves us so much and He still had a plan to fix their mistake — and we'll learn about it on our next reading adventure!"

- Read the verse together on page 44 on an "off" day.

Let's read the very first verse in the Bible together! I'll read most of it, but I see there is a word you know and can read. I'll point to each word as I read, when we get to the bold word, you can read that.

In the beginning, God created the heavens **ănd** the earth.

(Genesis 1:1)

S s

S is for Sin. Sin separates us from God, it's a very sad thing.

Color the uppercase and lowercase S!

Activity: Draw a line from the big picture to the little picture!

Writing: Let's practice writing the letter **S**!

Activity: Draw a sad face.

P is for **P**lan.
God had a **p**lan to **p**ay the **p**rice for our sin.

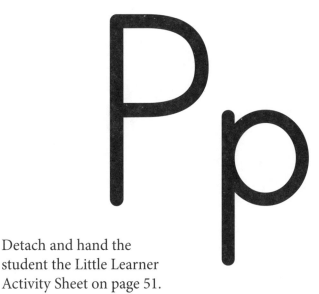

Detach and hand the
student the Little Learner
Activity Sheet on page 51.

LESSON NARRATIVE

This lesson covers the letter P. The sound of the letter P can be heard in the words paid, price, and pepper. As you read through this lesson, place emphasis on the sound of this letter where it is found in bold throughout the text.

Welcome back for another adventure. Do you remember what happened on our last sad adventure?

(Allow student time to answer. Answers should be related to sin, the Fall, etc.)

That's right, last time we learned about the letter S. The S says s. We learned that Adam and Eve disobeyed God's directions in the Garden of Eden. When we disobey God's directions, it is called sin. Sin separates us from God. It's a very sad thing.

In the very best book — called the Bible — we learn in the Book of Romans that we have all sinned:

Everyone has sinned. No one measures up to God's glory (Romans 3:23).

Because of Adam and Eve's sin, our world is no longer perfect the way God created it to be. We see sickness, sadness, and suffering. But worst of all, we all have sinned against God. And because of our sin, we can't be close to God because He is holy — God is sinless.

But your sins have separated you from your God. They have caused him to turn his face away from you. So he won't listen to you (Isaiah 59:2).

When we sin, there are consequences. Adam and Eve had to pay the consequences — the price — for their sinful decision to disobey God. And we must pay the consequences for our sin too. But there is good news! Let's read the good news from the Bible!

When you sin, the pay you get is death. But God gives you the gift of eternal life. That's because of what Christ Jesus our Lord has done (Romans 6:23).

God loves us so much, that even though we had disobeyed, He created a plan to save us! We will learn about God's plan through Jesus as we travel further into our adventure! But for now, we know that God had a **p**lan to **p**ay the **p**rice of sin.

Ooh, I heard a new sound. Did you hear it too? Our letter today is the letter **P**. The **P** says **p**. God had a plan to **p**ay the **p**rice of sin.

Can you say it with me?

The P says **p**. God had a **p**lan to **p**ay the **p**rice of sin.

(Repeat if necessary to reinforce the sound.)

Awesome! The letter **P** looks like this:

P p

(Ask student to trace uppercase and lowercase P with finger on the Little Learner Activity Sheet. Make sure the student points to the correct one.)

The uppercase **P** looks like this:

P

The lowercase **P** looks like this:

p

The uppercase and lowercase **P** look very similar, don't they?

P is for plan. God had a **p**lan to **p**ay the **p**rice of sin.

Now I'm going to read you some words: can you hear the **P** sound in them? If you hear the **P** sound, touch your nose! If you don't hear the **P** sound, don't do anything. Ready?

(Read the following words. Allow student time to answer after each.)

Pretty	Red
Popcorn	Adam
O**pp**osite	**P**op

Great job! We know that God had a **p**lan — we'll be learning more about it with each lesson we do! Let's go have some reading fun!

(Now begin the reading section below. If your child needs to take a break from the lesson, let him or her begin the first page of the Little Learner Activity Sheet. Be sure to go back to the reading section of this lesson to complete it.)

READING

Now you've learned a new letter, let's read a new word!

You remember how it's done! First, we'll start with a P. What sound does the P say?

(Point to letter; allow student time to answer.)

p

Next, we'll add the letter A! The letter A has a symbol to tell you what it says. Can you say the sounds?

(Point to each letter; help student blend sounds.)

And finish it off with a nice letter N! Can you read the word to me?

(Point to each letter. If necessary, help student with sounds and blending.)

Great job! Did you notice that word is part of the "an" word family? Let's try a few more!

I have just one more for you. This one has the "an" right in the middle. Let's try reading it together!

Dăn

tăn

păn

sănd

Wow! That was fun! Have you ever felt the sand between your toes?

(Allow student time to answer.)

(Have the student complete the Little Learner Activity Sheet.)

BONUS ACTIVITIES:

(Student has learned N, D, Ă, T, S, and P so far.)

- Give student a clean piece of paper. Use finger paints (or similar substance) and cover the student's fingers. Then ask the student to pick up the piece of paper without getting it dirty. Explain to student how just as their dirty fingers made the paper dirty and contaminated, sin also made the world dirty and contaminated. But Jesus loves us so much that He had a plan to fix it!

- Go on a letter P expedition! See how many objects at home or out and about you can find that start with the letter P!

- Using washi or painter's tape, tape letters the student has learned. Instruct student to jump onto a letter and say its sound as you call out its name.

- On an "off" day, have your student point out to all the uppercase, or lowercase, letters while saying their names and sounds on page 50.

Ask your student to point to each uppercase letter and say its name and sound. Then, do the same with the lowercase letters.

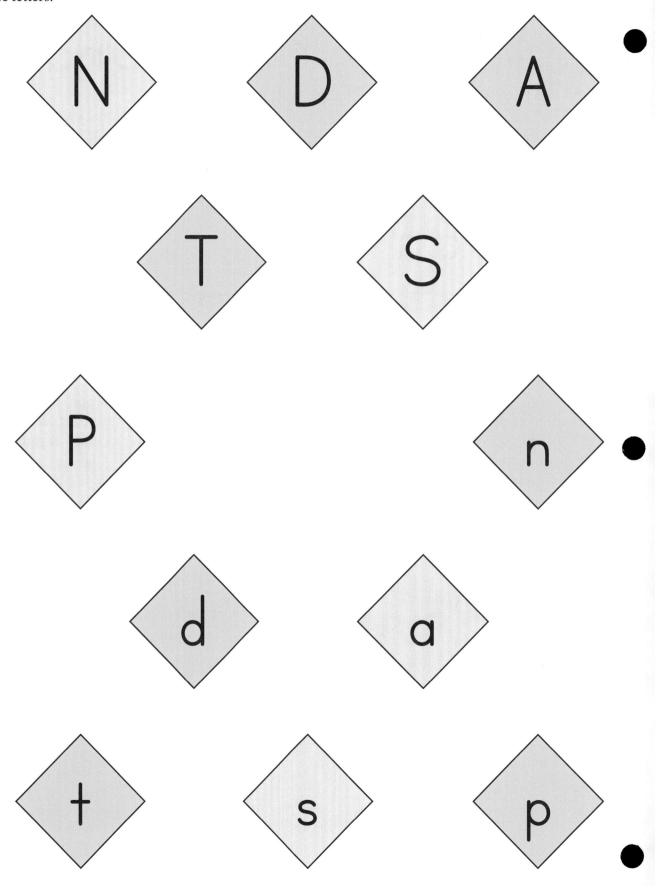

P p

P is for **P**lan. God had a **p**lan to **p**ay the **p**rice for our sin.

The P says p. Color the letter P below!

Letter Recognition: Match the uppercase letter to the lower case.

S

P

D

p

d

s

Writing: Let's practice writing the letter P!

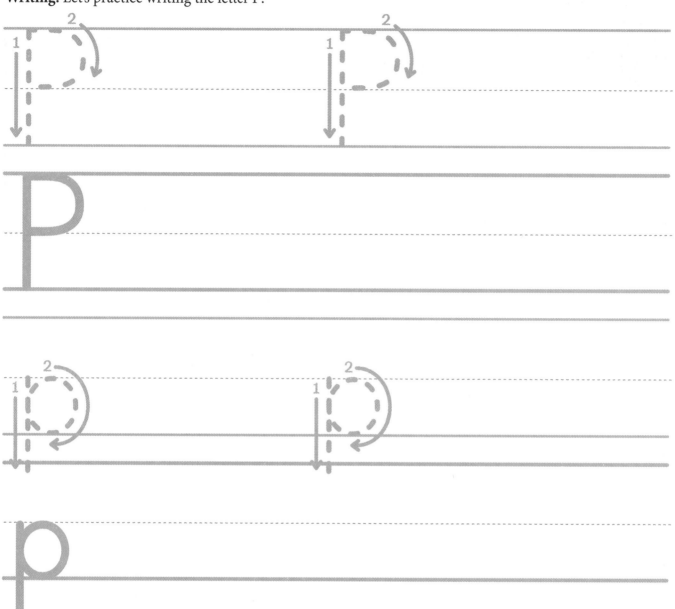

Activity: Purple starts with the letter P. Color the flower purple.

Ĭ is for Imperfect.
Because of sin, the world is now imperfect.

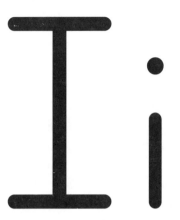

Detach and hand the student the
Little Learner Activity Sheet on page 57.

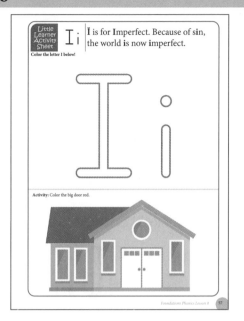

LESSON NARRATIVE

This lesson covers the short sound of the letter I. The short sound is designated within the lesson with the following symbol above the letters: Ĭĭ. The short sound of the letter I can be heard in the words ĭmperfect, ĭll, and ĭs. As you read through this lesson, place emphasis on the sound of this letter where it is found in **bold** *throughout the text.*

Why hello there. Are you back for another reading adventure? Hurray! Did you bring your imagination? Today we are going to explore the world after the Fall of man. As you've already learned, because of sin, the world is now **i**mperfect.

Ooh, did you hear our new sound for today?

I is our new letter today. The **I** says **Ĭ**. Can you say it with me? The **I** says **Ĭ**. Great!

(Repeat if necessary to reinforce the sound.)

Repeat after me: Because of s**i**n, the world **i**s now **i**mperfect.

Yes, after Adam and Eve's sin, the world no longer worked perfectly like God had created it to. Creation became **i**mperfect. Like we've talked about in the last couple lessons, there are consequences for our sins. In Genesis chapter 3, we learn about the consequences God gave for man's sin:

So the LORD God spoke to the serpent. He said, "Because you have done this, you are set apart from all livestock and all wild animals. I am putting a curse on you. You will crawl on your belly. You will eat dust all the days of your life. I will make you and the woman hate each other. Your children and her children will be enemies. Her son will crush your head. And you will bite his heel."

The LORD God said to the woman, "I will increase your pain when you give birth. You will be in great pain when you have children. You will long for your husband. And he will rule over you."

The LORD God said to Adam, "You listened to your wife's suggestion. You ate fruit from the tree I warned you about. I said, 'You must not eat its fruit.' So I am putting a curse on the ground because of what you did. All the days of your life you will have to work hard. It will be painful for you to get food from the ground. You will eat plants from the field, even though the ground produces thorns and prickly weeds. You will have to work hard and sweat a lot to produce the food you eat. You were made out of the ground. You will return to it when you die.

You are dust, and you will return to dust" (Genesis 3:14–19).

Because of sin, things would no longer be easy. Sin had contaminated and broken God's perfect creation. Now there were thorns and thistles. Have you ever been pricked by a thorn?

(Allow student time to answer.)

Everything now required hard work, and there was pain. Because of sin, the world **is** now **i**mperfect. **I** is for imperfect, the **I** says **Ĭ**.

The letter **I** looks like this:

I i

(Help student trace uppercase and lowercase I with finger on the Little Learner Activity Sheet. Make sure the student points to the correct one.)

The uppercase **I** looks like this:

I

And the lowercase **I** looks like this:

i

Remember how we talked about vowels and how vowels can make different sounds? The letter **I** is also a vowel and it makes two special sounds. Today, we will learn just one of those sounds!

We use symbols to tell us what sound the letter **I** makes, so when you see an **I** that looks like this:

Ĭ ĭ

You can be sure that that letter **I** says **ĭ** as in **i**mperfect. We call this sound the "short" I sound.

Adam and Eve's sin had a high cost — they lost the ability to be close with God, the world became an imperfect place to live, they would have to work and experience pain, one day they would die, and they also had to leave their home in the Garden of Eden. Can you imagine how sad they must have been? But like we talked about in our last lesson, God had a plan and He would pay the ultimate price for our sins through Jesus. But before we continue learning about His plan, we need to finish learning about the letter **I**!

Let's play a game. Stand up in front of me. I'm going to read you some words. If you can hear the **ĭ** sound, jump! If the word does not have the **ĭ** sound, don't jump. Ready? Let's go!

Ill	Sound	Try
Imperfect	This	Sour
Hit	Hat	Sit

Great job! That was a lot of fun! Now use your imagination one last time for now. Imagine the garden of Eden and say goodbye. Our next lesson adventure will take us further into the story!

(Begin the reading section. If your child needs to take a break from the lesson, let him or her begin the first page of the Little Learner Activity Sheet. Be sure to go back to the reading section of this lesson to complete it.)

Now, let's try reading some new words! The letter **I** is so much fun, and we can learn a new word family!

(Point to each letter and say the sound, then blend the letters together to sound out the word.)

ĭn

ĭt

ĭs

Those are all words we use quite a lot! Here are some examples:

I am **in** the house.

It is nice outside.

What **is** for dinner?

Let's try reading a few words from the "in" family! We already know the ending, so these won't be hard to read!

pĭn

sĭn

tĭn

Great job! Let's try one more family. How about two more words from the "it" word family? We already know the ending, so these won't be hard to read!

pĭt

sĭt

(Have the student complete the Little Learner Activity Sheet.)

BONUS ACTIVITIES:

(Student has learned N, D, Ă, T, S, P, and Ĭ so far.)

- Write letters the student has learned on sticky tabs, place tabs throughout house. Call out a letter or sound and have student locate it!
- Use sticky tabs to create words; read words with the student.

- Letter bowling: write letters the student has learned on paper or plastic cups. Set up cups in a room and call out a letter or sound. Have student kick a soft ball at the matching letter.
- Practice reading sight words on page 56 on an "off" day with your child.

Practice reading these words.

ăt   ĭt

ăn   ĭn

ăs   ĭs

ănd

I i

Ĭ is for Imperfect. Because of sin, the world is now imperfect.

Color the letter I below!

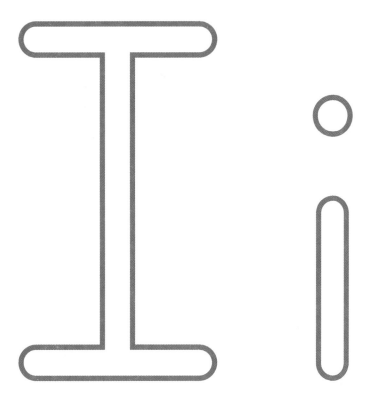

Activity: Color the big door red.

Writing: Let's practice writing the letter I!

Writing: We use these words so much! Read and copy them below.

it   in   is

F is for **F**lood.
During the **F**lood, the earth was **f**illed with water.

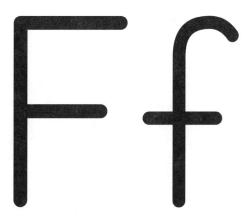

Detach and hand the student the
Little Learner Activity Sheet on page 63.

LESSON NARRATIVE

*This lesson covers the letter F. The sound of the letter F can be heard in the words flood, filled, and fan. As you read through this lesson, place emphasis on the sound of this letter where it is found in **bold** throughout the text.*

Here we are again, ready for another adventure! Put on your seat belt; we are leaving the Fall and traveling over 1,600 years further into the story!

After Adam and Eve left the Garden, they had kids, and then their kids had kids, and their kids had kids. It wasn't long before there were a lot of people on the earth. But sadly, it also wasn't long before man's sinful nature got worse and worse. Things sure weren't pretty — but don't take my word for it; let's read from the very best book. Can you tell me what it is?

(Allow student time to answer "the Bible.")

That's right! Here is what we learn in Genesis 6:5–10:

The LORD saw how bad the sins of everyone on earth had become. They only thought about evil things. The LORD was very sad that he had made human beings on the earth. His heart was filled with pain. So

the LORD said, "I created human beings, but I will wipe them out. I will also destroy the animals, the birds in the sky, and the creatures that move along the ground. I am very sad that I have made human beings." But the LORD was very pleased with Noah.

Here is the story of Noah's family line. Noah was a godly man. He was without blame among the people of his time. He walked faithfully with God. Noah had three sons. Their names were Shem, Ham and Japheth.

Noah was serving God and doing what God had asked of him.

In Genesis 6:11–14 we learn more of the story. Close your eyes and imagine Noah hearing these directions from the Lord:

The earth was very sinful in God's eyes. It was full of people who did mean and harmful things. God saw how sinful the earth had become. All its people were living very sinful lives. So God said to Noah, "I am going to put an end to everyone. They have filled the earth with their harmful acts. I am certainly going to destroy them and the earth. So make yourself an ark out of cypress wood. Make rooms in it. Cover it with tar inside and out."

Noah obeyed God's commands because he had faith that God's word was true — even though there would be years and years before he would see it come to pass.

As we read further, we learn about more directions the Lord gave to Noah:

> Then the LORD said to Noah, "Go into the ark with your whole family. I know that you are a godly man among the people of today. Take seven pairs of every kind of 'clean' animal with you. Take a male and a female of each kind. Take one pair of every kind of animal that is not 'clean.' Take a male and a female of each kind. Also take seven pairs of every kind of bird. Take a male and a female of each kind. Then every kind will be kept alive. They can spread out again over the whole earth. Seven days from now I will send rain on the earth. It will rain for 40 days and 40 nights. I will destroy from the face of the earth every living creature I have made." Noah did everything the LORD commanded him to do (Genesis 7:1–5).

There it is again — Noah trusted God and did just as God had told him to do. How do you think you can start trusting God?

(Allow student time to answer; guide as necessary.)

Finally, the ark was completed and loaded with food, supplies, and animals. Noah and his family entered the ark, and the Bible tells us that God shut the door behind them.

And then, just as God had said it would, it began to rain. And the earth tore apart as the fountains of the deep broke open. For 40 days and 40 nights, it rained. Can you imagine nothing but heavy rain day and night for over a month?

During the **F**lood, the earth was **f**illed with water.

Hmm, there was a new sound in that sentence. Did you hear it?

During the Flood, the earth was filled with water.

F is our letter for today!

The **F** says **f**.

Can you say it with me?

The **F** says **f**. During the **F**lood, the earth was **f**illed with water.

The Bible tells us that the water was higher than even the mountains!

> The waters continued to rise until they covered the mountains by more than 20 feet. Every living thing that moved on land died. The birds, the livestock and the wild animals died. All of the creatures that fill the earth also died. And so did every human being. Every breathing thing on dry land died. Every living thing on earth was wiped out. People and animals were destroyed. The creatures that move along the ground and the birds in the sky were wiped out. Everything on earth was destroyed. Only Noah and those with him in the ark were left. The waters flooded the earth for 150 days (Genesis 7:20–24).

During the **F**lood, the earth was **f**illed with water.

The letter **F** looks like this:

(Ask student to trace uppercase and lowercase F with finger on the Little Learner Activity Sheet. Make sure the student points to the correct one.)

The uppercase **F** looks like this:

The lowercase **F** looks like this:

The **F** says **f**. During the **F**lood, the earth was **f**illed with water. In our next lesson we will learn about a special promise from God. But for today, let's go have some letter fun!

(Now begin the reading section below. If your child needs to take a break from the lesson, let him or her begin the first page of the Little Learner Activity Sheet. Be sure to go back to the reading section of this lesson to complete it.)*

READING

Are you ready to read some new words? Let's practice words from the "it" word family!

sĭt

fĭt

pĭt

Great job! Now let's try words from the "an" word family. We already know the ending, so these won't be hard!

păn

făn

tăn

sănd

(Have the student complete the Little Learner Activity Sheet.)

BONUS ACTIVITIES:

(Student has learned N, D, Ă, T, S, P, Ĭ, and F so far.)

- Write letters the student has learned on blue sheets of paper. Cut paper into "puddle"-like shapes. Tell the student there has been a rainstorm and the room is full of puddles. Call out a letter and have student jump "in" the puddle as they call out the sound!

- Use the puddle sheets from above to spell out simple words for the student to read. See how many puddle words you can read together.

- Call out a letter the student has learned. See if you can find an object that starts with that letter together!

- Read the review on page 62 with your student on an "off" day.

We've learned so much. Let's see how much we can remember. Look at the words below. I see lots of words that you know! I'll point to each word as I read, and when we get to the large word, you can read those ones.

Ăt the start, there was nothing, none, not even a bit. But ĭt wasn't for long, because God started creating. Throughout all of creation, God placed grand design—from the itty-bitty ănt to all of mankind. A is for Adam, who God told to obey. But Adam ănd Eve turn to their own way. Sin separates us from God; it is a very săd thing. Though the world is now imperfect by sin, God still had a plan to pay the high price.

Little Learner Activity Sheet

F f

F is for **Flood**. During the **Flood**, the earth was **filled** with water.

Color the upper and lowercase F.

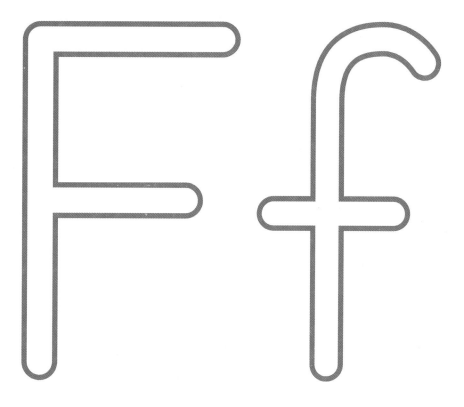

Activity: Fish starts with the letter F. Color the fish below green and yellow.

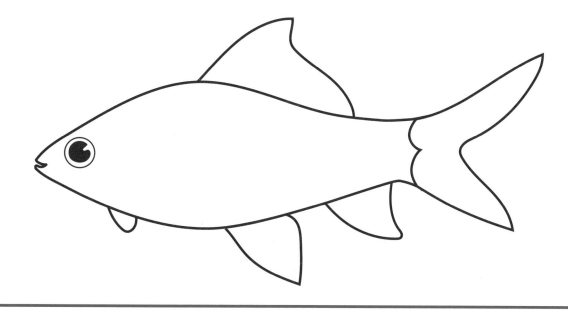

Writing: The ability to write is a special skill God gave us, so let's practice writing the letter F!

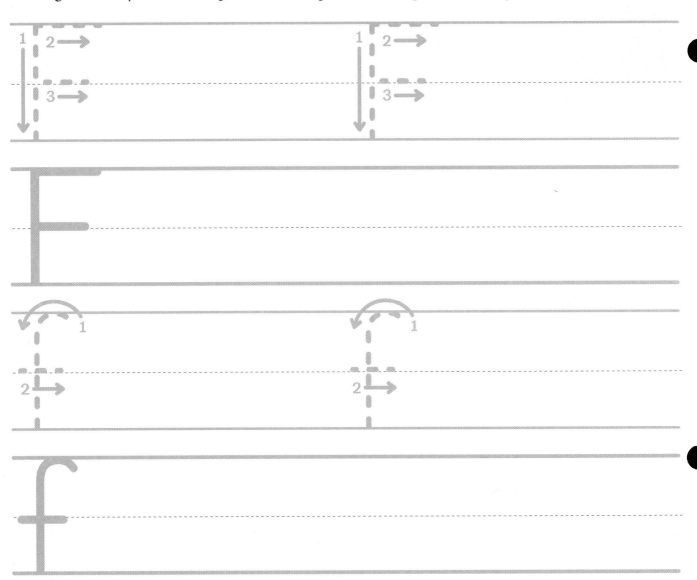

Reading: Do you remember these words? Can you read them for me?

ăs   ăn

ăt   ănd

Ŏ is for **Offered**. After the waters went down, Noah **offered G**o**d** a sacrifice.

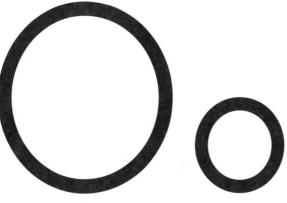

Detach and hand the student the Little Learner Activity Sheet on page 69.

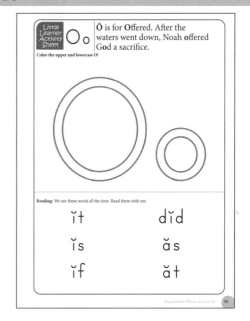

LESSON NARRATIVE

*This lesson covers the short sound of the letter O. The short sound is designated within the lesson with the following symbol above the letters: Ŏŏ. The short sound of the letter O can be heard in the words ŏffer, dŏwn, and ŏdd. As you read through this lesson, place emphasis on the sound of this letter where it is found in **bold** throughout the text.*

We've been learning a lot these last few weeks! I hope you've brought your imagination with you again today. We will be finishing the story of Noah and the ark! When we left off last time, it had rained for 40 days and 40 nights — and the earth was covered in water!

But God showed concern for Noah. He also showed concern for all the wild animals and livestock that were with Noah in the ark. So God sent a wind to sweep over the earth. And the waters began to go down. The springs at the bottom of the oceans had been closed. The windows of the sky had also been closed. And the rain had stopped falling from the sky. The water on the earth continued to go down. At the end of the 150 days the water had gone down. On the 17th day of the seventh month, the ark came to rest on the mountains of Ararat. The waters continued to go down until the tenth month. On the first day of that month, the tops of the mountains could be seen (Genesis 8:1–5).

It took time for the water to dry and for dry land to appear. Noah and his family continued to wait in the ark until the earth was dry again. And then finally, the Bible tells us about what must have been a very exciting day for Noah and his family:

It was the first day of the first month of Noah's 601st year. The water on the earth had dried up. Then Noah removed the covering from the ark. He saw that the surface of the ground was dry. By the 27th day of the second month the earth was completely dry. Then God said to Noah, "Come out of the ark. Bring your wife and your sons and their wives with you. Bring out every kind of living thing that is with you. Bring the birds, the animals, and all the creatures that move along the ground. Then they can multiply on the earth. They can have little ones and the number of them can increase (Genesis 8:13–17).

Can you imagine what it must have been like as they left the ark? The world was completely different from what they had always known. Everything they once knew had been destroyed in the Flood. But rather than be sad, angry, or afraid, Noah took time to worship the Lord.

Then Noah built an altar to honor the LORD. He took some of the "clean" animals and birds. He sacrificed them on the altar as burnt offerings. The smell of the offerings pleased the LORD. He said to himself, "I will never put a curse on the ground again because of human beings. I will not do it even though their hearts are always directed toward evil. Their thoughts are evil from the time they are young. I will never destroy all living things again, as I have just done (Genesis 8:20–21).

God put the rainbow in the sky to remind us of His promise to never flood the earth again. After the waters went down, Noah offered God a sacrifice.

O is our new sound for today! The O says Ŏ. After the waters went down, Noah **o**ffered G**o**d a sacrifice.

Can you say it with me? The O says Ŏ.

The letter O looks like this:

(Ask student to trace uppercase and lowercase O with finger on the Little Learner Activity Sheet. Make sure the student points to the correct one.)

The uppercase O looks like this:

The lowercase O looks like this:

They both look very similar, don't they? One is just bigger than the other! O is another vowel, which means it can make different sounds. When you see an O with this symbol on top, you can be sure that the O says Ŏ! We call this the "short" sound.

After the waters went down, Noah offered God a sacrifice. Now it's time to wave goodbye to Noah and his family. It's time for some more letter fun!

(Now begin the reading section. If your child needs to take a break from the lesson, let him or her begin the first page of the Little Learner Activity Sheet. Be sure to go back to the reading section of this lesson to complete it.)

Let's read some words, including some with our new letter O!

Sometimes, words have two of the same letter right in a row. When we see two of the same letters right in a row, we just say the letter's sound once. Let's give it a try!

ŏff

Great job! We use that word when we say, "Turn **off** the light," or "Take **off** your coat." How do you think you could use the word **off**?

(Allow student time to answer.)

Some words are very silly and their letters don't like to follow the rules. The letters in these silly words say different sounds. Let's learn one of these words!

"Of" is a silly word—when we read it, it sounds like "uh-v". The o and the f in "of" don't say their usual sounds. When we see the word

we say "uh-v".

> *When you reach the word "of" on the following page, pause and give your student a moment to recognize and read this silly word. If your student is unsure, that is ok! Read "of" together (you can even make a silly face while reading it!) and continue through the rest of the verse. "Of" should now be added to the list of sight words the student is practicing.*

(Have the student complete the Little Learner Activity Sheet.)

BONUS ACTIVITIES:

(Student has learned N, D, Ă, T, S, P, Ĭ, F, and Ŏ so far.)

- Write letters the student has learned on pieces of paper. Spread the papers out on the floor, and give the student a bean-bag (or similar object). Instruct the student to toss the beanbag onto the letter sheet and say the sound as you call out the letter's name.

- Use sheets from above to create words for the student to read.

- Spread play-dough out flat and have student use a plastic butter knife to carve letters into the clay! Alternatively, carve words into the clay and ask student to read the word, then roll up the clay and start again!

- On an "off" day, read the verse on page 68 with your child and let him or her read the large words throughout.

Faith is trusting that God will do what He says He will. Noah had faith when he built the ark and that God would take care of them. Let's read a Bible verse about faith. I'll point to each word as I read, and when we get to the large words, you can read those.

Faith ĭs being sure of what we hope for. Ĭt ĭs being sure of what we do nŏt see. (Hebrews 11:1)

When you are doing these bonus activities that include Bible verses, it is a great idea to take time and ask the student simple questions such as what they think about the verse or discuss the meaning of it to make sure they are understanding these important concepts. On a longer verse, go through each line and discuss it.

Ŏ is for **Offered**. After the waters went down, Noah **offered** G**o**d a sacrifice.

Color the upper and lowercase O!

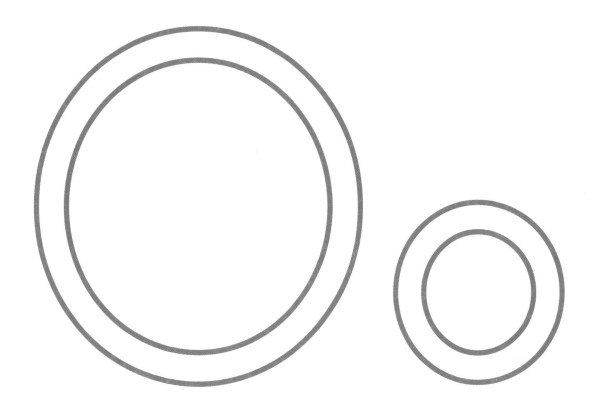

Reading: We see these words all the time. Read them with me.

ĭt   dĭd

ĭs   ăs

ĭf   ăt

Writing: The letter O is so much fun to write because it is a circle, so let's practice!

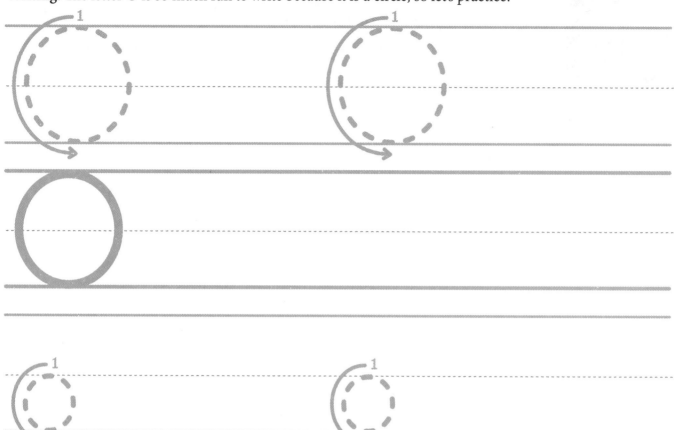

Activity: Draw a line from the uppercase letter to the matching lowercase letter!

D   t   S   o

N   a   I   f

T   p   O   s

A   n   F   i

P   d

B is for **B**abel.
Men **b**uilt a tower at **B**abel with **b**ricks.

Bb

Detach and hand the student the
Little Learner Activity Sheet on page 75.

LESSON NARRATIVE

This lesson covers the letter B. The sound of the letter B can be heard in the words built, Babel, and bricks. As you read through this lesson, place emphasis on the sound of this letter where it is found in bold throughout the text.

Get your imagination started. We've got another adventure today! After the Flood, Noah and his family worked hard. They had children, and their children had children, and their children had children — and it wasn't long before there were a lot of people on the earth again, just like before the Flood. However, it didn't take long before man's sin nature got in the way again. We can read the whole story in Genesis chapter 11:

> The whole world had only one language, and everyone spoke it. They moved to the east and found a broad valley in Babylon. There they made their home.
>
> They said to one another, "Come on! Let's make bricks and bake them well." They used bricks instead of stones. They used tar to hold the bricks together. Then they said, "Come on! Let's build a city for ourselves. Let's build a tower that reaches to the sky.

> We'll make a name for ourselves. Then we won't be scattered over the whole earth."
>
> But the LORD came down to see the city and the tower the people were building. He said, "All these people are united and speak the same language. That is why they can do all this. Now they will be able to do anything they plan. Come on! Let us go down and mix up their language. Then they will not be able to understand one other."
>
> So the LORD scattered them from there over the whole earth. And they stopped building the city. There the LORD mixed up the language of the whole world. That's why the city was called Babel. From there the LORD scattered them over the whole earth (Genesis 11:1–9).

Men **b**uilt a tower at **B**abel with **b**ricks.

Oh my, did you hear that new sound? Hmm, let's read that again: Men **b**uilt a tower at **B**abel with **b**ricks.

The letter **B** is our new letter for the day! The **B** says **b**. Men **b**uilt a tower at **B**abel with **b**ricks.

Can you say it with me?

The **B** says **b**.

(Repeat if necessary to reinforce the sound to the student.)

The letter **B** looks like this:

B b

(Ask student to trace uppercase and lowercase B with finger on the Little Learner Activity Sheet. Make sure the student points to the correct one.)

The uppercase **B** looks like this:

B

The lowercase **B** looks like this:

b

Men **b**uilt a tower at **B**abel with **b**ricks. But God **b**roke their plan by confusing their languages!

Can you imagine how confusing it must have been? Imagine as I am talking to you, if all of a sudden I started speaking in a language you couldn't

understand! And when you tried to tell me you couldn't understand, I couldn't understand you either! How do you think you would have felt?

(Allow student time to answer.)

It must have been very frustrating and confusing! Pretty soon, one person found someone who spoke the same language, and someone else found a few people speaking the same language. As groups of people found others who spoke the same language, they left the city at Babel together and spread out into different parts of the world. We are still reminded of what happened at the Tower of **B**abel today when we study different countries and their languages. Not only did God make people all different, He also made our languages all different! Can you think of another language?

(Allow student time to answer; guide as necessary, e.g., Spanish, French, etc.)

Men **b**uilt a tower at **B**abel with **b**ricks. **B**ut God **b**roke their plan by confusing their languages! The **B** says **b**. Wow, what an adventure! Now it's time for some more letter fun!

(Now begin the reading section. If your child needs to take a break from the lesson, let him or her begin the first page of the Little Learner Activity Sheet. Be sure to go back to the reading section of this lesson to complete it.)

READING

Let's practice reading. Let's try this sound first:

(Point to each letter and say the sound, then blend the letters together to sound out the word.)

Now, we know what those two letters say when they are together. Let's add different starting sounds to make a new word family!

Great job! Do you remember the sound these letters make together?

We already know the ending sound in these words. Now let's add different sounds at the start and make new words!

(Have the student complete the Little Learner Activity Sheet.)

BONUS ACTIVITIES:

(Student has learned N, D, Ă, T, S, P, Ĭ, F, Ŏ, and B so far.)

- Build a tower with letter blocks using letters the student has learned. Ask student to say the name and sound on each block as you build the tower.

- See how many objects the student can find that start with the letter B either at home or while you are out and about!

- Form simple words on the fridge using letter magnets for the student to read.

- Call out letter sounds and ask student to say the name of each letter.

- Look at a globe or world map that shows the various languages spoken in each country.

- Complete activity on page 74 on an "off" day.

Point to each brick with the letter B!

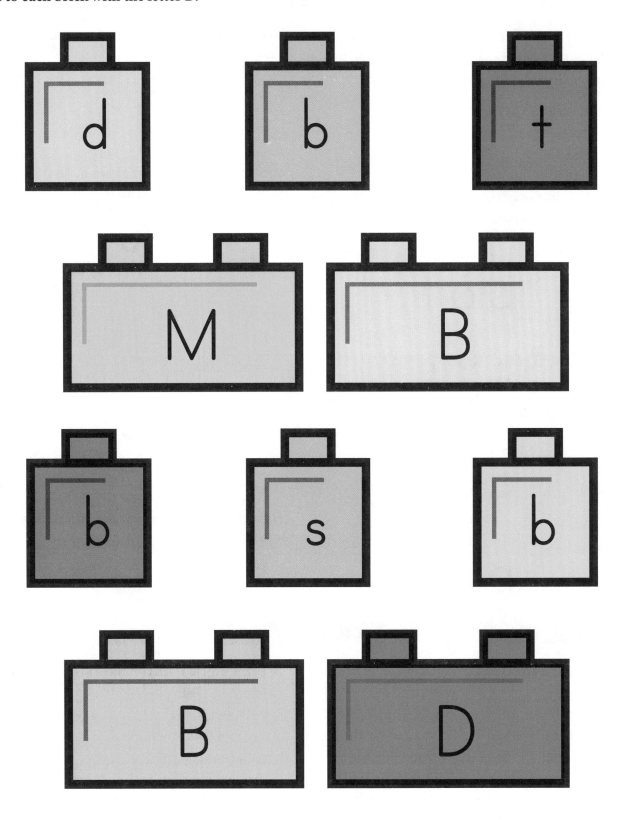

B b

B is for **Bab**el. Men **b**uilt a tower at **Bab**el with **b**ricks.

Color the upper and lowercase B!

Activity: Circle the pictures that start with the letter B.

Activity: Can you think of another "an" word that goes with this picture? Write the letter in the space.

Writing: Writing is a special skill God gave us, so let's practice writing the letter B!

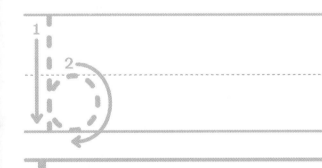

Review

N D Ă

T S P Ĭ

F Ŏ B

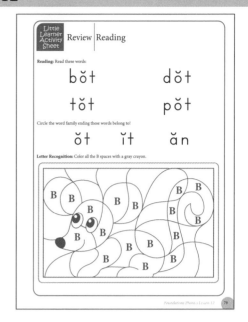

Detach and hand the student the Little
Learner Activity Sheet on page 79.

LESSON NARRATIVE

Whew! We have learned so very much on our reading adventure so far! We've learned about the letter T. What sound does the T say?

(Allow student time to answer.)

Right! The T says t. God told Adam to obey. Do you remember what letter we learned next?

(Allow student time to answer; answer should be S.)

Next was the letter S. The letter S says s. Sin separates us from God — it's a very sad thing. Though it is sad, we also learned there is hope, because God had a plan! What letter makes the p sound?

(Allow student time to answer; answer should be P.)

The letter P! God had a plan to pay the price for our sin.

But what happened to the world after sin?

(Allow student time to answer.)

Because of sin, the world is now imperfect. Imperfect starts with the letter I! The I says ĭ. Can you tell me what kind of special letter the letter I is?

(Allow student time to answer; answer should be "vowel.")

The letter I is a vowel; vowels can make different sounds! After we learned the letter I we traveled much further into history — can you tell me what happened next?

(Allow student time to answer; "Flood" or "Babel" are correct answers.)

Next came the Flood — what happened during the Flood?

(Allow student time to answer.)

During the Flood, the earth was filled with water. The letter F says f. Next we learned that after the waters went down, Noah offered God a sacrifice. Do you remember what letter we learned in that lesson?

(Allow student time to answer; answer is O.)

We learned the letter O! The O says ŏ! The letter O is also a vowel — what does that mean?

(Allow student time to answer; answer should be it can make different sounds.)

O is a vowel. It makes different sounds! Vowels are super cool, aren't they? And finally, can you tell me what we learned in our last lesson?

(Allow student time to answer; answer should be about the Tower of Babel or letter B)

We learned that men built a tower at Babel with bricks. The letter B says b.

Now, can you point to each letter and tell me the name and the sound?

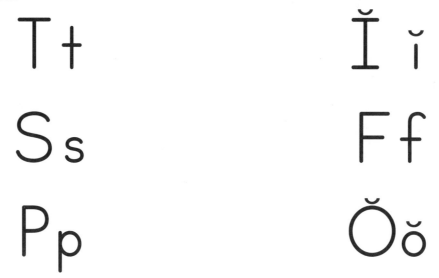

Tt

Ss

Pp

Ĭ ĭ

Ff

Ŏ ŏ

(Student has learned N, D, Ă, T, S, P, Ĭ, F, Ŏ, and B so far.)

- Use letter fridge magnets or similar loose letters to practice word families with student. Read each new word you create.

- Point out words the student has read when he/she uses them in conversation to reinforce the connection between speech and reading, and have the student point out when he/she hears or sees one of the words discussed in daily life.

Review | Reading

Reading: Read these words:

bŏt   dŏt

tŏt   pŏt

Circle the word family ending these words belong to!

 ŏt   ĭt   ăn

Letter Recognition: Color all the B spaces with a gray crayon.

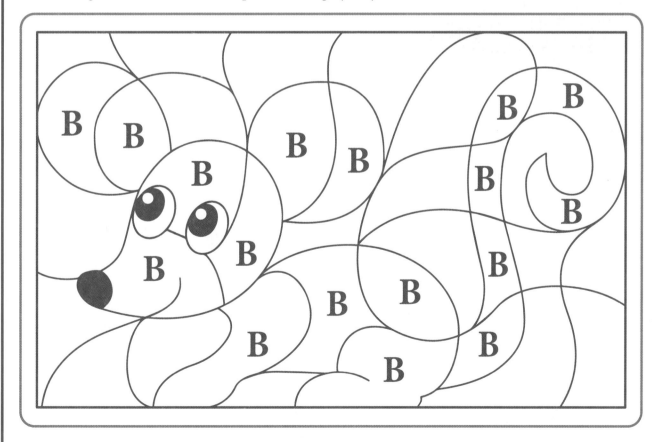

Activity: Let's practice "an" words! Look at each picture and choose the right beginning letter. Write it in the space.

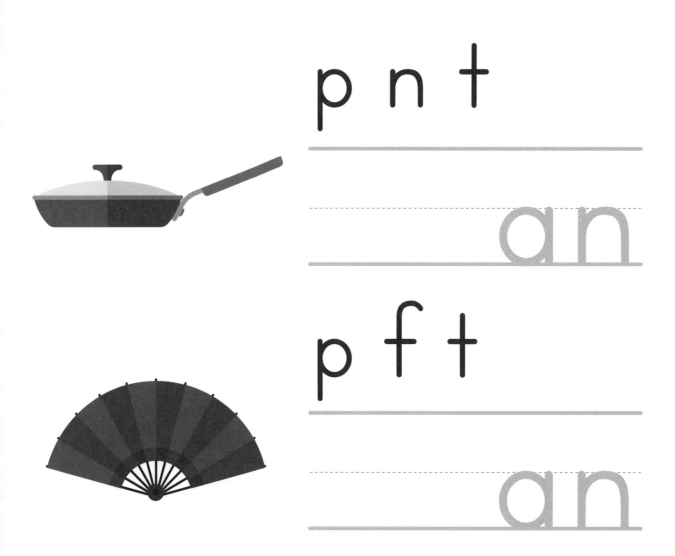

p n t

_____

_____ an

p f t

_____

_____ an

Letter Recognition: Draw a line from each uppercase letter to its matching lowercase letter!

F   s

P   p

N   f

D   d

S   n

Ā is for **Abraham**.
God changed **Abram**'s name to **Abraham**.

Detach and hand the student the
Little Learner Activity Sheet on page 85.

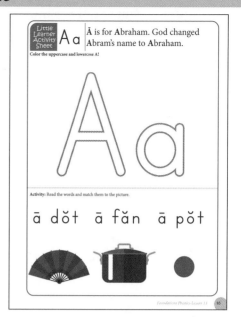

LESSON NARRATIVE

This lesson covers the long sound of the letter A. The long sound is designated within the lesson with the following symbol above the letters: Āā. The long sound of the letter A can be heard in the words Ābraham, pāid, and bāit. As you read through this lesson, place emphasis on the sound of this letter where it is found in **bold** *throughout the text.*

It's a new week, and we'll be learning about some special people this week! As we continue reading the very best book, the Bible, we meet a special man named Abram. As we meet Abram, we find out that God gave him a special promise:

> The LORD had said to Abram, "Go from your country, your people and your father's family. Go to the land I will show you. I will make you into a great nation. And I will bless you. I will make your name great. You will be a blessing to others. I will bless those who bless you. I will put a curse on anyone who puts a curse on you. All nations on earth will be blessed because of you" (Genesis 12:1–3).

How do you think Abram felt when the Lord told him to leave his country? That meant leaving everything he knew and traveling to places he didn't know, and maybe didn't understand. What would you have done?

(Allow student time to answer.)

Like Noah before him, Abram was faithful to the Lord. He followed God's directions and trusted that the promise God had given him was true. So Abram went out and did as the Lord instructed him. He had many adventures, more than I can tell you about in this little lesson! As a man, sometimes Abram got scared, he lied and made mistakes — but we know that he also continued to believe the Lord. Genesis 15:6 (NKJV) says:

> And he believed in the LORD, and He accounted it to him for righteousness.

We read about another amazing promise the Lord gave Abram:

> The LORD took Abram outside and said, "Look up at the sky. Count the stars, if you can." Then he said to him, "That's how many children will be born into your family" (Genesis 15:5).

When we look at the night sky — and all the amazing stars the Lord created, we are also reminded of this promise God gave to Abram!

God gave Abram many special promises, and God changed Abram's name to Abraham.

This is my covenant with you. You will be the father of many nations. You will not be called Abram anymore. Your name will be Abraham, because I have made you a father of many nations. I will greatly increase the number of your children after you. Nations and kings will come from you. I will make my covenant with you last forever. It will be between me and you and your family after you for all time to come. I will be your God. And I will be the God of all your family after you. You are now living in Canaan as an outsider. But I will give you the whole land of Canaan. You will own it forever and so will all your family after you. And I will be their God (Genesis 17:4–8).

God changed **Abram's** name to **Abraham**. Huh — did you hear a new sound? Let's listen again. God changed **Abram's** name to **Abraham**. Our letter today is the letter A! Remember, the A is a vowel; it makes different sounds. Today's A says its name. The A says **ā**, as in **Abraham**!

The letter A looks like this:

(Ask student to trace uppercase and lowercase A with finger on the Little Learner Activity Sheet.)

The letter A is a vowel, it makes different sounds. When you see a letter A that looks like this:

You can be sure that that letter A says **ā** as in **Abraham**. We call that sound the "long" A sound. God changed **Abram's** name to **Abraham**.

Can you tell me what sound "short" letter A says?

Great! Now what sound does the "long" A say?

Awesome! Let's go have some fun!

(Now begin the reading section. If your child needs to take a break from the lesson, let him or her begin the first page of the Little Learner Activity Sheet. Be sure to go back to the reading section of this lesson to complete it.)

The letter A often comes before another word. When the A comes first, it makes the long A sound. Let's give it a try. Read the phrases below:

(Point to each letter and say the sound, then blend the letters together to sound out the word.)

ā dǒt

ā fǎn

ā pǒt

ā tǒt

Can you think of other words or sentences you use the letter A in?

Sometimes in a word, letters don't say anything at all. When you see a letter that is gray in these lessons, that letter is silent. You can skip right over it as you sound out the word. Ready? Let's give it a try:

pāid

Great job! Let's try another one:

bāit

(Have the student complete the Little Learner Activity Sheet.)

BONUS ACTIVITIES:

(Student has learned N, D, Ǎ, T, S, P, Ǐ, F, Ǒ, B, and Ā so far.)

- Make sugar cookie dough, and use letter cookie cutters or shape into letters the student has learned. Bake cookies and enjoy after putting together some words to read!

- Use washi or painter's tape on the floor (test inconspicuous area first) to make letters the student has learned. Call out a letter or sound and have student jump on the letter.

- Using letters taped to the floor, call out a letter and have student jump on the letter and think of a work that starts with that sound. Help as necessary.

- Finger paint letters the student has learned thus far.

- Read review on page 84 with your student on an "off" day.

Children may feel intimidated by the size of this passage. If so, read the whole passage out-loud to them first. Then point out the words they know as you read through it a second time. Take a break and return if necessary; don't feel pressured to complete it all in one sitting.

But mankind continued to **sĭn** and disobey God, so God sent the flood. During the flood the earth was filled with water. After the water had gone down, Noah offered God a sacrifice. God blessed his family **ănd** the family grew **ănd** grew. Before long, there were many people. But they still didn't listen to God, they built a tower with bricks. **Ăt** the tower of Babel, God confused their languages. The people went out all over the earth.

A a

Ā is for Abraham. God changed Abram's name to Abraham.

Color the uppercase and lowercase A!

Activity: Read the words and match them to the picture.

ā dŏt   ā făn   ā pŏt

Activity: Let's practice our letters! Use your finger or a crayon to trace from letter to letter as you sing the alphabet song!

Ī is for **I**saac.
Isaac was Abraham's son.

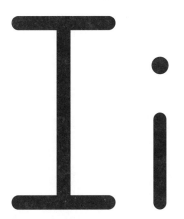

Detach and hand the student the
Little Learner Activity Sheet on page 89.

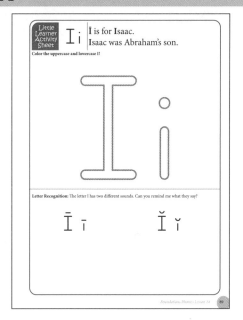

LESSON NARRATIVE

> *This lesson covers the long sound of the letter I. The long sound is designated within the lesson with the following symbol above the letters: Īī. The long sound of the letter I can be heard in the words Īsaac and īce. As you read through this lesson, place emphasis on the sound of this letter where it is found in* **bold** *throughout the text.*

Phew, we've covered a lot of ground this week so far, and today we are going to cover much more! After God changed Abram's name to Abraham, He gave Abraham and his wife another special promise:

> God also said to Abraham, "Do not continue to call your wife by the name Sarai. Her name will be Sarah. I will give her my blessing. You can be sure that I will give you a son by her. I will bless her so that she will be the mother of nations. Kings of nations will come from her."

Abraham fell with his face to the ground. He laughed and said to himself, "Can a 100-year-old man have a son? Can Sarah have a child at the age of 90?" (Genesis 17:15–17)

Sometimes when God gives us a promise we don't see the promise — we see all the reasons it couldn't

happen, just like Abraham did. But we know that when God says something, it is true and we can believe it. Later on, when Sarah heard of God's promise, she also laughed, because she could not see how God could fulfill His word to them. But Abraham and Sarah learned an important lesson — when God speaks, it is true!

> The LORD was gracious to Sarah, just as he had said he would be. The LORD did for Sarah what he had promised to do. Sarah became pregnant. She had a son by Abraham when he was old. The child was born at the exact time God had promised. Abraham gave the name Isaac to the son Sarah had by him (Genesis 21:1–3).

Isaac was Abraham's son. Did you hear that new sound? I is our new letter for today! The letter I says ī. **I**saac was Abraham's son.

Can you say it with me? The **I** says ī.

(Repeat if necessary to reinforce the sound to the student.)

Great! The letter I looks like this:

Ii

(Ask student to trace uppercase and lowercase I with finger on the Little Learner Activity Sheet. Make sure the student points to the correct one.)

The letter I is a vowel, remember? Vowels can make different sounds. We've already learned the I says ĭ as in imperfect. The letter I can also say its name as it does in Isaac. The I says ī. When you see a letter I that looks like this:

Ī ī

You can be sure it says its name! When a vowel says its name, that is called the "long" sound.

God's promises to Abraham were true, and God gave Abraham and Sarah a son — just like He said He would! We learn in the Bible that God's promises are true — we can trust what He says! Now close your eyes and imagine — wave goodbye to baby Isaac! In our next lesson he will be all grown up. But for now, we've learned a new letter and it's time for some fun!

(Now begin the reading section below. If your child needs to take a break from the lesson, let him or her begin the first page of the Little Learner Activity Sheet. Be sure to go back to the reading section of this lesson to complete it.)

READING

When the letter I is all alone, it makes the long I sound; it says its name! We use the I to talk about ourselves. Let's take a look. Can you read these phrases?

Ī dĭd

Ī sĭt

Ī bĭt

Great job! Can you think of some other phrases you would use the letter I in?

(Have the student complete the Little Learner Activity Sheet.)

BONUS ACTIVITIES:

(Student has learned N, D, Ă, T, S, P, Ĭ, F, Ŏ, B, Ā, and Ī so far.)

- Use fridge magnets to spell words for the student to practice reading.
- Help student finger paint words using letters he/ she has learned (see list above).

- Cut a pool noodle into 26 pieces. Use a permanent marker to write the letters of the alphabet on them (set aside letters the student hasn't learned for now). Use the pieces to put together words for the student to read, or practice letters and sounds by having the student toss the letter into a bin while saying its name and sound.

Little Learner Activity Sheet

I i | **Ī** is for **I**saac.
Isaac was Abraham's son.

Color the uppercase and lowercase I!

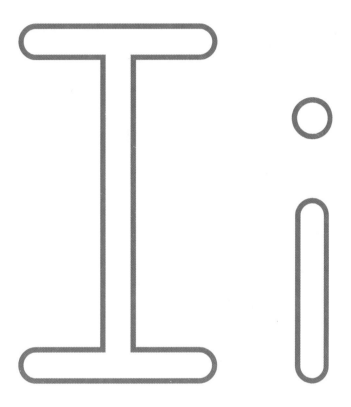

Letter Recognition: The letter I has two different sounds. Can you remind me what they say?

Letter Recognition: Oh no! These letters have forgotten their sound! Can you point to each one and say the sound to remind them?

n   d   ă

t   s   p

ĭ   f   ŏ

b   ā   ī

Å is for **Altar**.
A lamb was provided for the **altar**.

Detach and hand the student the
Little Learner Activity Sheet on page 93.

LESSON NARRATIVE

> 💡 *This lesson covers the final sound of the letter A. This sound is designated within the lesson with the following symbol above the letters: Åå. This sound can be called the schwa or neutral sound, and the proper pronunciation can be heard in the words ǻltar, ǻrm, and tǻr. As you read through this lesson, place emphasis on the sound of this letter where it is found in **bold** throughout the text.*

We are going further into our Bible adventure today, and it's a special day! Vowels are special letters because they make different sounds. We've already learned two of the sounds the letter A makes; can you tell me what they are?

(Allow student time to answer Ā, Ă; remind if necessary.)

Well, the letter A makes one more special sound — today we will learn the last sound!

We've learned about Abraham and how though he was a man who sometimes made mistakes, he trusted and followed God. We also learned that God gave Abraham many special promises; one of them was that Abraham would finally have a son. We learned about his son, Isaac, in our last lesson. Today we will learn a little bit more about Isaac's story.

Sometimes we take our focus off of God and we make other things more important than Him. And sometimes God asks us to give up things that are important to us, so that we can be reminded that God is really the most important thing in our lives.

Isaac grew and must have had many, many adventures! But when he was older, he had a very strange adventure and God showed him and his father Abraham something very special about His plan.

> Some time later God tested Abraham. He said to him, "Abraham!"
>
> "Here I am," Abraham replied.
>
> Then God said, "Take your son, your only son. He is the one you love. Take Isaac. Go to the place called Moriah. Give your son to me there as a burnt offering. Sacrifice him on the mountain I will show you" (Genesis 22:1–2).

This must have seemed very strange to Abraham! Abraham had waited a long time to have a son. He had trusted in God's promise and now that it had finally come to pass, God was asking him to give up his son. Abraham had learned many times in his life that God could be trusted, so he followed God's directions again.

Now Isaac must have seen his father offer many sacrifices to God before, but on this day he noticed something odd. As they walked, he called out:

Then Isaac said to his father Abraham, "Father?"

"Yes, my son?" Abraham replied.

"The fire and wood are here," Isaac said. "But where is the lamb for the burnt offering?"

Abraham answered, "God himself will provide the lamb for the burnt offering, my son." And the two of them walked on together (Genesis 22:7–8).

Finally, they reached the top of the mountain together and built the altar. Abraham did as the Lord had instructed him and laid Isaac on the altar — and then, something amazing happened! Let's read it from the Bible!

But the angel of the LORD called out to him from heaven. He said, "Abraham! Abraham!" "Here I am," Abraham replied. "Do not lay a hand on the boy," he said. "Do not harm him. Now I know that you would do anything for God. You have not held back from me your son, your only son." Abraham looked around. There in a bush he saw a ram caught by its horns. He went over and took the ram. He sacrificed it as a burnt offering instead of his son. So Abraham named that place The LORD Will Provide. To this day people say, "It will be provided on the mountain of the LORD" (Genesis 22:11–14).

God had given Abraham and Isaac special promises, and the adventure they had on this day was a picture of another special promise. You see, years and years further along into the story, God would send His Son — His only Son named Jesus — to the world to be the sacrifice for our sins. Jesus was called the "Lamb of God." The Lord provided the ultimate lamb for the altar to save us from sin — and we will learn more about that as we continue learning!

But for today, we have learned that a lamb was provided for the **a**ltar. Our letter for today is the letter A again! The letter A is a vowel, and it makes three different sounds! We've already learned it says ă as in Adam, and ā as in Abraham. The last sound the letter A can make is å as in altar. When you see a letter A that looks like this

you can be sure it says å as in altar! Let's play a game; if you hear the Å sound in a word, put your finger on your nose! Ready, set go!

C**a**r	Set	**A**re
Leap	F**a**r	Can
M**a**r	T**a**r	

Awesome! Today we learned that a lamb was provided for the **a**ltar, and many years later God would send Jesus Christ, who was called the Lamb of God, to save us from our sins. Now let's go have some more letter fun!

(Have the student complete the Little Learner Activity Sheet.)

BONUS ACTIVITIES:

(Student has learned N, D, Ă, T, S, P, Ĭ, F, Ŏ, B, Ā, Ī, and Å so far.)

- Help student draw or paint three pictures of objects that have a letter A in their name (e.g., car, can, cape).

- Practice reading more words together using letters the student has learned.

- Use building blocks to practice letters the student has learned. Help student form words and read them together!

A a

Å is for **A**ltar.
A lamb was provided for the **a**ltar.

In our lesson today, we learned a lamb was provided for the altar. Color the picture of the lamb!

Letter Recognition: On no! Something got scrambled. I can't seem to remember the sounds! Can you point to each letter A and tell me its sound? Remember to look at the symbol. It will remind you what sound each one says!

Ăă

Åå

Āā

Letter Recognition: Color the circles that have the letter A inside!

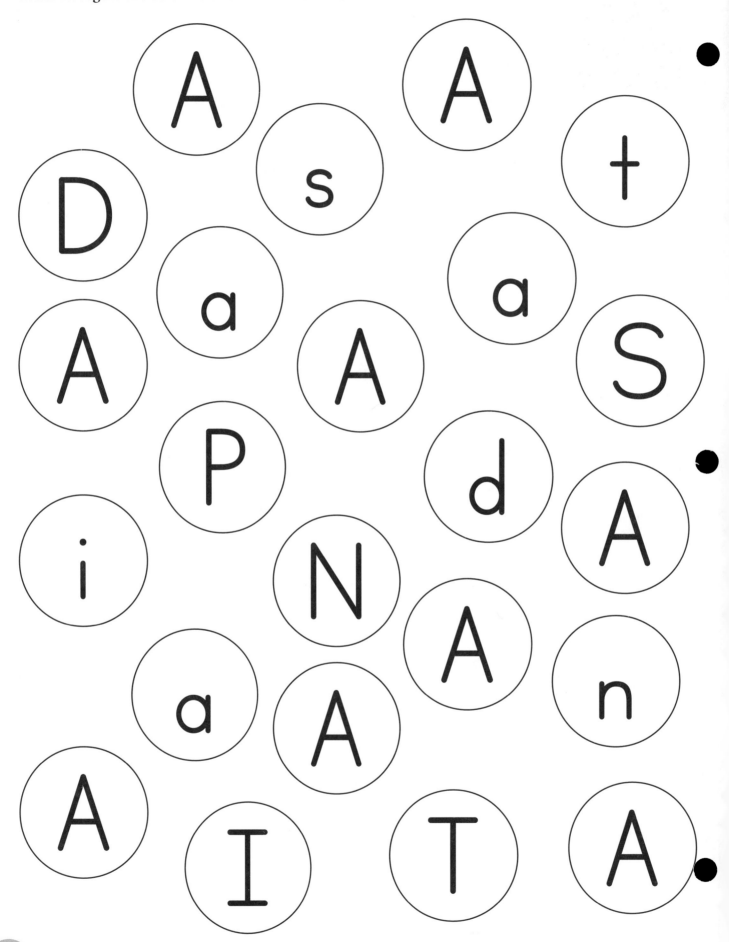

Foundations Phonics

J is for Jacob.
God changed Jacob's name to Israel.

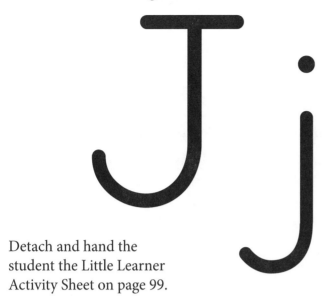

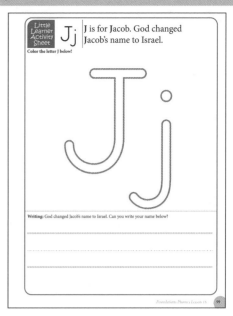

Detach and hand the student the Little Learner Activity Sheet on page 99.

LESSON NARRATIVE

This lesson covers the letter J. The sound of the letter J can be heard in the words Jacob, jump, and job. As you read through this lesson, place emphasis on the sound of this letter where it is found in bold throughout the text.

Here we are, ready to go! We've already learned about Abraham, and his son Isaac. Today we will learn about Isaac's son Jacob! Are you ready? Well what are we waiting for!

Isaac married a woman named Rebekah, and God blessed them with twin boys named Esau and Jacob. Esau was the older brother, and Jacob was younger. Jacob was a schemer. Jacob convinced Esau to give up his birthright. He stole Esau's blessing, lied to his father, and was often running away from trouble!

But even though Jacob did many bad things, God had a special purpose and promise for him as well. After Jacob lied to his father, Isaac, and stole Esau's blessing, he had to leave home because Esau was very, very angry with him. So Jacob left home, and as the sun set, he took a stone and used it as a pillow so he could sleep. Can you imagine trying to sleep on a stone? Do you think it would be comfortable?

(Allow student time to answer.)

Your pillow is much, much softer! As he slept that night, he had a special dream and God gave him a promise. We read about it in the Bible!

In a dream he saw a stairway standing on the earth. Its top reached to heaven. The angels of God were going up and coming down on it. The LORD stood beside the stairway. He said, "I am the LORD. I am the God of your grandfather Abraham and the God of Isaac. I will give you and your children after you the land you are lying on. They will be like the dust of the earth that can't be counted. They will spread out to the west and to the east. They will spread out to the north and to the south. All nations on earth will be blessed because of you and your children after you. I am with you. I will watch over you everywhere you go. And I will bring you back to this land. I will not leave you until I have done what I have promised you (Genesis 28:12–15).

Jacob was just a man — a man who often struggled to do the right thing — but God loves and uses ordinary men and women as part of His plan! Isn't it wonderful how much God loves us, even though we are imperfect?

Now, many, many years later, Jacob had a large family and it was time for him to travel back to his home. He was scared of what Esau might do to him — after all, Jacob had treated him very badly! As he was traveling back home, something surprising happened. Let's read about it in the very best book, the Bible!

> So Jacob was left alone. A man wrestled with him until morning. The man saw that he couldn't win. So he touched the inside of Jacob's hip. As Jacob wrestled with the man, Jacob's hip was twisted. Then the man said, "Let me go. It is morning."

> But Jacob replied, "I won't let you go unless you bless me."

> The man asked him, "What is your name?"

> "Jacob," he answered.

> Then the man said, "Your name will not be Jacob anymore. Instead, it will be Israel. You have wrestled with God and with people. And you have won."

> Jacob said, "Please tell me your name."

> But he replied, "Why do you want to know my name?" Then he blessed Jacob there.

> So Jacob named the place Peniel. He said, "I saw God face to face. But I'm still alive!"

> The sun rose above Jacob as he passed by Peniel. He was limping because of his hip (Genesis 32:24–31).

Jacob wrestled with God, and God changed Jacob's name to Israel. Jacob became the father of the nation of Israel, God's chosen nation. Hmm, I think I heard our new sound for today. Can you guess which one it is? God changed Jacob's name to Israel.

(Allow student time to answer.)

Our letter for today is the letter J. The J says **j**. God changed Jacob's name to Israel. The letter J looks like this:

J j

(Ask student to trace upper and lowercase J with finger on the Little Learner Activity Sheet. Make sure the student points to the correct one.)

Don't they look similar? One has a line; the other has a dot. The uppercase J looks like this:

J

The lowercase J looks like this:

j

The J says **j**. God changed Jacob's name to Israel.

(Repeat if necessary to reinforce the sound to the student.)

God was working out His promises to Abraham, Isaac, and Jacob. Just as God had promised, Abraham's descendants were many — and they became the nation of Israel. God worked out His plan for salvation through Abraham's descendants many, many, many years into the future. We'll learn about that in another lesson. But for today, we've learned a new letter, and it's time for some fun!

(Now begin the reading section. If your child needs to take a break from the lesson, let him or her begin the first page of the Little Learner Activity Sheet. Be sure to go back to the reading section of this lesson to complete it.)

Now it's time to read some fun words!

Let's practice some words from the ŏt word family! We already know the ending sound, so we can read them quickly!

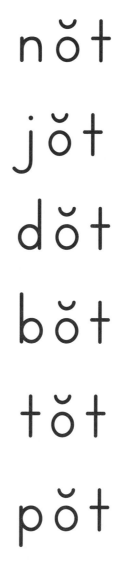

(Have the student complete the Little Learner Activity Sheet.)

BONUS ACTIVITIES:

(Student has learned N, D, Ă, T, S, P, Ĭ, F, Ŏ, B, Ā, Ī, Å, and J so far.)

- J is for jump! Have student jump in place and see how many letters he/she can name from the list he/she has learned.

- Write letters on sticky tabs and place on floor. Call out a sound and have student jump to the letter.

- Arrange sticky tabs from above activity into words and practice reading with student. Jump after each correct word!

- Review letters and sounds on page 98 on an "off" day.

Ask student to point to each letter and say its sound.

N n

D d

Ǎ ǎ

T t

S s

P p

Å å

Ĭ ĭ

F f

Ǒ ǒ

B b

Ā ā

Ī ī

J j

J j

J is for Jacob. God changed Jacob's name to Israel.

Color the letter J below!

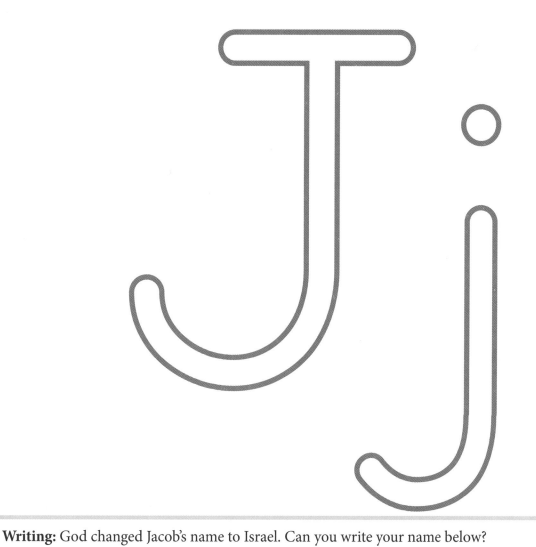

Writing: God changed Jacob's name to Israel. Can you write your name below?

Writing: The J is so much fun to write. Let's practice it!

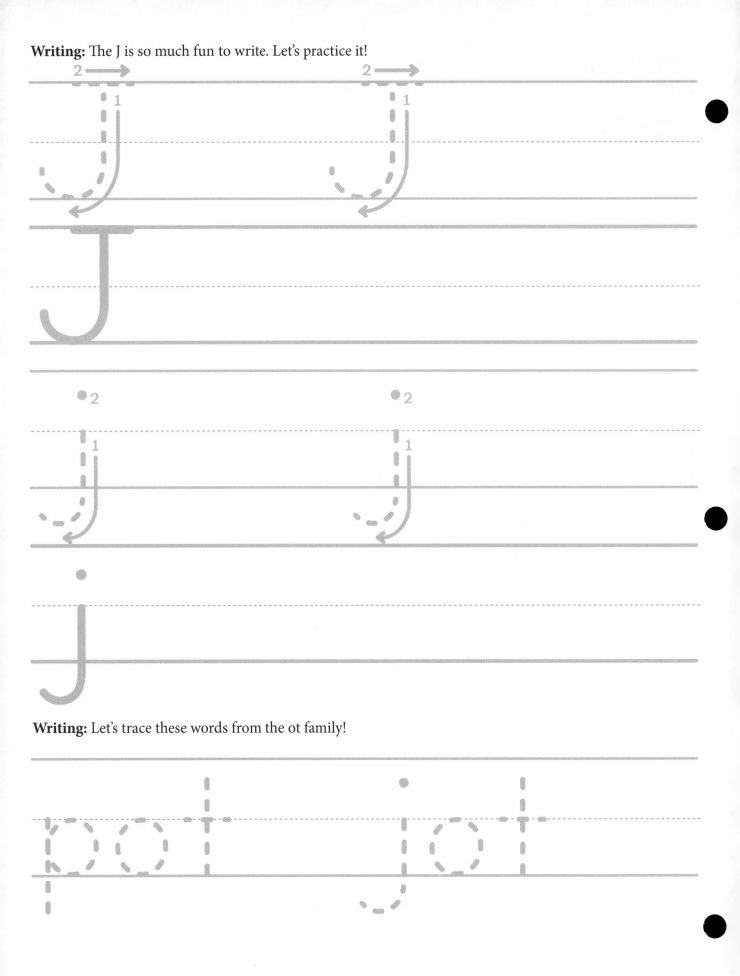

Writing: Let's trace these words from the ot family!

Ē is for **E**gypt.
Joseph was sent to **E**gypt.

Detach and hand the student the
Little Learner Activity Sheet on page 105.

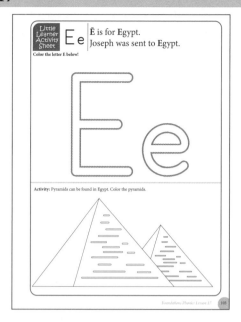

LESSON NARRATIVE

> *This lesson covers the long sound of the letter E. This sound is designated within the lesson with the following symbol above the letters: Ēē. This long sound can be heard in the words Ēgypt, sēēd, and bēan. As you read through this lesson, place emphasis on the sound of this letter where it is found in bold throughout the text.*

Phew, we've traveled quite far in this great big adventure, and we've sure learned a lot! But there is more to learn and much more ground to cover! Are you ready for today? Let's get started!

Jacob had many sons — 12 to be exact! Jacob had a big family. But Jacob made a mistake — rather than love everyone the same, he loved one son more than all the others. Everyone knew it, and it made them angry and very jealous. Jacob loved his son Joseph more than all the others.

God gave Joseph special dreams, and when Joseph told his brothers about them, it made them even angrier!

> Joseph had a dream. When he told it to his brothers, they hated him even more. He said to them, "Listen to the dream I had. We were tying up bundles of grain out in the field. Suddenly my bundle stood up straight. Your bundles gathered around my bundle and bowed down to it." His brothers said to him, "Do you plan to be king over us? Will you really rule over us?" So they hated him even more because of his dream. They didn't like what he had said (Genesis 37:5–8).

When Joseph's brothers were caring for their father's flocks far away, Jacob (whose name was now Israel, remember?) asked Joseph to go and check on them. So Joseph went out, and when his brothers saw him coming, they became angry and decided they would kill him. Reuben, one of Joseph's older brothers, heard what they were planning and convinced the others not to kill him, but to throw him into an empty pit instead. After the others had calmed down, Reuben planned to help Joseph out of the pit and take him back home safely. But things didn't go exactly according to his plan.

Joseph's brothers threw him into the empty pit and left him there as they went to eat dinner. Reuben was away, and as they were eating, they devised another cruel plan:

> Then they sat down to eat their meal. As they did, they saw some Ishmaelite traders coming from Gilead. Their camels were loaded with spices, lotion and myrrh. They were on their way to take them down to

Egypt. Judah said to his brothers, "What will we gain if we kill our brother and try to cover up what we've done? Come. Let's sell him to these traders. Let's not harm him ourselves. After all, he's our brother. He's our own flesh and blood." Judah's brothers agreed with him. The traders from Midian came by. Joseph's brothers pulled him up out of the well. They sold him to the Ishmaelite traders for eight ounces of silver. Then the traders took him to Egypt (Genesis 37:25–28).

When Reuben returned to find Joseph gone, he was very upset. But it was too late; Joseph was sent to Egypt. His brothers pretended Joseph had been killed by a wild animal and tricked Jacob into believing Joseph was dead. But Joseph was sent to Egypt, and though a bad thing had happened, God had an amazing plan for his life. Joseph was sent to **Egypt**.

I heard a new sound there. Did you hear it too? E is our letter for today! The E says ē. Joseph was sent to **Egypt**. The letter E is another vowel — it can make two special sounds, but we will learn just one today. The E says **ē**. This is called the long sound. It's the sound the letter makes when it says its name! Joseph was sent to **Egypt**.

The letter E looks like this:

E e

(Ask student to trace upper and lowercase E with finger on the Little Learner Activity Sheet. Make sure the student points to the correct one.)

The uppercase E looks like this:

E

The lowercase E looks like this:

e

When you see a letter E that looks like this:

Ē ē

you can be sure the E says ē. Joseph was sent to **Egypt**.

(Repeat if necessary to reinforce the sound to the student.)

Now, sometimes bad things happen in our lives, just like in Joseph's. But we know that the bad things aren't the end of the story! God uses even the bad things to work out His plan for our lives, and for the lives of the people around us. When bad things happen, we can remember this special verse from the Bible:

And we know that all things work together for good to those who love God, to those who are the called according to His purpose (Romans 8:28; NKJV).

God was working out a good plan for Joseph's life. We'll learn more about it in our next lesson. But for now, let's go have some fun with the letter E!

(Now begin the reading section. If your child needs to take a break from the lesson, let him or her begin the first page of the Little Learner Activity Sheet. Be sure to go back to the reading section of this lesson to complete it.)

Now, it's time to read! When two of the same letters are right next to each other, they say their name and we read it as one sound. Let's take a look:

bēē

sēē

These words have two e's at the end! The E says its name since there are two, and we read it as one sound. Let's try. Look at the words and sound them out with me.

(Point to the words above and sound them out this the student.)

Great! Let's try another word!

sēēd

The letter E can also be a very tricky letter. It likes to play silent games! When we see the letter E at the end of a word, it plays a silly game — it won't say anything at all! When the E doesn't talk, the other letters have to do more work, so the vowel in the middle says its name. The silent letter in each of these words is grey to remind you it is playing a silly game. Let's read some of these silly words!

fīne

tāpe

nīne

(Have the student complete the Little Learner Activity Sheet.)

BONUS ACTIVITIES:

(Student has learned N, D, Ă, T, S, P, Ĭ, F, Ŏ, B, Ā, Ī, Å, J, and Ē so far.)

- Find Egypt on a map or globe for the student. Remind student of Joseph's story and the letter E's sound!

- Using letters the student has learned, write different words on popsicle sticks. Place sticks upside down in a container, then have student draw a stick and read the word.

- Quiz students on letters and sounds as you go about your day.

- Practice reading sight words on page 104.

Read the sight words.

at

an

as

it

in

is

if

not

of

on

A

I

Little Learner Activity Sheet

E e | Ē is for **Egypt**.
Joseph was sent to **Egypt**.

Color the letter E below!

Activity: Pyramids can be found in Egypt. Color the pyramids.

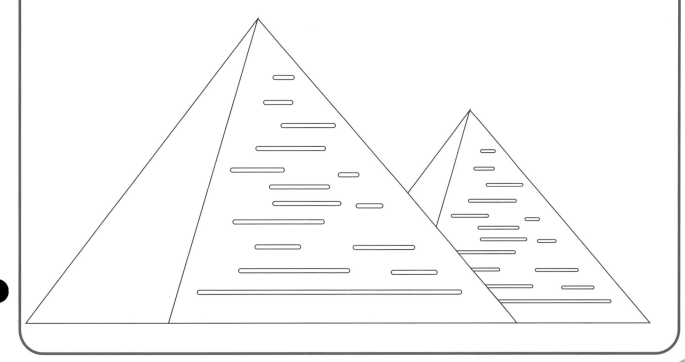

Writing: The tricky E is such a great letter. Let's write it!

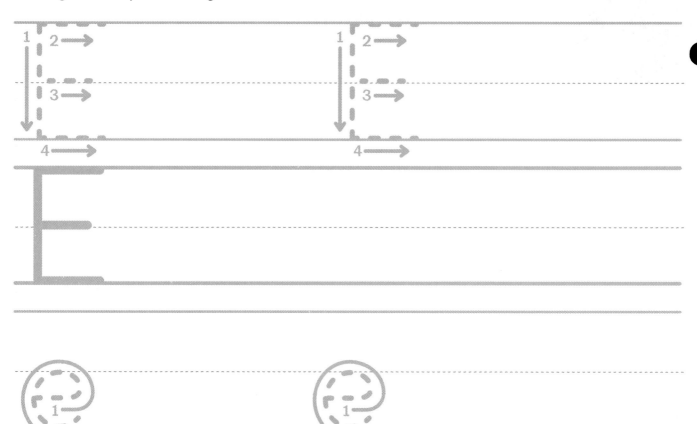

Review

N D Ă T
S P Ĭ F Ŏ
B Ā Ī Å
J Ē

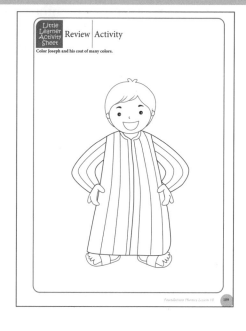

Detach and hand the student the Little Learner Activity Sheet on page 109.

LESSON NARRATIVE

We've learned so much and it is time for review! Can you tell me about your favorite letter we have learned so far?

(Allow student time to answer.)

I like that one too! We've learned about Abraham; can you tell me something about him?

(Allow student time to answer; guide as necessary.)

God changed Abram's name to Abraham. The letter A says ā. Next we learned about Abraham's son Isaac. What sound does the I say?

(Allow student time to answer.)

The I says ī. Great job! Next came the altar. A lamb was provided for the altar. The letter A is a vowel and it says three different sounds: Ă, Ā, and Å. What a special letter! Do you remember who came next in our story? It starts with a J!

(Allow student time to answer.)

Jacob! God changed Jacob's name to Israel. The J says j. And finally, we learned about Joseph. Joseph was sent to Egypt. The E says ē as in Egypt. After Joseph got to Egypt, he became a slave to Potiphar. Joseph worked hard and the Lord blessed him, so Potiphar put Joseph in charge of his whole house! But then Joseph was accused of something he didn't do, and though he was innocent, he was sent to

prison. How do you think Joseph felt as he sat alone in prison?

(Allow student time to answer.)

Joseph may have been sad, confused, or afraid, but he continued to trust in the Lord. And the Lord blessed him even in prison — let's read from the Bible!

> The LORD was with him. He was kind to him. So the man running the prison was pleased with Joseph (Genesis 39:21).

Soon, Joseph was even put in charge of the prison! He remained in prison for years until one night the Pharaoh had a dream that scared him. Joseph had interpreted dreams while he was in prison. When people remembered that he could tell the meaning of a dream they brought Joseph to Pharaoh. So Pharaoh told Joseph about his dream. Joseph told him the meaning — and it wasn't the best news for Egypt! Joseph told him there would be 7 years of plenty where the crops would be bountiful, but then there would be 7 years of terrible famine.

Pharaoh put Joseph in charge of gathering food and making sure Egypt would have enough food to survive the famine. Joseph worked hard and the Lord blessed him! Joseph saved enough food to feed

Egypt and even people from other countries for those seven years of famine! Eventually, Joseph was reunited with his family, and his father and brothers lived in Egypt for the rest of their days.

Sometimes, bad things happen in our lives. Romans 8:28 (NKJV) in the Bible tells us

> And we know that all things work together for good to those who love God, to those who are the called according to His purpose.

Even though bad things happened to Joseph, he continued to trust God and do his best. And God took those bad things and used them as part of His plan to use Joseph in an amazing way! What do you think you can learn from Joseph?

(Allow student time to answer; guide as necessary.)

I think that is a good lesson!

(Have the student complete the Little Learner Activity Sheet.)

BONUS ACTIVITIES:

(Student has learned N, D, Ă, T, S, P, Ĭ, F, Ŏ, B, Ā, Ī, Å, J, and Ē so far.)

- Go have some fun with your student! Look for objects in his or her play that start with letters from today's review. Or look for objects that look like letters he or she has already learned (e.g., the top of a cup or bowl looks like an O, a staircase or gate spindle could be an I, etc.).

Color Joseph and his coat of many colors.

Letter Recognition: Color the upper and lowercase Es with a red crayon. Color the upper and lowercase Fs with a green crayon.

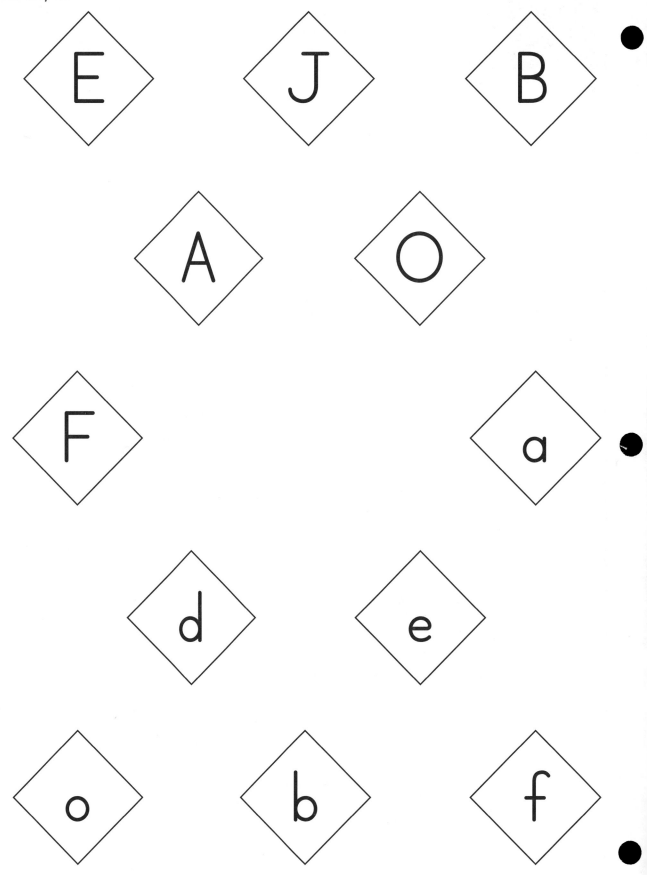

M is for Moses.
God saved Moses for a special mission.

Mm

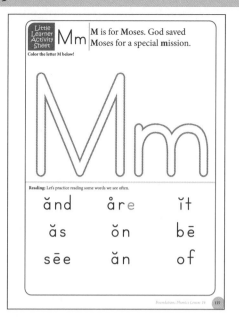

Detach and hand the student the
Little Learner Activity Sheet on page 115.

*This lesson covers the letter M. The sound of the letter M can be heard in the words Moses and mission. As you read through this lesson, place emphasis on the sound of this letter where it is found in **bold** throughout the text.*

I'm so excited to start our adventure today. The Bible is a big book that is divided into many smaller books. Each book in the Bible has a name. The first book of the Bible is called "Genesis." We've already traveled through the history recorded in the Book of Genesis. Today, we start our adventure in the next book of the Bible! Are you excited? For our next few lessons, our reading adventures come from the Book of Exodus. Exodus is the second book in the Bible. Let's get started!

After Joseph died, the years went by and a new pharaoh came to power in Egypt. No one remembered all the good Joseph had done in Egypt anymore. Let's read what happened from the very best book, the Bible!

Then a new king, to whom Joseph meant nothing, came to power in Egypt. "Look," he said to his people, "the Israelites have become far too numerous for us. Come, we must deal shrewdly with them or they will become even more numerous and, if war breaks out, will join our enemies, fight against us and leave the country." So they put slave masters over them to oppress them with forced labor, and they built Pithom and Rameses as store cities for Pharaoh. But the more they were oppressed, the more they multiplied and spread; so the Egyptians came to dread the Israelites and worked them ruthlessly. They made their lives bitter with harsh labor in brick and mortar and with all kinds of work in the fields; in all their harsh labor the Egyptians worked them ruthlessly (Exodus 1:8–14 NKJV).

The Israelites were forced to work hard for the Egyptians — but that wasn't the worst of it! When the pharaoh saw that the Israelite families continued to grow in spite of all the hard work, he decided that all the new baby boys should be killed. It was a very sad time for the Israelites.

When Moses was born, his parents were very brave, and they hid him to keep him safe. After three months they couldn't keep him hidden much longer. So his mom made a basket for Moses, placed him inside, and put the basket in the river. Moses' older sister must have cared very much and watched from a distance to see what would happen to her brother.

God had a special plan for Moses' life — just like He has for yours! Pharaoh's daughter came to the river that day and saw the basket. When she opened it, baby Moses cried and she had compassion on him. She adopted Moses and raised him as her son! How incredible!

When Moses was older, he saw how his people were being treated and he wanted to help. But he forgot to ask God what he could do to help, and instead, he took matters into his own hands. Let's read from the Bible!

> One day, after Moses had grown up, he went out to where his own people were and watched them at their hard labor. He saw an Egyptian beating a Hebrew, one of his own people. Looking this way and that and seeing no one, he killed the Egyptian and hid him in the sand. The next day he went out and saw two Hebrews fighting. He asked the one in the wrong, "Why are you hitting your fellow Hebrew?" The man said, "Who made you ruler and judge over us? Are you thinking of killing me as you killed the Egyptian?" Then Moses was afraid and thought, "What I did must have become known." When Pharaoh heard of this, he tried to kill Moses, but Moses fled from Pharaoh and went to live in Midian, where he sat down by a well (Exodus 2:11–15 NKJV).

God saved **M**oses for a special **m**ission — and we will learn about that in our next lesson. But for now, I think I heard a new sound. Hmm, can you hear it too? God saved **M**oses for a special **m**ission. M is our letter for today! The letter M says **m**. God saved **M**oses for a special **m**ission.

The letter M looks like this:

(Ask student to trace uppercase and lowercase M with finger on the Little Learner Activity Sheet. Make sure the student points to the correct one.)

The uppercase M looks like this:

The lowercase M looks like this:

They look very similar, don't they? The M says **m**. God saved **M**oses for a special **m**ission. What do you think will happen in our next adventure?

(Allow student time to answer.)

I guess we'll find out! For now, wave goodbye to Moses as he is hiding from Pharaoh in Midian! Now it's time for some fun!

(Now begin the reading section. If your child needs to take a break from the lesson, let him or her begin the first page of the Little Learner Activity Sheet. Be sure to go back to the reading section of this lesson to complete it.)

Let's practice reading!

măt	mē
măst	Săm
jăm	sāme

Now it's time to put all this learning to work! Let's read a little story together, I know you can do it!

Mŏm māde jăm.

Săm āte jăm.

Ī săt ănd āte jăm.

Great job! Now, can you answer these questions? Who made jam? Who ate the jam?

(Have the student complete the Little Learner Activity Sheet.)

BONUS ACTIVITIES:

(Student has learned N, D, Ă, T, S, P, Ĭ, F, Ŏ, B, Ā, Ī, Å, J, Ē, and M so far.)

- See how many objects you can find in the house that start with the letter M! When you find an object, write its name on paper and read together (e.g., mat, mitten, map, milk, etc.).

- Read a simple story together. Have student read simple M words.
- Send student on a mission to find objects that start with the letter M!
- Look at map of Egypt on page 114 with your student on an "off" day.

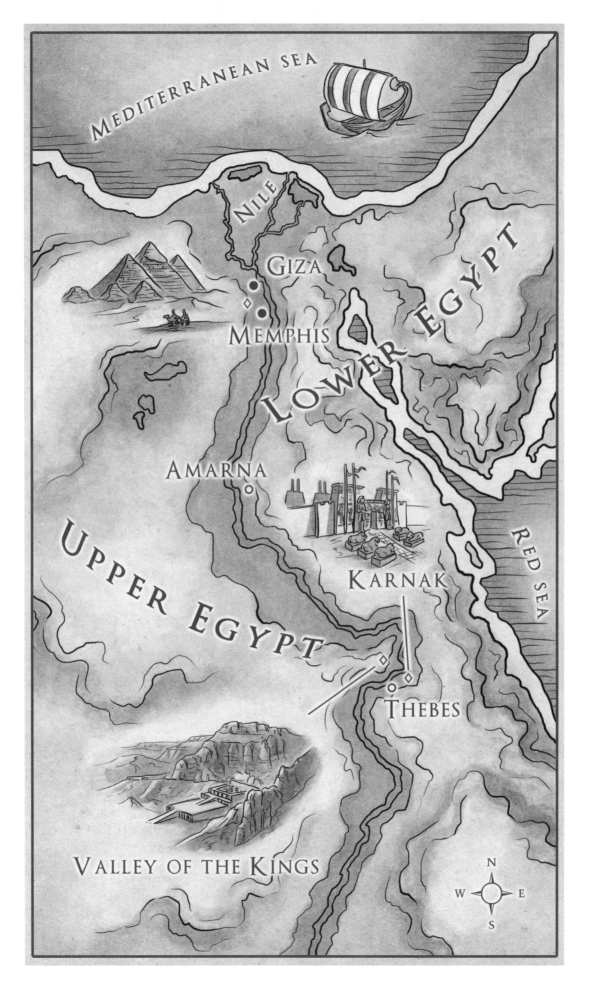

Mm

M is for **Moses**. God saved Moses for a special **m**ission.

Color the letter M below!

Reading: Let's practice reading some words we see often.

ănd   åre   ĭt

ăs   ŏn   bē

sēe   ăn   of

Writing: The M is so much fun to write. Show me how it's done!

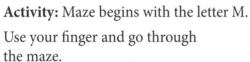

Activity: Maze begins with the letter M.
Use your finger and go through
the maze.

L is for Led.
God **l**ed His people as they **l**eft Egypt.

Detach and hand the student the
Little Learner Activity Sheet on page 121.

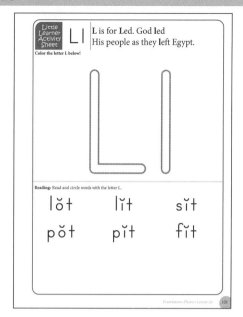

LESSON NARRATIVE

*This lesson covers the letter L. The sound of the letter L can be heard in the words led, left, and lot. As you read through this lesson, place emphasis on the sound of this letter where it is found in **bold** throughout the text.*

Our last adventure was so exciting! Are you ready to learn about the special mission God gave to Moses today? Let's get started on our adventure from the Bible!

You remember from our last adventure, Moses was living in Midian. One day, something really strange happened! What do you think it was?

(Allow student time to answer.)

That's a really good guess! Let's read the story from the Bible and find out:

Moses was taking care of the flock of his father-in-law Jethro. Jethro was the priest of Midian. Moses led the flock to the western side of the desert. He came to Horeb. It was the mountain of God. There the angel of the LORD appeared to him from inside a burning bush. Moses saw that the bush was on fire. But it didn't burn up. So Moses thought, "I'll go over and see this strange sight. Why doesn't the bush burn up?"

The LORD saw that Moses had gone over to look. So God spoke to him from inside the bush. He called out, "Moses! Moses!"

"Here I am," Moses said.

"Do not come any closer," God said. "Take off your sandals. The place you are standing on is holy ground." He continued, "I am the God of your father. I am the God of Abraham. I am the God of Isaac. And I am the God of Jacob." When Moses heard that, he turned his face away. He was afraid to look at God.

The LORD said, "I have seen how my people are suffering in Egypt. I have heard them cry out because of their slave drivers. I am concerned about their suffering. So I have come down to save them from the Egyptians. I will bring them up out of that land. I will bring them into a good land. It has a lot of room. It is a land that has plenty of milk and honey. The Canaanites, Hittites, Amorites, Perizzites, Hivites and Jebusites live there. And now Israel's cry for help has reached me. I have seen how badly the Egyptians are treating them. So now, go. I am sending you to Pharaoh. I want you to bring the Israelites out of Egypt. They are my people" (Exodus 3:1–10).

Though things had been hard, God hadn't forgotten the special promises He had given to Abraham, Isaac, Jacob, and their children. Sometimes God gives us special promises too. Though we may go through hard times, God never forgets what He promised, and we can know that in the right time, His promises will be fulfilled!

God sent Moses back to Egypt to tell the Pharaoh to let the Israelites go. So Moses went and did as the Lord had told him to. But there was a problem. Pharaoh wouldn't listen and he made things even harder for the Israelites! So God sent miracles and signs, and finally ten terrible plagues to Egypt to change Pharaoh's mind. Finally, Pharaoh let Moses and his people go, and God led His people as they left Egypt.

> By day the LORD went ahead of them in a pillar of cloud to guide them on their way and by night in a pillar of fire to give them light, so that they could travel by day or night (Exodus 13:21 NKJV).

God **l**ed His people as they **l**eft Egypt. Oh my! I think we found our new sound for today! L is our letter today. The L says **l**. Can you say it with me? The L says **l**. The letter L looks like this:

L l

(Ask student to trace upper and lowercase L with finger on the Little Learner Activity Sheet. Make sure the student points to the correct one.)

The uppercase L looks like this:

L

The lowercase L looks like this:

l

They look very similar, don't they? The L says **l**. God led His people as they **l**eft Egypt. God performed many more miracles for the Israelites, and He saved them when Pharaoh came back to take them as slaves again. We can read the story in the Bible later, but for now we have some fun activities with our new letter **L**!

(Now begin the reading section. If your child needs to take a break from the lesson, let him or her begin the first page of the Little Learner Activity Sheet. Be sure to go back to the reading section of this lesson to complete it.)

Let's practice reading! Remember this ending sound?

ŏt

We know the ending sound. Now let's try different beginning letters!

bŏt

lŏt

pŏt

jŏt

dŏt

Great job! What about this ending sound? Read the words below!

ĭt

bĭt

lĭt

pĭt

sĭt

fĭt

Fantastic!

(Have the student complete the Little Learner Activity Sheet.)

BONUS ACTIVITIES:

(Student has learned N, D, Ă, T, S, P, Ĭ, F, Ŏ, B, Ā, Ī, Å, J, Ē, M, and L so far.)

- Cut up 5 sheets of construction paper into fourths and write a letter the student has learned on each fourths. Put pieces together to form words to read together.

- On an "off" day, read the verse on page 120 with your child and let him or her read the large words throughout.

God led the Israelites through the wilderness. Let's read the verse that tells us about how He led them together! I'll point to each word as I read, and when we get to large words, you can read those.

 This passage contains several sight words. Your student may recognize these words; however, longer passages to read can feel intimidating. Symbols for these words have been included as a gentle reminder for these words.

The word "pillar" is also a large word — encourage your student to sound it out and help them blend it together. Explain that when we see a larger word we don't know, we can sound it out!

By day the LORD went ahead **of** them ĭn a **pĭllȧr of** cloud to guide them **ŏn** their way **ănd** by night ĭn a pillar **of** fire to give them light, so that they could travel by day or night. (Exodus 13:21)

L l

L is for **L**ed. God **l**ed
His people as they **l**eft Egypt.

Color the letter L below!

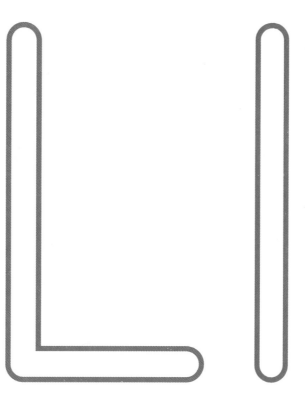

Reading: Read and circle words with the letter L.

lŏt   lĭt   sĭt

pŏt   pĭt   fĭt

Writing: I love to write the letter L, so let's practice!

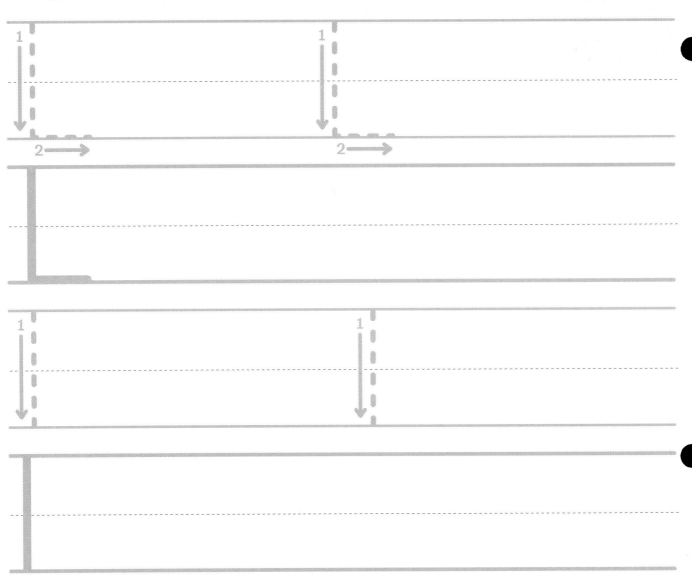

Color the lizard green.

Ŭ is for **U**nder.
Men were **u**nder the law in the Old Testament.

Detach and hand the student the
Little Learner Activity Sheet on page 127.

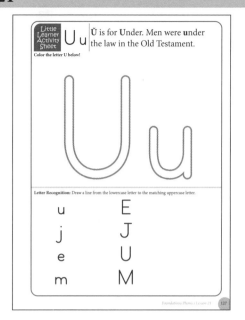

LESSON NARRATIVE

💡 *This lesson covers the short sound of the letter U. This sound is designated within the lesson with the following symbol above the letters: Ŭŭ. This short sound can be heard in the words ŭnder, ŭmbrella, and ŭp. As you read through this lesson, place emphasis on the sound of this letter where it is found in* **bold** *throughout the text.*

Here we are, ready for a brand new adventure! Get your imagination started. Let's go! After God led Moses and the Israelites out of Egypt, He provided, cared for, and protected them on their journey for three months. Finally they arrived in the Wilderness of Sinai and camped below the mountain. Now, let's read from the very best book — the Bible!

On the morning of the third day there was thunder and lightning. A thick cloud covered the mountain. A trumpet gave out a very loud blast. Everyone in the camp trembled with fear. Then Moses led the people out of the camp to meet with God. They stood at the foot of the mountain. Smoke covered Mount Sinai, because the LORD came down on it in fire. The smoke rose up from it like smoke from a furnace. The whole mountain trembled and shook. The sound of the trumpet got louder and

louder. Then Moses spoke. And the voice of God answered him. The LORD came down to the top of Mount Sinai. He told Moses to come to the top of the mountain. So Moses went up (Exodus 19:16–20).

Wow! Can you imagine what it must have been like? How do you think you would have felt if you had been there and seen it?

(Allow student time to answer.)

After Moses had gone up the mountain, God spoke and gave Moses the law — we call it the Ten Commandments. Let read them from the Bible!

Do not put any other gods in place of me.

Do not make for yourself statues of gods that look like anything in the sky. They may not look like anything on the earth or in the waters either. Do not bow down to them or worship them. I, the LORD your God, am a jealous God. I cause the sins of the parents to affect their children. I will cause the sins of those who hate me to affect even their grandchildren and great-grandchildren. But for all time to come I show love to all those who love me and keep my commandments.

Do not misuse the name of the LORD your God. The LORD will find guilty anyone who misuses his name.

Remember to keep the Sabbath day holy. Do all your work in six days. But the seventh day is a sabbath to honor the LORD your God. Do not do any work on that day. The same command applies to your sons and daughters, your male and female servants, and your animals. It also applies to any outsiders who live in your towns. In six days the LORD made the heavens, the earth, the sea and everything in them. But he rested on the seventh day. So the LORD blessed the Sabbath day and made it holy.

Honor your father and mother. Then you will live a long time in the land the LORD your God is giving you.

Do not murder.

Do not commit adultery.

Do not steal.

Do not be a false witness against your neighbor.

Do not want to have anything your neighbor owns. Do not want to have your neighbor's house, wife, male or female servant, ox or donkey (Exodus 20:3–17).

The Bible is divided into two sections. The first section is called the "Old Testament." The second is called the "New Testament." "Testament" means covenant or agreement. So there is the old agreement and the new agreement. In the Old Testament, God gave us the law. The law, or Ten Commandments, shows us that no matter how hard we try, we can never measure up to God's standard. We have all broken the commandments. The Bible tells us:

> . . . for all have sinned and fall short of the glory of God (Romans 3:23; NKJV).

We have all broken God's laws. That is why God made a plan to save us from sin! In the New

Testament, God gave us grace through Jesus Christ. Romans 6:14 tells us:

> Sin will no longer control you like a master. That's because the law does not rule you. God's grace has set you free.

God gave us the law to show us we cannot keep it — we are imperfect. For today's lesson, you've learned that men were **u**nder the law in the Old Testament. Did you hear that sound?

(Allow student time to guess.)

The letter **U** is our new letter for today! The **U** says **ŭ**, as in **u**nder. Men were **u**nder the law in the Old Testament. The letter **U** looks like this:

(Ask student to trace upper and lowercase U with finger on the Little Learner Activity Sheet. Make sure the student points to the correct one.)

The uppercase U looks like this:

The lowercase U looks like this:

They look almost the same! The **U** says **ŭ**. Men were **u**nder the law in the Old Testament. The letter **U** is another vowel. It can make different sounds. When you see a U that looks like this:

you can be sure it says **ŭ** as in **u**nder! We call this the short sound.

In the Old Testament, men had to bring animal sacrifices to pay the price of breaking God's laws.

Breaking God's laws is called sin. But in the New Testament, God sent His Son Jesus to be sacrificed for us. Jesus would pay the price of sin forever. We'll be learning more about that later in our adventures though. For now, let's have some letter fun!

(Now begin the reading section below. If your child needs to take a break from the lesson, let him or her begin the first page of the Little Learner Activity Sheet. Be sure to go back to the reading section of this lesson to complete it.)

READING

Let's practice reading!

Jŭt

bŭd

sŭn

dŭd

mănn

Ŭp

Sŭd

pŭp

(Have the student complete the Little Learner Activity Sheet.)

BONUS ACTIVITIES:

(Student has learned N, D, Ă, T, S, P, Ĭ, F, Ŏ, B, Ā, Ī, Å, J, Ē, M, L, and Ŭ so far.)

- Place objects that start with same letter into container. Have student figure out what the mystery letter is based on the objects.
- Spread shaving cream onto a cookie sheet. Write letters or words.

- Say a simple word to the student (e.g., sun, man, etc.). Ask student if he/she can figure out which letters make up the word. Write the word.
- Review the Ten Commandments on page 126 with your student on an "off" day. Remind your student of today's lesson and how Jesus would come to pay the price of our sin.

Ten Commandments

1. Do not put any other gods in place of me.

2. Do not make for yourself statues of gods that look like anything in the sky. They may not look like anything on the earth or in the waters either. 5 Do not bow down to them or worship them. I, the Lord your God, am a jealous God. I cause the sins of the parents to affect their children. I will cause the sins of those who hate me to affect even their grandchildren and great-grandchildren. 6 But for all time to come I show love to all those who love me and keep my commandments.

3. Do not misuse the name of the Lord your God. The Lord will find guilty anyone who misuses his name.

4. Remember to keep the Sabbath day holy. Do all your work in six days. But the seventh day is a sabbath to honor the Lord your God. Do not do any work on that day. The same command applies to your sons and daughters, your male and female servants, and your animals. It also applies to any outsiders who live in your towns. In six days the Lord made the heavens, the earth, the sea and everything in them. But he rested on the seventh day. So the Lord blessed the Sabbath day and made it holy.

5. Honor your father and mother. Then you will live a long time in the land the Lord your God is giving you.

6. Do not murder.

7. Do not commit adultery.

8. Do not steal.

9. Do not be a false witness against your neighbor.

10. Do not want to have anything your neighbor owns. Do not want to have your neighbor's house, wife, male or female servant, ox or donkey.

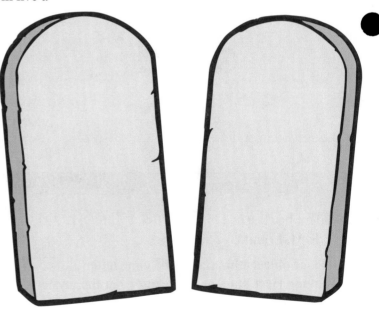

Exodus 20:3–17

Little Learner Activity Sheet

U u

Ŭ is for Under. Men were under the law in the Old Testament.

Color the letter U below!

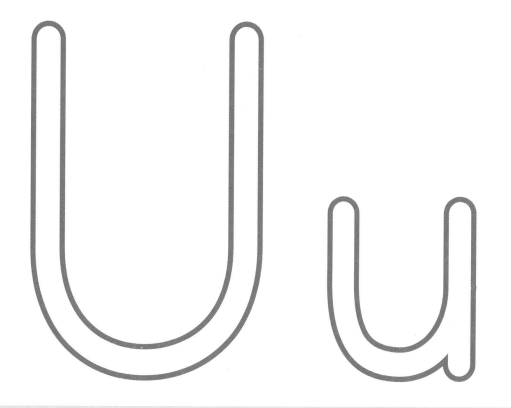

Letter Recognition: Draw a line from the lowercase letter to the matching uppercase letter.

u   E

j   J

e   U

m   M

Writing: Learning to write is very important! Let's practice the letter U.

Writing: Write the uppercase letter for each lowercase letter!

u

m

e

l

Ō is for **O**beyed.
Joshua served and **o**beyed God.

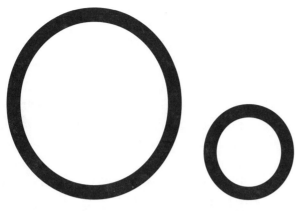

Detach and hand the student the
Little Learner Activity Sheet on page 133.

LESSON NARRATIVE

*This lesson covers the long sound of the letter O. This sound is designated within the lesson with the following symbol above the letters: Ōō. This long sound can be heard in the words ōbey, ōver, and sō. As you read through this lesson, place emphasis on the sound of this letter where it is found in **bold** throughout the text.*

Are you ready for an awesome adventure today? If you use your imagination, you may just feel sand in your shoes because we are going to spend some time way out in the desert! Are you ready to get started? Start your imagination and let's go!

Moses led the Israelites through the wilderness as they journeyed to the land God had promised to Abraham, Isaac, and Jacob. Can you imagine the sand and the hot, dry air? You would imagine the people would be so happy when they reached the Promised Land and would be ready to do whatever God told them to do! But, something else happened. When the people got close to the land God had promised them, they got scared of the people who were already living in the land. They refused to trust God's promises and do as He had commanded them.

This made God very angry, and the people suffered a very sad consequence for refusing to trust and

obey God — they were not allowed to enter into the land God had promised to their people so many years ago. God told the people that because of their sin, they would wander in the desert for 40 years until all the people who had refused to follow God died. But there were two men who had trusted God and who tried to convince the people to trust God as well. Their names were Caleb and Joshua. God gave them a special blessing; let's read it from the Bible!

> But not one of the people who came up out of Egypt will see the land except Caleb and Joshua. Caleb is the son of Jephunneh, the Kenizzite. And Joshua is the son of Nun. They will see the land. They followed the LORD with their whole heart (Numbers 32:12).

Caleb and Joshua trusted the Lord with their whole hearts — and the Lord told them they would enter into the land God had promised the Israelites!

Now, Moses had gotten frustrated one day and he didn't follow God's instructions exactly as God had told him. Because Moses hadn't obeyed God, he also died before the Israelites entered the Promised Land. After Moses died, Joshua led the Israelites. Joshua followed the Lord and obeyed God's instructions — even when it seemed a little crazy! With God's help, Joshua led the Israelites into the land God had promised to Abraham, Isaac, and Jacob (whose name God had changed to Israel, remember?).

One day, Joshua gathered the people together and he encouraged them to obey the Lord. We can read about it in Joshua 24:14–15:

"So have respect for the LORD. Serve him. Be completely faithful to him. Throw away the gods your people worshiped east of the Euphrates River and in Egypt. Serve the LORD. But suppose you don't want to serve him. Then choose for yourselves right now whom you will serve. You can choose the gods your people served east of the Euphrates River. Or you can serve the gods of the Amorites. After all, you are living in their land. But as for me and my family, we will serve the LORD."

Joshua served and **o**beyed the Lord. Did you hear our new letter for today? Joshua served and **o**beyed the Lord. Our new letter is the letter **O**! The letter **O** is a vowel. It can make different sounds! This **O** says its name, the **O** says ō, as in obeyed! The letter **O** looks like this:

They look very similar, don't they? One is just smaller than the other! When you see an O that looks like this

you can be sure that it says its name, **Ō**! We call this the long sound. Joshua obeyed the Lord, and we can make the choice to obey the Lord too. Sometimes it is hard to obey God, and other people may think God cannot be trusted, but we have seen that God never breaks His word or His promises. God can be trusted. He means what He says! Joshua obeyed the Lord, and we can too! Now, let's go have some more letter fun with the letter **O**!

(Now begin the reading section. If your child needs to take a break from the lesson, let him or her begin the first page of the Little Learner Activity Sheet. Be sure to go back to the reading section of this lesson to complete it.)

The letter O is our new letter. Let's read some new words together!

Bōat

tōe

bōnes

sō

Pŏt

ŏn

Nō

dŏt

Sometimes, letters don't always follow the rules. When two letter Os sit side by side, they make the sound "oo" as in "too" or "boo." Let's practice reading these types of words!

too

boo

moo

(Have the student complete the Little Learner Activity Sheet.)

BONUS ACTIVITIES:

(Student has learned N, D, Ă, T, S, P, Ĭ, F, Ŏ, B, Ā, Ī, Å, J, Ē, M, L, Ŭ, and Ō so far.)

- Bury alphabet magnets or similar loose letters in uncooked rice or sugar. Give student a small brush. Call out a letter and see how quickly student can find and excavate it!

- Write upper and lowercase letters on building

blocks or Easter eggs using a permanent marker. Give student letters he/she has learned thus far. Separate the pairs and ask student to match the upper and lowercase letters. Save for future use.

- On an "off" day, read the verse on page 132 with your child.

Joshua was a very brave and Godly man. He served God through his whole life! Let's read what Joshua said. I'll point to each word as I read, when we get to the large word, you can read those ones.

... Bŭt as fōr mē and my family, we will serve the LORD.

(Joshua 24:15)

What do you think that verse means?

Ō is for Obeyed. Joshua served and obeyed God.

Color the upper and lowercase O!

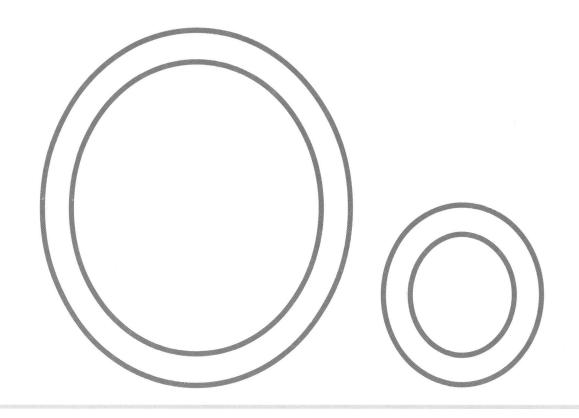

Activity: Circle the pictures if you hear the ō sound.

Writing: Let's practice writing some words!

toe

pot

dot

son

Activity: Write the first letter of each picture!

R is for **R**uth.
Ruth was blessed by the Lord.

Detach and hand the student the
Little Learner Activity Sheet on page 139.

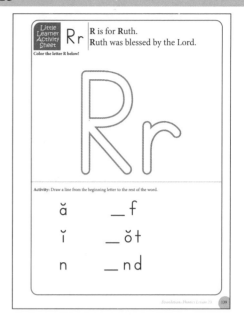

LESSON NARRATIVE

*This lesson covers the letter R. The sound of the letter R can be heard in the words Ruth, run, red. As you read through this lesson, place emphasis on the sound of this letter where it is found in **bold** throughout the text.*

I'm so glad you are here! Today, we have a special adventure and will learn a special new sound. Are you ready to learn? Well then, let's get started!

Close your eyes and imagine what a famine would be like. A famine is a time in which food becomes scarce, when the fields won't grow food, and when people become very hungry because there is nothing to eat. That is how our adventure opens today — the land was under a famine, and families were having a very hard time.

If there was no food here, what do you think we would do?

(Allow student time to answer; guide as necessary.)

We would probably have to leave our home and search for a place where food was plentiful. In our adventure today, we meet a man named Elimelech, his wife Naomi, and his sons, Mahlon and Chilion. Elimelech moved his family from Bethlehem where the famine was to the land of Moab.

After they arrived in Moab, Elimelech died and Mahlon and Chilion married Orpah and Ruth, two

women from Moab. They continued living in Moab for several years, and then more sadness struck the family. Mahlon and Chilion also died, leaving Naomi, Orpah, and Ruth all alone there.

How sad they must have felt! Naomi heard that there was food again in her land, so she decided to make the journey back home. Orpah and Ruth started to go with her, but Naomi counseled them to return to Moab with the blessing of the Lord. Orpah wept, kissed Naomi goodbye, and returned home. But Ruth decided to follow Naomi. Naomi tried again to convince Ruth to leave her, but here is what the Bible tells us:

> But Ruth replied, "Don't try to make me leave you and go back. Where you go I'll go. Where you stay I'll stay. Your people will be my people. Your God will be my God. Where you die I'll die. And there my body will be buried. I won't let even death separate you from me. If I do, may the LORD punish me greatly" (Ruth 1:16–17).

So Ruth and Naomi arrived home in Bethlehem together, and Ruth went to the fields to gather the leftover crops as they were harvested. Ruth found herself working in a relative's field — his name was Boaz. He had heard good things about Ruth and he treated her with favor and kindness.

Naomi noticed the kindness and favor Boaz treated Ruth with, and before too long she gave Ruth instructions for asking Boaz to marry her. Ruth followed Naomi's instructions, and Boaz was overjoyed!

Then he said, "Blessed are you of the LORD, my daughter! For you have shown more kindness at the end than at the beginning, in that you did not go after young men, whether poor or rich. And now, my daughter, do not fear. I will do for you all that you request, for all the people of my town know that you are a virtuous woman" (Ruth 3:10–11; NKJV).

So after Boaz worked out details with other relatives, he took Ruth to be his wife. The Lord then blessed Ruth and Boaz with a son named Obed. Obed grew up and became the father of Jesse, and Jesse was the father of David, who would later become king!

Ruth was blessed by the Lord for her choice of faithfulness. Remember God's plan to pay the price of sin? Ruth was included in the family Jesus would later be born into! How amazing! **R**uth was blessed by the Lord. Oh my! I heard a new sound. Did you hear it too? Our letter today is the letter R. The **R** says **r**. The letter R looks like this:

Rr

The uppercase R looks like this:

R

The lowercase r looks like this:

r

(Ask student to trace uppercase and lowercase R with finger on the Little Learner Activity Sheet. Make sure the student points to the correct one.)

The **R** says **r**. Can you say it with me? The **R** says **r**. **R**uth was blessed by the Lord. Our adventures are moving fast now! Wave goodbye to Boaz, Ruth, and baby Obed! It's time for some more letter fun with the letter R!

(Now begin the reading section. If your child needs to take a break from the lesson, let him or her begin the first page of the Little Learner Activity Sheet. Be sure to go back to the reading section of this lesson to complete it.)

Let's practice reading! Sound out this ending sound:

å r

Now we know the ending sound, let's add different beginning sounds to make new words!

b å r

t å r

p å r

j å r

(Have the student complete the Little Learner Activity Sheet.)

(Student has learned N, D, Ă, T, S, P, Ĭ, F, Ŏ, B, Ā, Ī, Å, J, Ē, M, L, Ŭ, Ō, and R so far.)

- Ask student to draw a picture of Ruth gathering wheat in the fields. Help student write the R at the top of the page.

- Write letters the student has learned on sticky tabs and place throughout house. Call out a letter or sound and ask student to find it.

- Use sticky tabs from above to form words for the student to read.

- Review sight words on page 138 on an "off" day.

We know these words! Let's read them together!

There are no symbols on these words. Your student may not recognize these words yet and may still try to sound them out. If your student forgets a sound, that is okay. Simply remind him or her what sound the letter makes and continue reading.

all

are

but

be

see

a

I

and

at

an

it

is

in

R r

R is for **Ruth**.
Ruth was blessed by the Lord.

Color the letter R below!

Activity: Draw a line from the beginning letter to the rest of the word.

ă   _ f

ĭ   _ ŏt

n   _ nd

Writing: Great job! Now let's practice writing!

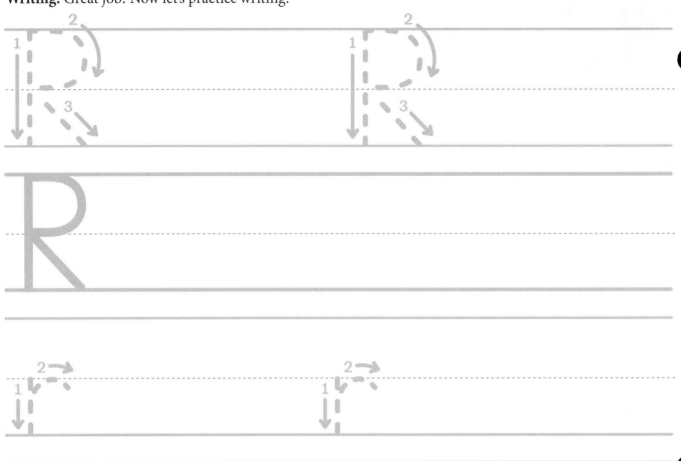

Activity: Circle the pictures that end in the R sound.

Review

N D Ă T S

P Ĭ F Ŏ B

Ā Ī Å J Ē

M L Ŭ Ō R

Detach and hand the student the Little Learner Activity Sheet on page 143.

LESSON NARRATIVE

(Review.)

Every adventure needs a day of rest! Today we catch our breath from all the learning we've been doing! We learned about Moses and how God saved Moses for a special mission. Can you tell me what sound the letter M makes?

(Allow student time to answer.)

That's right! The M says m. Then we learned how God led His people as they left Egypt. What sound does the L say?

(Allow student time to answer.)

Great! The L says l. Next we learned about the laws that God gave and how in the Old Testament men were under the law. Hmm, what letter makes the ŭ sound?

That's right, the letter U! Do you remember who came after Moses?

(Allow student time to answer.)

Joshua! Joshua chose to obey God. Obey starts with the letter O; can you tell me what sounds the letter O makes?

(Allow student time to answer; answer should be Ŏ and Ō.)

Wow! After Joshua, we learned about Ruth. The R says r. Phew, what a lot we've learned!

Let's practice reading some words! Ready to start? Let's start with this ending sound. Read it for me:

ă t

Now let's add different starting sounds! Read each word below:

băt făt măt
săt răt păt

Great job! Now what about this ending sound?

ăn

Now let's add different starting sounds! Read each word below:

tăn păn făn
băn măn răn

You are doing so well! Let's read these sentences, and then we are done!

Dăd răn.
Dăd răn făst.
I rŭn făst too!

Good job reading! (Have the student complete the Little Learner Activity Sheet.)

BONUS ACTIVITIES:

(Student has learned N, D, Ă, T, S, P, Ĭ, F, Ŏ, B, Ā, Ī, Å, J, Ē, M, L, Ŭ, Ō, and R so far.)

• Go, have some fun with your student! Look for objects in his or her play that start with letters from today's review. Or look for objects that look like letters he or she has already learned (e.g., the top of a cup or bowl looks like an O, a staircase or gate spindle could be an I, etc.).

Review | Activity

Activity: Help the dad win the race! Trace the path to his family with your finger or a crayon.

Activity: Trace the shape to make an umbrella! Use your finger to practice, and then use a purple crayon to trace the shape.

C is for **Cry**.
God heard Hannah's **cry**.

Detach and hand the student the
Little Learner Activity Sheet on page 149.

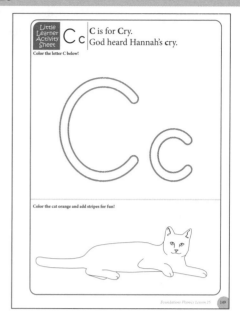

LESSON NARRATIVE

> *This lesson covers the letter C. The sound of the letter C can be heard in the words cry, car, and cat. As you read through this lesson, place emphasis on the sound of this letter where it is found in **bold** throughout the text.*

I'm ready to start another learning adventure — what about you?

(Allow student time to answer.)

You know, sometimes in life things don't work the way we want them to. Sometimes we want something so badly, it can make us cry. Sometimes, it can feel as though God does not see or hear us, but that isn't true. The Bible tells us that God says:

> "Call to Me, and I will answer you, and show you great and mighty things, which you do not know" (Jeremiah 33:3–NKJV).

God hears us when we call to Him. He also sees when we are sad. In Psalms it says:

> You number my wanderings; put my tears into Your bottle; are they not in Your book? (Psalm 56:8–NKJV).

I'm glad God sees and hears us, aren't you? In our adventure today we meet a woman named Hannah. When we meet her, Hannah is very, very sad.

Hannah had no children, but she had prayed and asked God to bless her with a child for years. Can you show me how Hannah's face might have looked?

(Allow student time to make a sad face; guide as necessary.)

Hannah was so sad, she didn't even want to eat anymore. One day when she was very sad, Hannah went to the tabernacle again to pray. Let's read her story from the very best book, the Bible!

> One time when they had finished eating and drinking in Shiloh, Hannah stood up. Eli the priest was sitting on his chair by the doorpost of the LORD's house. Hannah was very sad. She wept and wept. She prayed to the LORD. She made a promise to him. She said, "LORD, you rule over all. Please see how I'm suffering! Show concern for me! Don't forget about me! Please give me a son! If you do, I'll give him back to the LORD. Then he will serve the LORD all the days of his life. He'll never use a razor on his head. He'll never cut his hair."

As Hannah kept on praying to the LORD, Eli watched her lips. She was praying in her heart. Her lips were moving. But she wasn't making a sound. Eli thought Hannah was drunk. He said to her, "How long are you going to stay drunk? Stop drinking your wine."

"That's not true, sir," Hannah replied. "I'm a woman who is deeply troubled. I haven't been drinking wine or beer. I was telling the LORD all my troubles. Don't think of me as an evil woman. I've been praying here because I'm very sad. My pain is so great."

Eli answered, "Go in peace. May the God of Israel give you what you have asked him for."

She said, "May you be pleased with me." Then she left and had something to eat. Her face wasn't sad anymore" (1 Samuel 1:9–18).

Hannah recognized that the Lord had heard her, and as she went away she was no longer sad — even though the Lord hadn't answered her prayers yet. Even when things are hard in our lives, we can pray and know that the Lord hears us, just like Hannah. God heard Hannah's **c**ry. Ooh! There is our new sound for today! Our letter today is the letter **C**. The **C** says **c**. God heard Hannah's **c**ry. The letter C looks like this:

C c

(Ask student to trace uppercase and lowercase C with finger on the Little Learner Activity Sheet. Make sure the student points to the correct one.)

The uppercase C looks like this:

C

The lowercase C looks like this:

c

Say it with me, the **C** says **c**. God answered Hannah's prayer and blessed her with a son. His name was Samuel. When Samuel had grown into a little boy, Hannah fulfilled her promise to God and took him to the tabernacle to serve the Lord. Samuel grew up at the tabernacle and served God throughout his whole life — and God used Samuel to do some very special things too! God also blessed Hannah with more sons and daughters. Wow! What an amazing story. The **C** says **c**. God heard Hannah's **c**ry — and He hears us too! Now let's go have some more word fun!

(Now begin the reading section below. If your child needs to take a break from the lesson, let him or her begin the first page of the Little Learner Activity Sheet. Be sure to go back to the reading section of this lesson to complete it.)

READING

Let's practice reading! Let's start with the "at" word family!

căt

păt

făt

băt

răt

măt

Now let's read a little story!

This passage contains several sight words; see if your student can point them out! Symbols have been included on these sight words as a gentle reminder in case your student does need to sound out a word. Reading comprehension (reading and understanding what is read) is the focus of this passage and the questions that follow.

Ā căt săt ŏn ā măt.

Căt ĭs tăn ănd făt.

Ī căn păt căt!

Now, can you answer the questions about the story?

Where did the cat sit?

What color was the cat?

Who can pat the cat?

(Have the student complete the Little Learner Activity Sheet.)

BONUS ACTIVITIES:

(Student has learned N, D, Ă, T, S, P, Ĭ, F, Ŏ, B, Ā, Ī, Å, J, Ē, M, L, Ŭ, Ō, R, and C so far.)

- Write words on several different popsicle sticks using letters the student has learned. Place sticks into a cup, then have student draw a stick and read the word.

- Go on a letter scavenger hunt — see how many objects you can find that start with the letter C!

- Call out a letter sound. Ask student to name the letter.

- Use pillows, blankets, or other objects to make a big upper and lowercase C.

- Show student image of the tabernacle on page 148.

Samuel grew up in the Tabernacle. Can you imagine what that might have been like?

 **C c** | C is for **C**ry.
God heard Hannah's **c**ry.

Color the letter C below!

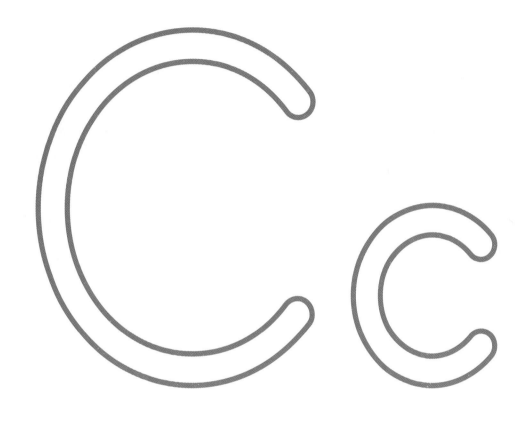

Color the cat orange and add stripes for fun!

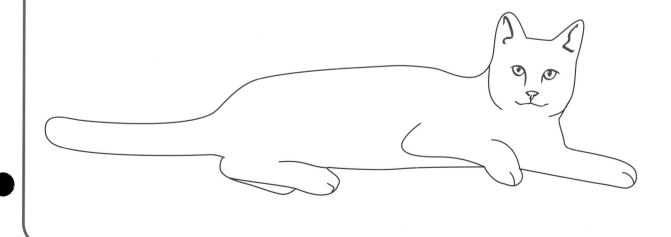

Writing: Now let's write the letter C!

Activity: Can you draw a cat?

W is for Would.
God would choose a new king.

Detach and hand the student the
Little Learner Activity Sheet on page 155.

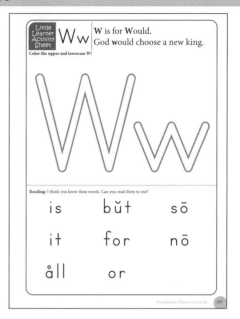

LESSON NARRATIVE

💡 *This lesson covers the letter W. The sound of the letter W can be heard in the words would, saw, and wet. As you read through this lesson, place emphasis on the sound of this letter where it is found in* **bold** *throughout the text.*

Are you ready for another adventure? Well then, what are we waiting for! Let's get started! Close your eyes and imagine as I tell you the tale. You remember Samuel from our last adventure, don't you?

(Allow student time to answer.)

By now, he was all grown up and was a prophet in the nation of Israel. When Samuel was old, the people of Israel decided they no longer wanted God to be their king. They wanted to be like other nations and have a king they could see. Samuel was upset by this, but when he prayed, the Lord said:

> The LORD told him, "Listen to everything the people are saying to you. You are not the one they have turned their backs on. I am the one they do not want as their king" (1 Samuel 8:7).

The people had rejected God as their king. Samuel warned them that a king would sometimes do

things that made the people sad, or angry, or even hurt them. A king may make poor choices and refuse to follow the Lord's commands. Samuel tried to change their minds, but the people would not listen, they wanted a man to be their king. So the Lord led Samuel to the man He chose to be the king over the people. Let's read what happened from the very best book, the Bible!

> When Samuel saw a man coming toward him, the LORD spoke to Samuel again. He said, "He is the man I told you about. His name is Saul. He will govern my people" (1 Samuel 9:17).

Samuel anointed Saul as king over Israel. For a while, Saul was a good king, and he sought the Lord. But then, Saul stopped listening to God and did things God had told him not to do. God gave Saul very specific instructions before a battle, but Saul rebelled and did what he wanted to do rather than what God had told him to do. When we rebel against God, we make a mess of things and it makes God very sad.

Because Saul rebelled against Him, God took away the kingdom from Saul and anointed another as king over Israel. When we reject God in our lives, there are consequences for our decisions, and it is very sad. Saul suffered the consequences for his rebellion against God for the rest of his life. Because of Saul's rebellion, God **would** choose a new king. Wait just a minute! Did you hear something? God **would** choose a new king. I think I hear our new sound! Do you know what letter would say **w** as in **would**?

(Allow student time to answer.)

The letter **W**! The **W** says **w**. God **would** choose a new king. Can you say it with me? The W says w. The letter W looks like this:

(Ask student to trace uppercase and lowercase W with finger on the Little Learner Activity Sheet. Make sure the student points to the correct one.)

They look very similar, don't they? One is just smaller than the other! The uppercase W looks like this and is big:

The lowercase W looks like this and is smaller:

The **W** says **w**. God **would** choose a new king. In our next lesson we will learn about the new king God had chosen — but for now, it is time for some more letter fun!

(Now begin the reading section. If your child needs to take a break from the lesson, let him or her begin the first page of the Little Learner Activity Sheet. Be sure to go back to the reading section of this lesson to complete it.)

The W is a pretty cool letter. Let's try reading some new W words together!

wås

When the letter W is at the end of a word, it can also be a sneaky silent letter. Let's read some words with the sneaky silent W!

Såw

Påw

jåw

Great job! When we add a letter S to the end of a word, it makes the word "plural" — that means there is more than one! So, just one paw becomes paws. That means there is more than one paw! Let's try reading some plural words!

jåws

såws

påws

(Have the student complete the Little Learner Activity Sheet.)

BONUS ACTIVITIES:

(Student has learned N, D, Ă, T, S, P, Ĭ, F, Ŏ, B, Ā, Ī, Å, J, Ē, M, L, Ŭ, Ō, R, C, and W so far.)

- Print letters the student has learned onto pieces of paper. Spread the papers out onto the floor and give the student a beanbag (or similar object). Instruct the student to toss the beanbag onto the letter sheet and say the sound as you call out the letter's name (or vice versa).

- Use play-dough to shape the letter W. If desired, shape additional letters and practice reading words together.

- Read verse on page 154 on an "off" day.

A human king can never be perfect because our world is now imperfect. Do you remember why? Yes, because of sin. Let's read the verse below together. I'll point to each word as I read, and when we get to the large words, you can read those.

Fōr åll have sĭnned and fåll short of the glory of God.

(Romans 3:23 NKJV)

Ww

W is for **W**ould.
God **w**ould choose a new king.

Color the upper and lowercase W!

Reading: I think you know these words. Can you read them to me?

is	bŭt	sō
it	for	nō
åll	or	

Writing: The W is so much fun to write. Let's practice!

Activity: Write the first letter of each picture!

_____ in

_____ at.

H is for **H**ad. David **h**ad been a shepherd boy before God chose him to be the new king.

Detach and hand the student the
Little Learner Activity Sheet on page 159.

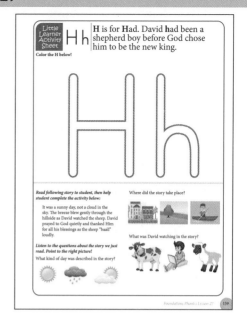

LESSON NARRATIVE

*This lesson covers the letter H. The sound of the letter H can be heard in the words had, held, and hat. As you read through this lesson, place emphasis on the sound of this letter where it is found in **bold** throughout the text.*

Are you ready to meet someone else very special in history on our adventure today? All right — let's get started! After the Lord rejected Saul as king, the Bible says that Samuel never went to see Saul again, and he was very sad. Then the Lord spoke to Samuel and said,

"How long will you be filled with sorrow because of Saul? I have refused to have him as king over Israel. Fill your animal horn with olive oil and go on your way. I am sending you to Jesse in Bethlehem. I have chosen one of his sons to be king" (1 Samuel 16:1).

So Samuel obeyed, and he traveled to Bethlehem. Now, you remember Ruth, don't you?

(Allow student time to answer; guide as necessary.)

Ruth married Boaz, and they had a son name Obed. Obed grew up and became the father of Jesse, the same Jesse the Lord sent Samuel to! When Samuel came to Jesse, he asked to see all of Jesse's sons. So

Jesse brought seven of his sons to Samuel, but the Lord told Samuel none of them were chosen to be king. So what do you think happened next?

(Allow student time to answer.)

Hmm, that's a good guess! Let's read from the Bible!

Jesse had seven of his sons walk in front of Samuel. But Samuel said to him, "The LORD hasn't chosen any of them." So he asked Jesse, "Are these the only sons you have?"

"No," Jesse answered. "My youngest son is taking care of the sheep."

Samuel said, "Send for him. We won't sit down to eat until he arrives."

So Jesse sent for his son and had him brought in. He looked very healthy. He had a fine appearance and handsome features.

Then the LORD said, "Get up and anoint him. This is the one."

So Samuel got the animal horn that was filled with olive oil. He anointed David in front of his brothers. From that day on, the Spirit of the LORD came powerfully on David. Samuel went back to Ramah (1 Samuel 16:10–13).

David had watched the sheep before God chose him as king. David **had** been a shepherd boy. I heard our sound for today — did you hear it too? Our letter for today is the letter **H**. The **H** says **h**. David **had** been a shepherd boy. The letter H looks like this:

(Ask student to trace uppercase and lowercase H with finger on the Little Learner Activity Sheet. Make sure the student points to the correct one.)

The uppercase H looks like this:

The lowercase H looks like this:

The H says **h**. Say it with me; the **H** says **h**. David **had** been a shepherd before God chose him as the new king. We'll be learning more about David in our next few lessons. Now, let's go learn more about the letter **h**!

(Now begin the reading section below. If your child needs to take a break from the lesson, let him or her begin the first page of the Little Learner Activity Sheet. Be sure to go back to the reading section of this lesson to complete it.)

READING

Let's read!

Hŏt

hăt

hē

hĭs

as

is

(Have the student complete the Little Learner Activity Sheet.)

BONUS ACTIVITIES:

(Student has learned N, D, Ă, T, S, P, Ĭ, F, Ŏ, B, Ā, Ī, Å, J, Ē, M, L, Ŭ, Ō, R, C, W, and H so far.)

- Help student draw letters he/she has learned onto construction paper. Glue cotton balls over the top of the letter. Add ears, eyes, and mouth to the picture to make sheep letters!

- Use sticky tabs or sheets of paper from above and write letters the student has learned. Place tabs or sheets on the floor. Give student a straw and mini pom-pom/ball fringe. Call out a letter or sound and ask student to blow the pom-pom onto the correct sheet.

H h

H is for **Had**. David **h**ad been a shepherd boy before God chose him to be the new king.

Color the H below!

Read following story to student, then help student complete the activity below:

It was a sunny day, not a cloud in the sky. The breeze blew gently through the hillside as David watched the sheep. David prayed to God quietly and thanked Him for all his blessings as the sheep "baa'd" loudly.

Listen to the questions about the story we just read. Point to the right picture!

What kind of day was described in the story?

Where did the story take place?

What was David watching in the story?

Writing: Let's write the letter H!

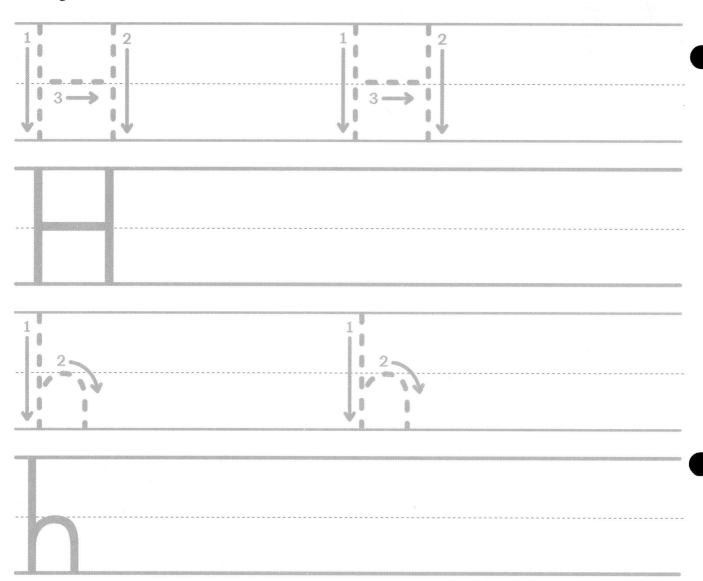

Letter Recognition: Color the circles with the letter H.

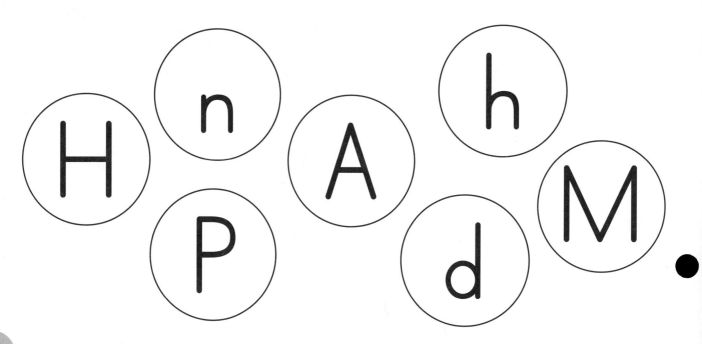

G is for **G**reater.
God is **g**reater than fear!

Detach and hand the
student the Little Learner
Activity Sheet on page 165.

LESSON NARRATIVE

> 💡 *This lesson covers the letter G. The sound of the letter G can be heard in the words God, get, and gate. As you read through this lesson, place emphasis on the sound of this letter where it is found in **bold** throughout the text.*

Today's adventure is a super exciting one! It will be so much fun! Did you bring your imagination with you? Well, get it started, and let's dive right in!

After Samuel anointed David as the new king of Israel, another nation called the Philistines gathered their army and came for war against the Israelites. So Saul gathered his armies and went to meet the Philistine army in the valley of Elah. Now, close your eyes and imagine the scene as I read the next part of the story!

> Goliath stood there and shouted to the soldiers of Israel. He said, "Why do you come out and line up for battle? I'm a Philistine. You are servants of Saul. Choose one of your men. Have him come down and face me. If he's able to fight and kill me, we'll become your slaves. But if I win and kill him, you will become our slaves and serve

us." Goliath continued, "This day I dare the soldiers of Israel to send a man down to fight against me." Saul and the whole army of Israel heard what the Philistine said. They were terrified (1 Samuel 17:8–11).

The whole Israelite army was scared of Goliath! Day after day he came and issued the same challenge. He taunted the army and was very disrespectful to God. Every morning and night for 40 days Goliath taunted the men of Israel.

Some of David's brothers were part of the army, and after they had been gone for a while, their father, Jesse, asked David to take them food and find out how they were doing. As David reached the camp, Goliath stepped forward to issue his challenge and all the men cowered in fear. David couldn't believe it! So David came to Saul and said,

> "Don't let anyone lose hope because of that Philistine. I'll go out and fight him."

> Saul replied, "You aren't able to go out there and fight that Philistine. You are too young. He's been a warrior ever since he was a boy."

> But David said to Saul, "I've been taking care of my father's sheep. Sometimes a lion

or a bear would come and carry off a sheep from the flock. Then I would go after it and hit it. I would save the sheep it was carrying in its mouth. If it turned around to attack me, I would grab its hair. I would strike it down and kill it. In fact, I've killed both a lion and a bear. I'll do the same thing to this Philistine. He isn't even circumcised. He has dared the armies of the living God to fight him. The LORD saved me from the paw of the lion. He saved me from the paw of the bear. And he'll save me from the powerful hand of this Philistine too."

Saul said to David, "Go. And may the LORD be with you" (1 Samuel 17:32–37).

Saul tried to give David armor before he went to fight Goliath, but it made David clumsy since he wasn't used to wearing big, heavy armor. Rather than armor, David took his staff, five stones from the stream, and a sling, and then he ran to meet Goliath on the battlefield.

When Goliath saw David, he became angry and he insulted David. Goliath told David he would lose the battle. But David wouldn't be swayed. Rather than cower in fear, David said to Goliath,

> "You are coming to fight against me with a sword, a spear and a javelin. But I'm coming against you in the name of the LORD who rules over all. He is the God of the armies of Israel. He's the one you have dared to fight against. This day the LORD will give me the victory over you. . . . Then the whole world will know there is a God in Israel. The LORD doesn't rescue people by using a sword or a spear. And everyone here will know it. The battle belongs to the LORD. He will hand all of you over to us."

As the Philistine moved closer to attack him, David ran quickly to the battle line to meet him. He reached into his bag. He took out a stone. He put it in his sling. He slung it at Goliath. The stone hit him on the forehead and sank into it. He fell to the ground on his face.

So David won the fight against Goliath with a sling and a stone. He struck down the Philistine and killed him. He did it without even using a sword (1 Samuel 17:45–50).

David was courageous, and he showed the army of Israel that **G**od is **g**reater than fear! Hey, was that a new sound? **G**od is **g**reater than fear! Yes it was! Our new letter today is the letter G. **G** says **g**, as in **g**reater. Can you say it with me? **G** says **g**.

Great job! The letter G looks like this:

G g

(Ask student to trace uppercase and lowercase G with finger on the Little Learner Activity Sheet. Make sure the student points to the correct one.)

The uppercase G looks like this:

G

The lowercase G looks like this:

g

God is **g**reater than fear! **G** says **g**. Sometimes, there are things in our lives that make us afraid. But when we are afraid, we can remember that God is greater than fear and He is with us. The Bible tells us in Isaiah 41:10:

> So do not be afraid. I am with you.
>   Do not be terrified. I am your God.
> I will make you strong and help you.
>   I will hold you safe in my hands.
>   I always do what is right.

When you are afraid, you can remember Isaiah 41:10 and know that God is greater than your fear. Now, we've learned a new letter, and it's time for some fun! Let's get started!

(Now begin the reading section below. If your child needs to take a break from the lesson, let him or her begin the first page of the Little Learner Activity Sheet. Be sure to go back to the reading section of this lesson to complete it.)

READING

We've learned a new letter. Let's read some new words!

gō

tăg

Săg

băg

Jŏg

(Have the student complete the Little Learner Activity Sheet.)

BONUS ACTIVITIES:

(Student has learned N, D, Ă, T, S, P, Ĭ, F, Ŏ, B, Ā, Ī, Å, J, Ē, M, L, Ŭ, Ō, R, C, W, H, and G so far.)

- Go on a letter hunt either at home or out and about. See how many G words you can locate together.

- Read a story together. See if student can find any G words as you read.

- Read verse on page 164 together on an "off" day.

Let's read the verse below together. I'll point to each word as I read, when we get to the large words, you can read those.

The larger words below may intimidate a child. If students need a challenge, let them sound each out. If they aren't quite ready for a word this big, simply sound it out for them and blend the sounds all together to form the word. Explain that when we see a large word we don't know, we can sound it out and find out! Then just move on through the text.

Sō do nŏt bē afraid. Ī ăm with you. Do nŏt bē terrified. Ī ăm your God. Ī wĭll make you strong ănd hĕlp you. Ī wĭll hold you safe ĭn my hănds.

I always do what ĭs right.

(Isaiah 41:10)

G g

G is for **Greater**.
God is **g**reater than fear!

Color the letter G!

Reading: Let's read some words!

hē   hŏw   wē

hĭs   cǎn   wĭll

Writing: Let's practice writing the letter G!

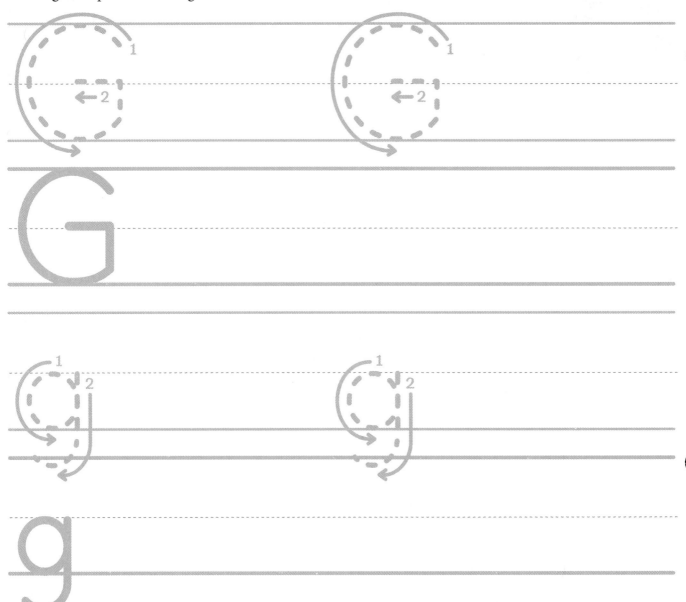

Activity: Flowers grow in a garden. Can you draw a small garden of flowers?

K is for **King**.
King David followed God.

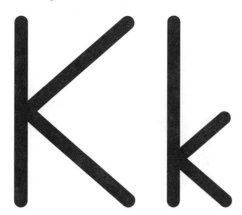

Detach and hand the student the
Little Learner Activity Sheet on page 169.

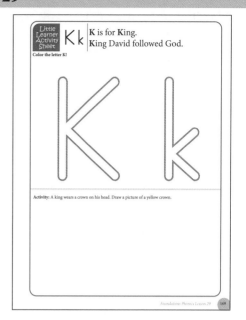

LESSON NARRATIVE

*This lesson covers the letter K. The
sound of the letter K can be heard in the
words king, kick, and kid. As you read
through this lesson, place emphasis on the
sound of this letter where it is found in **bold**
throughout the text.*

Wow! We've had some pretty amazing adventures
lately! Are you ready for our next one?

(Allow student time to answer.)

Although God had chosen David to be the new king
of Israel, David had to wait for God's timing. During
this time, David did a lot of running because Saul
wanted to kill him. Sometimes when God gives us
promises, we have to wait for them to be fulfilled —
but that doesn't mean God has forgotten!

After Saul died, David became the king of Israel.
King David was a good king, and he served and
followed God his whole life. In fact, the Lord called
David a "man after His own heart" in 1 Samuel
13:14!

Now David did make mistakes — sometimes some
very big mistakes — but once he realized he had
sinned against God, David also repented and asked

God to forgive him. **K**ing David followed God, and
he was even included in the family line of Jesus!
Hey, I heard a new sound. Did you hear it too? **K**ing
David followed God. There it is! Our new letter for
today is the letter **K**! The **K** says **k**, as in **k**ing. **K**ing
David followed God.

The letter K looks like this:

***(Ask student to trace uppercase and lowercase K
with finger on the Little Learner Activity Sheet.
Make sure the student points to the correct one.)***

The uppercase K looks like this:

The lowercase K looks like this:

They look very similar, don't they? The **K** says **k**. **K**ing David followed God. Can you say it with me? The **K** says **k**. David's life sure was amazing to learn about, wasn't it? But now it is time to move further along in our adventure. First though, we've learned a new letter, and I am so excited! It's time for some more letter fun!

(Now begin the reading section below. If your child needs to take a break from the lesson, let him or her begin the first page of the Little Learner Activity Sheet. Be sure to go back to the reading section of this lesson to complete it.)

READING

We've learned a new letter, so let's read some new words! When we see two of the same letter, we just make its sound once. One of these words is also playing a silly game—when you see the grey e, you'll know that e stays silent!

Kēēn

Kīnd

Kēēp

kĭd

kīte

(Have the student complete the Little Learner Activity Sheet.)

BONUS ACTIVITIES:

(Student has learned N, D, Ă, T, S, P, Ĭ, F, Ŏ, B, Ā, Ī, Å, J, Ē, M, L, Ŭ, Ō, R, C, W, H, G, and K so far.)

- Use construction paper to form a crown. Help student write the word "king" on it to remind him or her of King David!

- Read your favorite Psalm to the student. Tell the student David wrote many of the Psalms. Once you've read it, ask the student questions about what the Psalm was about.

- After you have read the Psalm together, ask the student to pick out words he or she can read. Guide student by pointing out some words if necessary.

K k | **K** is for **King.**
King David followed God.

Color the letter K!

Activity: A king wears a crown on his head. Draw a picture of a yellow crown.

Writing: Let's practice writing the letter K!

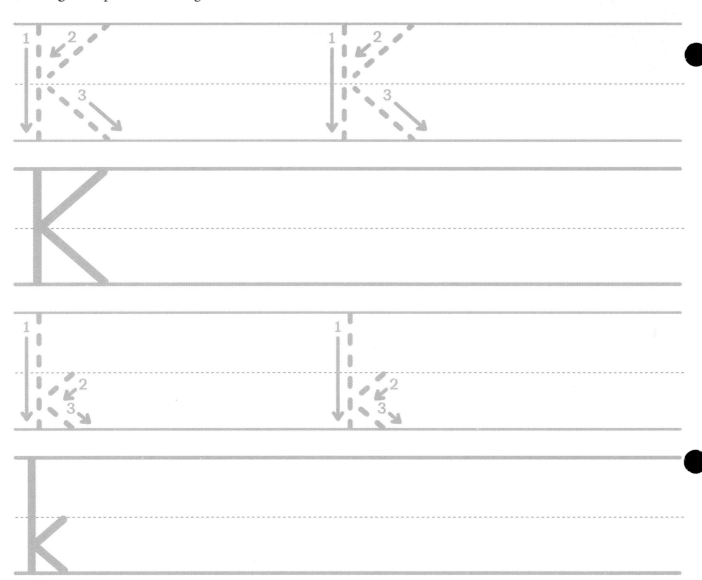

Activity: Draw a line from the picture to the first letter in its name!

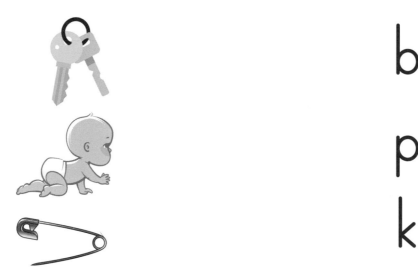

b

p

k

Review

N D Ă T S P Ĭ

F Ŏ B Ā Ī Å

J Ē M L Ŭ Ō

R C W H G K

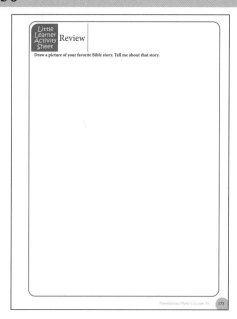

Detach and hand the student the Little Learner Activity Sheet on page 173.

LESSON NARRATIVE

Review.

Are you ready for our review day? Me too! Can you tell me about a letter you've learned recently?

(Allow student time to answer; guide as necessary.)

Well, we learned about Hannah and how God heard her cry. The letter C says c. Let's read some C words together!

căt

cŏt

căb

cår

Good job! Next we learned all about David and the letters H, G, W, and K! Can you tell me about David?

(Allow student time to answer; guide as necessary.)

Great job remembering! Let's read some words!

gāte

kĭd

Kēep

Såw

bēet

You did a great job reading! Let's try some sentences!

Ī ăm ā kĭd.
Ī căn sĭt.
Ī căn rŭn.
Ī căn rēad!

Awesome! Now, look at each sentence. See how each sentence begins with a capital letter? Sentences also have a special mark at the end called a punctuation mark. That was a big word!

See the dot at the end of the first sentence. That punctuation mark is called a period.

Which sentence has something different at the end of it?

(Allow the student time to point out the sentence with the exclamation point.)

That punctuation mark is an exclamation point. Now that we learned about sentences, let's have some fun!

(Have the student complete the Little Learner Activity Sheet.)

BONUS ACTIVITIES:

(Student has learned N, D, Ă, T, S, P, Ĭ, F, Ŏ, B, Ā, Ī, Å, J, Ē, M, L, Ŭ, Ō, R, C, W, H, G, and K so far.)

• Read a simple book with the student. Point out how the letters and sounds are working together to make words. Help student to read words he or she has learned.

Review

Draw a picture of your favorite Bible story. Tell me about that story.

Activity: Trace the shapes. Color the square blue, the triangle red, the car orange, and the circle yellow.

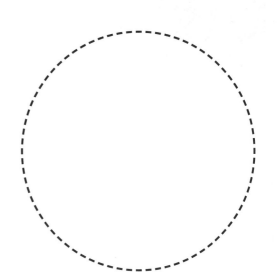

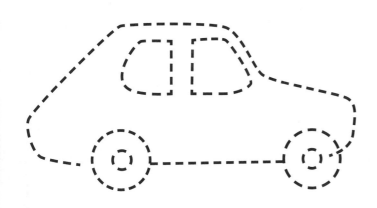

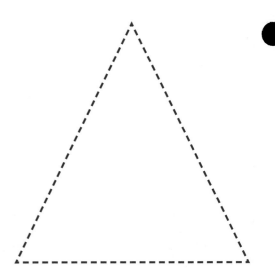

Th is for **The.**
Solomon built **the** temple.

Detach and hand the student the
Little Learner Activity Sheet on page 179.

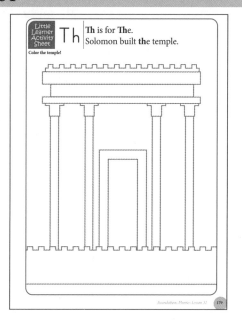

LESSON NARRATIVE

> 💡 *This lesson covers the Th blend. The sound of the Th blend can be heard in the words the, that, and then. As you read through this lesson, place emphasis on the sound of this blend where it is found in **bold** throughout the text.*

Let's get started on our new adventure for today! After King David died, his son Solomon became king of Israel. Solomon asked the Lord to give him wisdom, and the Lord made him a very wise and wealthy man! Solomon also built **th**e temple in Jerusalem. Ooh, there is our new sound for today! Today's sound is a blend. A blend is the sound two letters make when they sit side by side. When a T and an H sit side by side, they say **th**. The T and H blend looks like this:

th

Or like this:

Th

The T H blend says **th**. Do you remember Moses and what we learned about him?

(Allow student time to answer; guide as necessary.)

As Moses led the people through the wilderness, God gave very specific instructions for building what was called the "tabernacle." Since the children of Israel were still traveling through the desert, the tabernacle was designed so that it could be moved along with them as they traveled. It was the place the Israelites worshiped God, where sacrifices for their sins were made, and God's glory filled the tabernacle.

And so, from Moses' time all the way to Solomon, the children of Israel worshiped God at the tabernacle. During Solomon's time as king, he built the temple. The temple was a huge, permanent structure that replaced the tabernacle. Once construction was completed, the people held a feast, and sacrificed, and Solomon dedicated the temple to the Lord. The Lord's glory settled into the holy place in the temple, just as it had in the tabernacle. Then the Lord spoke to Solomon. Let's read what God promised him from the Bible!

> The LORD said to him, "I have heard you pray to me. I have heard you ask me to help you. You have built this temple. I have set it apart for myself. My Name will be there

forever. My eyes and my heart will always be there. But you must walk faithfully with me, just as your father David did. Your heart must be honest. It must be without blame. Do everything I command you to do. Obey my rules and laws. Then I will set up your royal throne over Israel forever. I promised your father David I would do that. I said to him, 'You will always have a son from your family line on the throne of Israel' " (1 Kings 9:3–5).

God gave Solomon a promise, but God also gave him a warning and severe consequences if he did not follow what God had commanded. We will find out what happened in another lesson, but for today, we learned that Solomon built the temple. "The" is a very special word; we use it all the time! The has the T H blend and looks like this:

(Point to the word and read it to the student.)

Or like this:

Look at the word and read it with me!

the

Great job! The T H blend says **th**. Solomon built **the** temple. Do you think Solomon will obey God's commands?

(Allow student time to answer.)

I guess we will have to wait to find out! It's time for some more letter fun!

(Now begin the reading section below. If your child needs to take a break from the lesson, let him or her begin the first page of the Little Learner Activity Sheet. Be sure to go back to the reading section of this lesson to complete it.)

READING

Let's use our new word "the" and practice reading!

the căt   the dŏg

the măn   the jăr

Let's read a story!

Sēē the căt?
The căt săt.
Căt såw ā dŏg.
The căt răn făst!

Great job! Point to the picture that answers the question.

What was the cat doing first?

  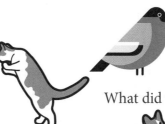

What did the cat see?

What did the cat do at the end?

(Have the student complete the Little Learner Activity Sheet.)

BONUS ACTIVITIES:

(Student has learned N, D, Ă, T, S, P, Ĭ, F, Ŏ, B, Ā, Ī, Å, J, Ē, M, L, Ŭ, Ō, R, C, W, H, G, K, and TH so far.)

- Use small, round candies like M&Ms® to construct letters or words. Enjoy a sweet treat after!

- Practice sight words from the front of the book with the student.

- Make words for student to read using alphabet stamps. Think of a word, then see if the student can sound it out and say what letters make up the word.

- Read Psalm on page 178 on an "off" day. Talk about what the passage means after you've read it together.

King David wrote many of the Psalms. Let's read part of a Psalm together!

(Read the passage with your student. Allow him or her to read the large words.)

This passage contains several sight words; see if your student can point them out! As this is a larger passage which may stretch your student, symbols have been included on these sight words as a gentle reminder in case your student does need to sound out a word. After reading, ask your student what these verses mean and discuss them together.

LŌRD, you have sēēn what ĭs ĭn my heart. You know åll about mē. You know when I sĭt dŏwn ănd when I get ŭp. You know what I'm thinking even though you åre får away. (Psalm 139:1-2)

Th

Th is for **The**.
Solomon built **th**e temple.

Color the temple!

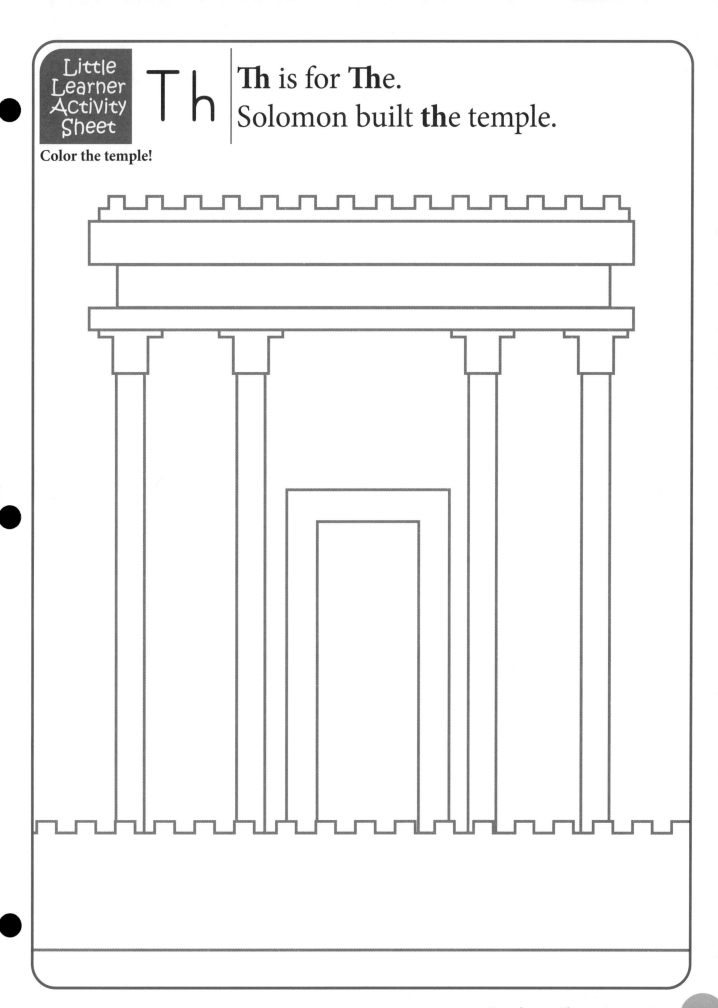

Writing: Write the following words.

the

at

to

so

if

Sp is for **Sp**lit.
The kingdom of Israel was **sp**lit apart.

Sp

Detach and hand the
student the Little Learner
Activity Sheet on page 185.

LESSON NARRATIVE

> *This lesson covers the Sp blend. The
> sound of the Sp blend can be heard in the
> words split, spot, and speck. As you read
> through this lesson, place emphasis on the
> sound of this blend where it is found in* **bold**
> *throughout the text.*

Here we are on adventure number 32! Can you
believe how far we've come? You've learned so many
letters, and you're reading so well! Are you ready for
today's adventure? Is your imagination set to go?

(Allow student time to answer.)

Well then, let's get started! We learned last time
about Solomon, the temple, and the promise God
gave him. Today we learn about the warning God
also gave him. Let's read it from the very best book,
the Bible! We'll start with the promise, and then
listen close:

> "I have heard you pray to me. I have heard
> you ask me to help you. You have built this
> temple. I have set it apart for myself. My
> Name will be there forever. My eyes and my
> heart will always be there.

> "But you must walk faithfully with me, just
> as your father David did. Your heart must

be honest. It must be without blame. Do
everything I command you to do. Obey my
rules and laws. Then I will set up your royal
throne over Israel forever. I promised your
father David I would do that. I said to him,
'You will always have a son from your family
line on the throne of Israel.'

"But suppose all of you turn away from me.
Or your children turn away from me. You
refuse to obey the commands and rules I
have given you. And you go off to serve
other gods and worship them. Then I will
remove Israel from the land. It is the land
I gave them. I will turn my back on this
temple. I will do it even though I have set it
apart for my Name to be there. Then Israel
will be hated by all the nations. They will
laugh and joke about Israel. This temple
will become a pile of stones. All those who
pass by it will be shocked. They will make
fun of it. And they will say, 'Why has the
LORD done a thing like this to this land
and temple?' People will answer, 'Because
they have deserted the LORD their God.
He brought out of Egypt their people of
long ago. But they have been holding on to
other gods. They've been worshiping them.

They've been serving them. That's why the LORD has brought all this horrible trouble on them' " (1 Kings 9:3–9).

Wow, God gave Solomon an amazing promise, but there was a condition — Solomon had to follow the Lord wholeheartedly. If he didn't, the consequences would be severe. What do you think Solomon did?

(Allow student time to answer.)

Well, I'm sad to say that Solomon didn't listen to the Lord. The Bible says,

> Solomon did what was evil in the sight of the LORD. He didn't completely obey the LORD. He didn't do what his father David had done (1 Kings 11:6).

How very sad! Solomon knew the right things to do, but he did not do them. God had warned Solomon what would happen if he chose not to obey God. Let's read what happened from the Bible:

> So the LORD said to Solomon, "You have chosen not to keep my covenant. You have decided not to obey my rules. I commanded you to do what I told you. But you did not do it. So you can be absolutely sure I will tear the kingdom away from you. I will give it to one of your officials. But I will not do that while you are still living. Because of your father David I will wait. I will tear the kingdom out of your son's hand" (1 Kings 11:11–12).

When we choose not to obey the Lord, there are consequences. After Solomon died, the kingdom of Israel was split apart, just as God said it would be. Now there would be two kingdoms, Israel and Judah. Because of Solomon's choice not to follow God's ways, the kingdom was **sp**lit apart. Hey, did you hear something?

(Allow student time to answer.)

I heard our new sound for today! Today's sound is another blend. When the S and the P are right next to each other, the sound they make is **sp**. The kingdom of Israel was **sp**lit apart. The S P blend says **sp**. Can you say it with me? **Sp**.

The S P blend looks like this:

s p

Or like this:

S p

God gives us all choices to make. When we choose to follow God's ways, God promises to take care of us. But when we make the choice to disobey God's ways, there are consequences to our decision. Consequences are the price we have to pay. Solomon chose not to follow God's ways, and paid the price for his decision. The kingdom of Israel was **sp**lit apart, just like God had warned. I wonder if the kingdoms will choose to follow God's ways. What do you think?

(Allow student time to answer.)

I guess we'll find out! Now, we've learned a new sound, and it's time for some fun!

*(**Now begin the reading section. If your child needs to take a break from the lesson, let him or her begin the first page of the Little Learner Activity Sheet. Be sure to go back to the reading section of this lesson to complete it.**)*

We've learned a new sound, sp! Let's read some words!

spăn   spŏt

spĭt

Let's read a story!

The dŏg ĭs tăn.

Hĭs nāme ĭs Fīdō.

Fīdō hăs ā spŏt.

The spŏt ĭs bĭg.

Fīdō hăs ā bĭg spŏt!

Great job! Point to the correct answer to the questions.

What is the dog's name?

Fīdō   Spŏt

(Have the student complete the Little Learner Activity Sheet.)

(Student has learned N, D, Ă, T, S, P, Ĭ, F, Ŏ, B, Ā, Ī, Å, J, Ē, M, L, Ŭ, Ō, R, C, W, H, G, K, TH, and SP so far.)

- Use toothpicks and marshmallows to construct letters. Turn letters into words.

- Use a computer word processor, and type one letter or sight word per page. Print out each page and insert into a page protector. Give student a dry erase marker and have him/her practice writing the letters or words.

Sp

Sp is for **Sp**lit. The kingdom of Israel was **sp**lit apart.

Color the map of Israel and Judah below!

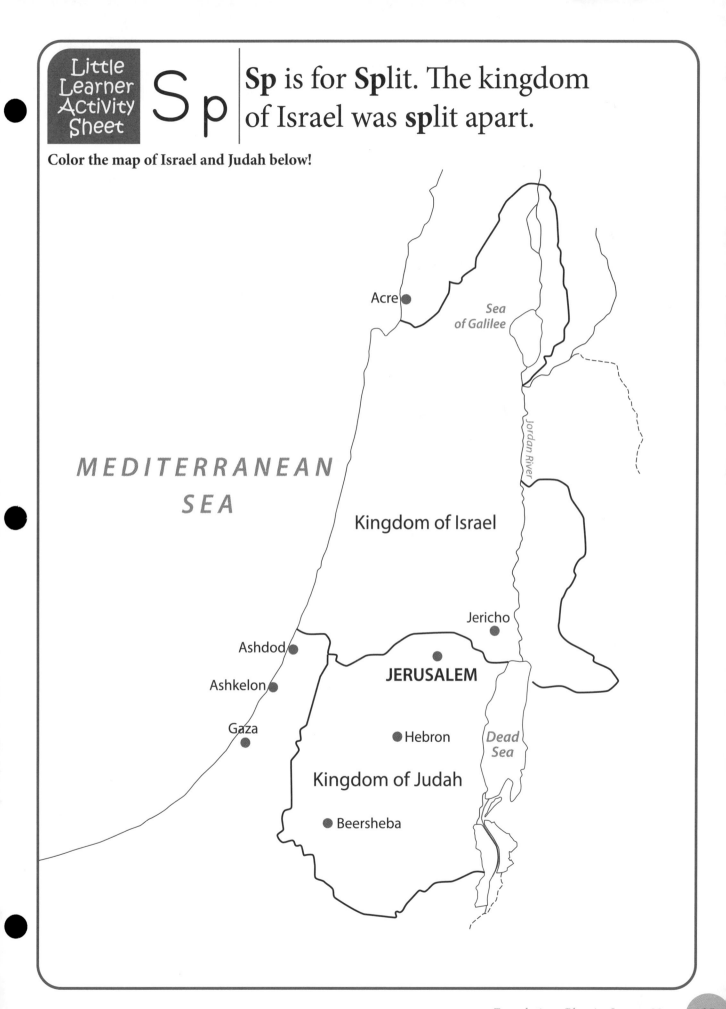

Acre

Sea of Galilee

Jordan River

MEDITERRANEAN SEA

Kingdom of Israel

Jericho

Ashdod

JERUSALEM

Ashkelon

Gaza

Hebron

Dead Sea

Kingdom of Judah

Beersheba

Activity: What color do you think his spot is? Draw his spot, and color it the color you think it is. Color the rest of Fido tan.

Foundations Phonics

Ck is for Ba**ck**. Israel was
sent ba**ck** into captivity and exile.

Detach and hand the student the
Little Learner Activity Sheet on page 189.

LESSON NARRATIVE

> *This lesson covers the Ck blend. The sound of the Ck blend can be heard in the words back, sack, and lack. As you read through this lesson, place emphasis on the sound of this blend where it is found in* **bold** *throughout the text.*

Why hello there! It is time for another adventure! Last time, we learned that Solomon did not heed God's warning, and the kingdom was split apart. Now, there were two kingdoms, the northern kingdom of Israel and the southern kingdom of Judah. Each kingdom now had different kings.

The Lord sent prophets, just like Samuel, to the kingdoms. The prophets warned the people that the Lord would punish their sin if they did not repent. They warned the people that the kingdom would be destroyed, and the people would be taken far away from their homes. Sometimes the people listened; many times they did not. In the northern kingdom of Israel, the many kings did evil in the sight of the Lord. They led the people to disobey God. Because of their disobedience, God allowed the nation of Assyria to conquer Israel and the people were taken from their homes. It was very, very sad.

In the southern kingdom of Judah, some kings were good and showed the people how to follow God, but some kings were bad and did evil things. Because the southern kingdom also did not listen to God's warnings to turn from their sin, God allowed the nation of Babylon to conquer Judah, destroy the temple Solomon had built, and take the people far away from their homes. Both kingdoms were now in captivity, just like the people had been in Egypt.

Israel and Judah were sent ba**ck** into captivity and exile. I heard a new sound; did you hear it too? Israel and Judah were sent ba**ck** into captivity and exile. Our sound today is another blend. This blend is the sound that the C and the K make when they are right next to each other; **ck**, as in ba**ck**. The Ck blend looks like this:

$$ck$$

(Point to the blend and say the sound with student.)

Israel and Judah did wrong in the sight of the Lord. Though it was very sad when the nations went into captivity, God was still working out His plan. God gives us consequences because He loves us — He knows that allowing us to continue sinning hurts us. Eventually, God brought His people back into their land and the cities were rebuilt. God sent men to remind and teach them the ways of the Lord. We will continue our adventure on another day, but for today we've learned a new sound, and it is time for some fun!

(Now begin the reading section below. If your child needs to take a break from the lesson, let him or her begin the first page of the Little Learner Activity Sheet. Be sure to go back to the reading section of this lesson to complete it.)

READING

We've learned a new sound, ck! Let's read some words!

bǎck

tǎck

dǔck

lǔck

trǔck

kǐck

lǐck

(Have the student complete the Little Learner Activity Sheet.)

BONUS ACTIVITIES:

(Student has learned N, D, Ǎ, T, S, P, Ǐ, F, Ǒ, B, Ā, Ī, Å, J, Ē, M, L, Ǔ, Ō, R, C, W, H, G, K, TH, SP, and CK so far.)

- "Drive" toy cars through finger paint, then drive onto paper and make letter shapes.

- Call out a sound, and have the student write the letter.

- With your finger, "draw" a letter on the student's back. See if he/she can figure out which letter it was and write it on paper.

Ck is for Ba**ck**. Israel was sent ba**ck** into captivity and exile.

Color the picture of the Bible below!

Writing: Let's practice writing some words! Read the words as you write them.

and   as

an   at

Activity: Draw a truck.

Ĕ is for Esther.
God had a very special plan for **Esther**.

Detach and hand the student the
Little Learner Activity Sheet on page 195.

Ĕ is for Esther. God had a very special plan for **Esther**.

LESSON NARRATIVE

*This lesson covers the short sound of the letter E. This sound is designated within the lesson with the following symbol above the letters: Ĕĕ. The short sound can be heard in the words Ĕsther, ĕgg, and lĕt. As you read through this lesson, place emphasis on the sound of this letter where it is found in **bold** throughout the text.*

Oh, here we are again, ready for a new reading adventure! Are you ready to learn an amazing story today?

(Allow student time to answer.)

Yay! Let's get started! Last time we learned how the Jews had been sent into captivity for the wrong they had done before the Lord. This was certainly a very sad, difficult time for the people, but God's promises to them were still true and He had not forgotten them! Eventually, the Jews were allowed to return back to their homes. However, because their homes were still destroyed in Jerusalem, many families decided to remain in exile. What do you think it would feel like to be so far away from your country?

(Allow student time to answer.)

In our adventure today, we meet a woman named Esther. When we meet Esther, she is living far away from home in Babylon. Esther's parents had died, so her cousin Mordecai had raised her.

Now close your eyes and imagine you can see her story as I tell it to you!

The king of Babylon, Xerxes, needed a new queen. So he called all the young women to the palace so he could pick a new queen. Can you imagine how Esther must have felt to have to leave her home to live in the palace while the king picked a new queen? Do you think she was scared or excited?

(Allow student time to answer.)

Esther was beautiful, and many people loved to be around her. When the king met her, he chose her to be the new queen! It must have been so exciting, but also scary for Esther because her life would change so much. A very bad man named Haman hated Mordecai and all of the Jews. He tricked the king into passing a law that would mean all the Jews in the land would be killed.

When Mordecai learned of this plan, he sent word to Esther and asked her to go before the king and ask him to save her people, the Jews. But there was a big problem! At that time, if the king had not invited you to appear before him, you could be put to death! Esther was afraid, but Mordecai reminded her that maybe God had placed her in the position of queen for just this purpose.

Yet who knows whether you have come to the kingdom for such a time as this? (Esther 4:14; NKJV)

So Esther went before the king — and he welcomed her in! With great wisdom, Esther revealed to the king that she herself was a Jew and that Haman had plotted to kill all the Jews. The king was very upset by this — Esther was his queen — so he punished Haman severely and made a new law that saved the Jewish people. How amazing! God had a very special plan for **Esther**. Did you hear that sound? I think we found our new letter for today! God had a very special plan for **Esther**.

Our letter for today is the letter **E**! The **E** says **ĕ**. Can you say it with me? The **E** says **ĕ**.

(Repeat with student as necessary to reinforce.)

God had a very special plan for Esther.

The letter E looks like this:

$$Ee$$

(Ask student to trace uppercase and lowercase E with finger on the Little Learner Activity Sheet.)

The uppercase E looks like this:

$$E$$

The lowercase E looks like this:

$$e$$

The **E** says **ĕ**. God had a very special plan for **Esther**. The letter **E** is another vowel! Vowels are special because they can make different sounds. When you see a letter E that looks like this:

you can be sure it says **ĕ** as in Esther! What an amazing adventure! Now it's time for some fun!

(Now begin the reading section below. If your child needs to take a break from the lesson, let him or her begin the first page of the Little Learner Activity Sheet. Be sure to go back to the reading section of this lesson to complete it.)

READING

I'm so excited to get started. Let's try reading some new words with our special new letter!

$$Fĕd$$

$$mĕn$$

$$dĕn$$

$$Bĕn$$

$$lĕd$$

(Have the student complete the Little Learner Activity Sheet.)

BONUS ACTIVITIES:

(Student has learned N, D, Ă, T, S, P, Ĭ, F, Ŏ, B, Ā, Ī, Å, J, Ē, M, L, Ŭ, Ō, R, C, W, H, G, K, TH, SP, CK, and Ĕ so far.)

- Gather sheets, costume jewelry, etc., and have students dress up. Girls can dress up like Queen Esther, boys can dress up as the king. Remind student of the story and how God had a very special plan for Esther (and for us too!).

- Have student trace the uppercase and lowercase letter E using his/her finger several times while repeating its sound.

- Gather toys and make a letter E shape, both uppercase and lowercase.

- Read the verse on page 194 together on an "off" day.

Proverbs 3:5 reminds us to trust in the Lord in everything with our whole hearts. Let's read it together!

(Read the passage with your student. Allow him or her to read the large words.)

 This is a passage with words your student may find difficult. Help him or her sound out the words when necessary.

Trŭst in the LŌRD wĭth åll your heart. Do nŏt dēpĕnd on your ōwn understanding.

(Proverbs 3:5)

E e

Ĕ is for Esther. God had a very special plan for Esther.

Color the picture below!

Writing: Great job! God had a very special plan for Esther. And we can be sure that God has a special plan for us too! Let's practice writing. Read and copy each word once on the lines below it.

the   in

I   at

was

Wh is for **Wh**en.
When Jonah disobeyed, things went wrong!

Detach and hand the student the
Little Learner Activity Sheet on page 201.

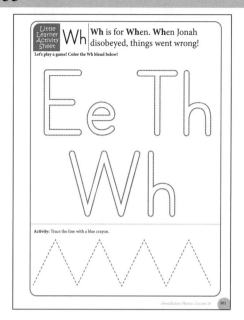

LESSON NARRATIVE

This lesson covers the Wh blend. The sound of the Wh blend can be heard in the words when, who, and what. As you read through this lesson, place emphasis on the sound of this blend where it is found in **bold** *throughout the text.*

Hmm, I smell something a little fishy today. What do you think our adventure will be about?

(Allow student time to guess.)

On our reading adventure today, we will learn about the prophet Jonah! Let's read the start of his story from the very best book, the Bible!

> A message from the LORD came to Jonah, the son of Amittai. The LORD said, "Go to the great city of Nineveh. Preach against it. The sins of its people have come to my attention." But Jonah ran away from the LORD. He headed for Tarshish. So he went down to the port of Joppa. There he found a ship that was going to Tarshish. He paid the fare and went on board. Then he sailed for Tarshish. He was running away from the LORD (Jonah 1:1–3).

Uh-oh, that doesn't sound very good. Can you tell me what Jonah did wrong?

(Allow student time to answer; guide as necessary.)

God gave Jonah instructions. God told him to go to Nineveh and warn them that they were very wicked in the sight of the Lord. But Jonah disobeyed God's instructions and traveled in the opposite direction. It isn't good when God gives us directions and we disobey Him. What do you think will happen?

(Allow student time to answer.)

Jonah got on the boat and fell asleep. As the boat sailed out to sea, God sent a huge storm — the Bible tells us that the ship was nearly broken apart! Can you show me what the sailors might have looked like as the boat rocked violently back and forth, and from side to side?

(Allow student time to act.)

Finally the shipmaster woke Jonah up and told him he better start to pray to his God to save them all. But then they discovered that Jonah had disobeyed God and the storm was God's punishment upon them. So Jonah told the men to throw him into the sea and God would calm the storm. What do you think happened next?

(Allow student time to answer.)

Hmm, let's read from the Bible and find out!

Now the LORD sent a huge fish to swallow Jonah. And Jonah was in the belly of the fish for three days and three nights (Jonah 1:17).

Wow! That must have been a huge fish! Can you imagine how Jonah may have felt? Do you think he was scared, angry, or sorry?

(Allow student time to answer.)

From the belly of the fish, Jonah called to God. God is merciful and compassionate. He heard Jonah and caused the fish to take him to dry land and spit him out there. So Jonah got up and went to Nineveh as the Lord had instructed him to. He told the people they had behaved wickedly, and in 40 days God would destroy the city. The people were afraid and sad; they repented for their sin and cried out to God to save them. Again, God heard and was compassionate and merciful to the people. Because they turned from their sin, God saved their city.

But Jonah was not happy that God had spared the city. God had shown Jonah much mercy, compassion, and grace when Jonah did wrong, but Jonah did not want God to do the same for others. It is important that we give mercy and compassion to others because God first gave mercy and compassion to us. Can you think of someone you could give mercy or compassion to?

(Allow student time to answer; guide as necessary.)

When Jonah disobeyed, things went wrong! Ooh, there was a new sound! Today's sound is another

blend. A blend is the special sound two letters make when they are together. Today's sound is the W H blend. When W and H are together, they make the sound **wh**.

The wh blend looks like this:

Or like this:

(Ask student to trace uppercase and lowercase wh with finger on the Little Learner Activity Sheet.)

When Jonah disobeyed, things went wrong! W and H say **wh** when they are together. We see stories throughout the Bible of people who obeyed or disobeyed God. It is important that we obey God because His way is the best way. Are you ready for some fun?

(Now begin the reading section. If your child needs to take a break from the lesson, let him or her begin the first page of the Little Learner Activity Sheet. Be sure to go back to the reading section of this lesson to complete it.)

Now let's read some new words! Are you ready?
Let's go!

Whĕn   whåt

Let's read a sentence.

Ī wĭll fŏllōw Gŏd.

Sometimes, words are a little silly. They don't follow the rules at all! "Where" is a word we use a lot. Where looks like this:

where

(Point to "where" and read the word with student.)

When we see this word, we read it as where. Shall we try it?

Where ăm Ī?

Good job!

(Have the student complete the Little Learner Activity Sheet.)

BONUS ACTIVITIES:

(Student has learned N, D, Ă, T, S, P, Ĭ, F, Ŏ, B, Ā, Ĭ, Å, J, Ē, M, L, Ŭ, Ō, R, C, W, H, G, K, TH, SP, CK, Ĕ, and WH so far.)

- Eat fish for dinner. Ask student to tell the story of Jonah and reinforce lesson as you eat.

- Ask student to draw and color a picture of the fish God sent to swallow Jonah. Help student draw the Wh blend at the top of the sheet.

- On an "off" day, read the verse on page 200 with your child and let him or her read the large words throughout.

- Ask student to tell you a story, then work through the following prompts with student as you point out the wh blend of each question:

  ~ Who was the story about?

  ~ What was the story about?

  ~ When did the story take place?

  ~ Where did the story happen?

  ~ Why did it happen?

The story of Jonah is pretty amazing, and it reminds us to obey God. Let's read one of the verses from Jonah's story together!

Nŏw the LŌRD sĕnt a huge fish to swȧllōw Jōnȧh. And Jōnȧh wȧs in the belly of the fish for thrēē days and thrēē nights.

(Jonah 1:17)

Wh

Wh is for **Wh**en. **Wh**en Jonah disobeyed, things went wrong!

Let's play a game! Color the Wh blend below!

Activity: Trace the line with a blue crayon.

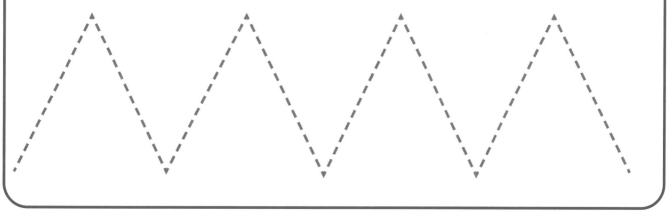

Reading: Let's read a sentence.

Ī wĭll fŏllōw Gŏd.

Writing: Let's practice writing. Help the student space words properly by putting a finger after the "I" so that they know where to start the new word, "will." Now write the sentence you read below!

I will

follow

God.

Review

N D Ă T S P Ĭ
F Ŏ B Ā Ī Å J
Ē M L Ŭ Ō R
C W H G K TH
SP CK Ĕ WH

Reading: Good! Let's read a story!

Where ĭs Spŏt?
Spŏt ĭs ā dŏg.
Hē ĭs ā good dŏg.
Where ĭs he?
Wē wĭll look
nēar the trēē.
There Spŏt ĭs!

You read really well! Can you answer the questions about what we just read?
What is Spot?
Was Spot missing?
Where was Spot?

Foundations Phonics Lesson 36 205

Detach and hand the student the Little Learner Activity Sheet on page 205.

LESSON NARRATIVE

Phew! We've done a lot of learning lately! Can you tell me about your favorite story so far?

(Allow student time to answer; guide as necessary.)

We've learned about the temple that Solomon built. Can you read the words below?

the

thĕn

thăt

Here is another silly word — it is like "where." It doesn't follow the rules.

there

(Point to the word and say it with student.)

there

where

Good!

(Student has learned N, D, Ă, T, S, P, Ĭ, F, Ŏ, B, Ā, Ī, Å, J, Ē, M, L, Ŭ, Ō, R, C, W, H, G, K, TH, SP, CK, Ĕ, and WH so far.)

- Have student draw a picture of his/her favorite Bible story thus far. Ask student to tell you about that story in his or her own words.

- Read a simple book with the student. Point out how the letters and sounds are working together to make words. Help student to read words he or she has learned.

Reading: Good! Let's read a story!

Where ĭs Spŏt?

Spŏt ĭs ā dŏg.

Hē ĭs ā good dŏg.

Where ĭs he?

Wē wĭll look

nēar the trēē.

There Spŏt ĭs!

You read really well! Can you answer the questions about what we just read?

What is Spot?

Was Spot missing?

Where was Spot?

Activity: Draw a picture of Spot and a tree with green leaves and a brown trunk from the story we just read!

Good job. Now we are all done!

Ou is for Ab**ou**t. The prophecies ab**ou**t God's plan would be fulfilled.

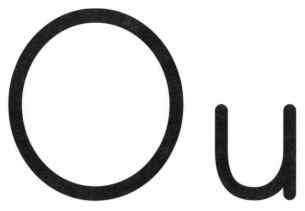

Detach and hand the student the Little Learner Activity Sheet on page 211.

LESSON NARRATIVE

*This lesson covers the Ou blend. This blend sounds like "ow" and can be heard in the words about and house. As you read through this lesson, place emphasis on the sound of this blend where it is found in **bold** throughout the text.*

Welcome back. Here we go yet again! We've got a really neat adventure in store for today; but first, can you tell me about your favorite letter we've learned on the way?

(Allow student time to answer; guide as necessary.)

That is really cool; I like that letter too! Remember when we learned about the prophets? The prophets gave warnings and encouragement from the Lord. Many times they predicted what would happen in the future as the Lord revealed it to them. When that happened, it was called a "prophecy." There are some extra special prophecies in the Bible that tell us about God's special plan to pay the price for our sin. Let's read some of these very special prophecies from the Bible!

Therefore the Lord Himself will give you a sign: Behold, the virgin shall conceive and bear a Son, and shall call His name Immanuel (Isaiah 7:14; NKJV).

For unto us a Child is born, unto us a Son is given; and the government will be upon His shoulder. And His name will be called Wonderful, Counselor, Mighty God, Everlasting Father, Prince of Peace" (Isaiah 9:6; NKJV).

But the servant was pierced because we had sinned. He was crushed because we had done what was evil. He was punished to make us whole again. His wounds have healed us (Isaiah 53:5).

The Bible is true, and God's Word can be trusted. There are many, many prophecies in the Bible like the ones we just read! God's Word is truth, and the prophecies about God's plan would be fulfilled. We will learn about that in another lesson, but for right now I think I heard a new sound! The prophecies ab**ou**t God's plan would be fulfilled. We are learning another blend today! A blend is the sound two letters make when they are next to each other. When the O and the U are next to each other, they make a sound like "ow." The O U blend looks like this:

Or like this:

o u

(Ask student to trace uppercase and lowercase ou with finger on the Little Learner Activity Sheet.)

Let's compare. Read the words — they both make the same sound!

(Point to each one and say "ow" with the student.)

o w

o u

Wonderful! I'm so very proud! The prophecies about God's plan would be fulfilled. As we continue our adventure, you will learn to read more and more, and we'll learn more and more about God's plan! Now let's go have some more word fun!

(Now begin the reading section below. If your child needs to take a break from the lesson, let him or her begin the first page of the Little Learner Activity Sheet. Be sure to go back to the reading section of this lesson to complete it.)

READING

Let's read some words!

mouse

house

cŏw

cloud

loud

out

Awesome! Sometimes, silly words don't follow the rules. Here are two new words that don't follow the rules:

do

to

(Point to word and read to student.)

The O "do" says oo, like it does in the word "moo." The "O" in "to" also says oo like it does in the word "moo"! When you see these words, you know that they say "oo" as in "moo."

Let's try reading a sentence with these silly words:

The Bīble tĕlls mē whåt to do. Ī līke to do whåt the Bīble tĕlls ŭs to do. Ī fŏllōw Gŏd!

(Have the student complete the Little Learner Activity Sheet.)

BONUS ACTIVITIES:

(Student has learned N, D, Ă, T, S, P, Ĭ, F, Ŏ, B, Ā, Ī, Å, J, Ē, M, L, Ŭ, Ō, R, C, W, H, G, K, TH, SP, CK, Ĕ, WH, and OU so far.)

- Together, look up additional prophecies about the coming of Jesus. Read them as a family, and talk about how God's Word would be fulfilled through Jesus.

- Gather a baking sheet and sugar or flour. Spread an even layer of sugar or flour onto the sheet, and draw words in it for the student to read. Guide as necessary. Once a word has been read, affirm the student and spread the sugar/flour back out and draw another. See how many words the student can read!

Review the alphabet. Have the student say each letter. For a special challenge, see if they can spell out their first name by pointing to the letters.

Aa Bb Cc Dd Ee

Ff Gg Hh Ii Jj

Kk Ll Mm Nn Oo

Pp Qq Rr Ss Tt Uu

Vv Ww Xx Yy Zz

Ou is for Ab**ou**t. The prophecies ab**ou**t God's plan would be fulfilled.

Color the letters Ou!

Writing: Let's write some words.

out

loud

Now let's color the picture below!

Ch is for **Ch**ild.
A **ch**ild was born, just as God said.

Detach and hand the student the
Little Learner Activity Sheet on page 217.

LESSON NARRATIVE

*This lesson covers the Ch blend. The Ch blend can be heard in the words child, check, and cheer. As you read through this lesson, place emphasis on the sound of this blend where it is found in **bold** throughout the text.*

Today we start the best part of our adventure! In our next few lessons, we will learn all about how God's plan to save us from the Fall and our sin was fulfilled! Are you ready to start? Well here we go!

In our last lesson, we learned about the prophecies that told how God's plan to save men would work. Remember the prophecies we read in our last lesson? They would be fulfilled through Jesus Christ. Oh, but wait, we are getting a little ahead of the story!

Put on your imagination. Get it started and ready. God chose a special young woman named Mary to be a part of His plan. Close your eyes and imagine a quiet day. Maybe Mary was quietly working on chores — but then, an angel appeared all of a sudden! Can you imagine the scene? How do you think Mary felt?

(Allow student time to answer.)

Those are all good guesses. Let's read from the very best book, the Bible, to find out what happened!

God sent the angel Gabriel to Nazareth, a town in Galilee. He was sent to a virgin. The girl was engaged to a man named Joseph. He came from the family line of David. The virgin's name was Mary. The angel greeted her and said, "The Lord has blessed you in a special way. He is with you."

Mary was very upset because of his words. She wondered what kind of greeting this could be. But the angel said to her, "Do not be afraid, Mary. God is very pleased with you. You will become pregnant and give birth to a son. You must call him Jesus. He will be great and will be called the Son of the Most High God. The Lord God will make him a king like his father David of long ago. The Son of the Most High God will rule forever over his people. They are from the family line of Jacob. That kingdom will never end" (Luke 1:26–33).

Mary wasn't sure how this could happen, and she was probably still a little scared! But Mary served the Lord and trusted Him, even though she didn't understand. So she accepted the angel's words and replied,

"I serve the Lord," Mary answered. "May it happen to me just as you said it would." Then the angel left her (Luke 1:38).

So it happened, just like the angel said it would! God had started working out His plan to save us from our sins. Ready to read the next part of the story? Get your imagination started — here we go!

In those days, Caesar Augustus made a law. It required that a list be made of everyone in the whole Roman world. It was the first time a list was made of the people while Quirinius was governor of Syria. Everyone went to their own town to be listed.

So Joseph went also. He went from the town of Nazareth in Galilee to Judea. That is where Bethlehem, the town of David, was. Joseph went there because he belonged to the family line of David. He went there with Mary to be listed. Mary was engaged to him. She was expecting a baby. While Joseph and Mary were there, the time came for the child to be born. She gave birth to her first baby. It was a boy. She wrapped him in large strips of cloth. Then she placed him in a manger. That's because there was no guest room where they could stay (Luke 2:1–7).

Mary named the baby Jesus, just as the angel had told her to do. Remember the prophecy we read from Isaiah 9:6?

A child will be born to us. A son will be given to us. He will rule over us. And he will be called Wonderful Adviser and Mighty God. He will also be called Father Who Lives Forever and Prince Who Brings Peace.

It happened, just as God said it would! How wonderful that God always keeps His promises — we can trust Him. A **ch**ild was born, just as God said. Hey, I heard a new sound there. Did you hear it too? A **ch**ild was born, just as God said. Today we are learning another blend. It is the sound the C and H make when they are together. The C H blend says **ch**, as in **ch**ild! Say it with me, **ch, ch, ch**!

The C H blend looks like this:

Ch

Or like this:

ch

A child was born, just as God said. God's word is true, and He always keeps His promises. Now let's read some more!

(Now begin the reading section. If your child needs to take a break from the lesson, let him or her begin the first page of the Little Learner Activity Sheet. Be sure to go back to the reading section of this lesson to complete it.)

Let's read together! Some of these words are big, but we know what to do! We'll sound them out and read the word:

A chīld wås bōrn, jŭst as Gŏd prŏmĭsed. Thĭs wås Gŏd's plăn. Jēsŭs cāme to sĕt ŭs frēē!

(Have the student complete the Little Learner Activity Sheet.)

(Student has learned N, D, Ă, T, S, P, Ĭ, F, Ŏ, B, Ā, Ī, Å, J, Ē, M, L, Ŭ, Ō, R, C, W, H, G, K, TH, SP, CK, Ĕ, WH, OU, and CH so far.)

- Practice sight words with student.
- Practice writing sight words. Write word in pencil and have student trace in marker.

- Have student act out the Christmas story for you!
- On an "off" day, read the verse on page 216 with your child and let him or her read the large words throughout.

God's promises are amazing! Let's read one about His plan. I'll point to each word as I read, and when we get to the large ones, you can read those words.

For ŭnto ŭs a Child is born,
ŭnto ŭs a Son is given;
and the government wĭll
bē ŭpŏn Hĭs shoulder.
And Hĭs nāme wĭll bē
cȧlled Wonderful, Counselor,
Mighty Gŏd, Everlasting Father,

Prince of Peace." (Isaiah 9:6; NKJV)

Go through the verse again line by line. Ask students questions about what it means, explaining any difficult concepts.

Ch

Ch is for **Child.**
A **ch**ild was born, just as God said.

Color the picture below.

Writing: Let's practice writing. Help the student space words properly by putting a finger after the "s" in "us" so that they know where to start the new word "free." Write the sentence below!

Jesus

sets

us free

from sin!

Y is for **Y**oung.
Jesus was **y**oung, just like **y**ou!

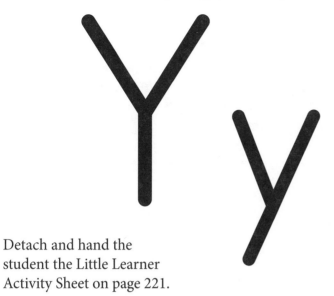

Detach and hand the
student the Little Learner
Activity Sheet on page 221.

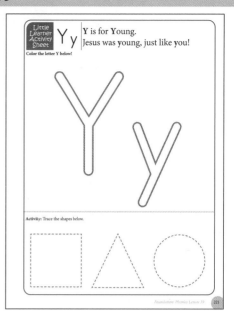

LESSON NARRATIVE

*This lesson covers the letter Y. The sound of the letter Y can be heard in the words young, yellow, and you. As you read through this lesson, place emphasis on the sound of this letter where it is found in **bold** throughout the text.*

In our last lesson, we learned about the birth of Jesus. Jesus was part of God's plan to save us from sin. Jesus came to the earth He had created as fully God and fully man. Jesus lived a life just like we do — but there was something different about Him. What do you think it was?

(Allow student time to answer.)

Unlike you and me, and everyone else on the earth since Adam and Eve, Jesus lived a sinless life. Jesus had the same choice Adam had to disobey and rebel against God, but Jesus chose differently than Adam did — Jesus obeyed God.

After Jesus was born, He grew, and grew, and grew, and grew! He had to learn to talk, and walk, just like you! I'm sure Jesus played games, and had chores to do too, just like you! He even had to learn and study, just like you! When we are excited, sad, lonely, happy, frustrated, or facing the temptation to

do something wrong, we can pray and talk to Jesus about it. The Bible tells us that Jesus understands because He lived life just like us.

> We have a high priest who can feel it when we are weak and hurting. We have a high priest who has been tempted in every way, just as we are. But he did not sin (Hebrews 4:15).

Jesus was **y**oung, just like **y**ou! Oh my, I think we found our new letter today! Today's letter is the letter **Y**. Now, the letter **Y** is different because sometimes it is a vowel, and sometimes it is a consonant, so it makes different sounds too. But today, we are learning just one! When the letter **Y** is at the start of a word, it usually says **y** as in **y**oung! When found at the start, the **Y** says **y**!

The letter **Y** looks like this:

(Ask student to trace uppercase and lowercase Y with finger on the Little Learner Activity Sheet. Make sure the student points to the correct one.)

The uppercase **Y** looks like this:

The lowercase **Y** looks like this:

Jesus was **y**oung, just like **y**ou! The **Y** says **y**. I can't wait to learn more about Jesus. What about **y**ou?

(Allow student time to answer)

We'll learn more in our next lesson! For now, it's time for some letter fun!

(Now begin the reading section below. If your child needs to take a break from the lesson, let him or her begin the first page of the Little Learner Activity Sheet. Be sure to go back to the reading section of this lesson to complete it.)

READING

Let's read!

(Have the student complete the Little Learner Activity Sheet.)

BONUS ACTIVITIES:

(Student has learned N, D, Ă, T, S, P, Ĭ, F, Ŏ, B, Ā, Ī, Å, J, Ē, M, L, Ŭ, Ō, R, C, W, H, G, K, TH, SP, CK, Ĕ, WH, OU, CH, and Y so far.)

- Let student think of a word. Write the word out and ask the student to copy on to lined paper.

- Give student an old magazine. Assign student a letter he or she has learned from above and ask him or her to find and cut out that letter. Glue the letter to construction paper if desired, and have student draw a picture of something that starts with that letter.

Y y

Y is for **Young**.
Jesus was **young**, just like **you**!

Color the letter Y below!

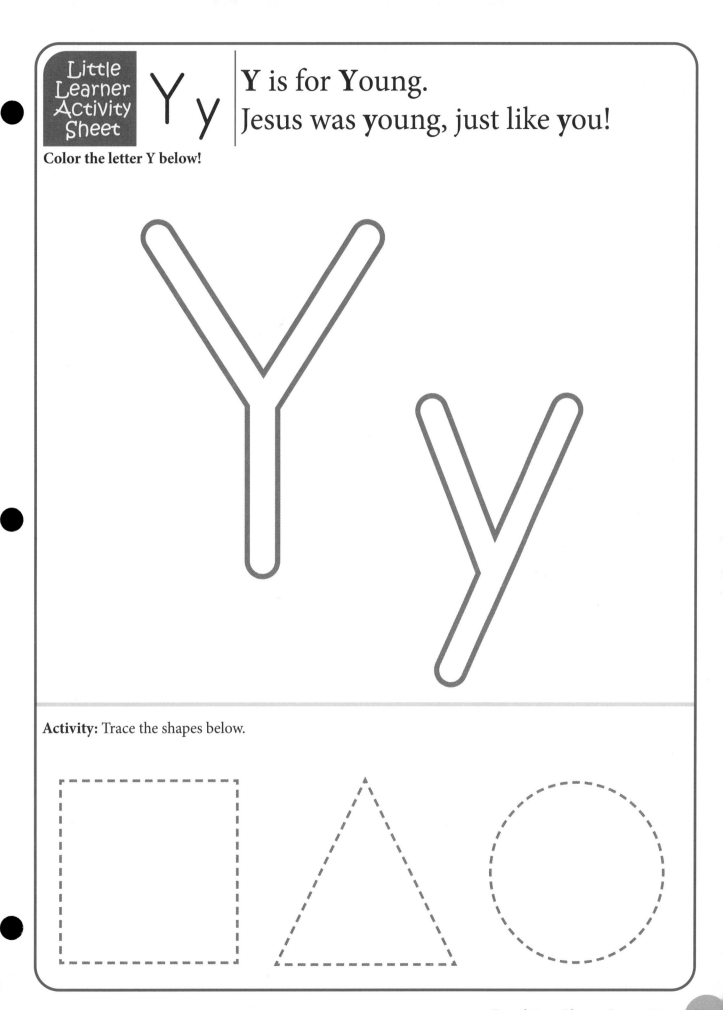

Activity: Trace the shapes below.

Writing: When we learn to write, we write things for people to read! Let's practice writing the letter Y.

Letter Recognition: Point to each letter and tell me its sound.

 Ā ā

 Ă ă

 Å å

C is for Voice.
A voice came from Heaven when Jesus was baptized.

Detach and hand the student the
Little Learner Activity Sheet on page 225.

*This sound sounds like "s" and can be heart in the words voice, choice, and face. As you read through this lesson, place emphasis on the sound of this letter where it is found in **bold** throughout the text.*

It's time for a new adventure today! Is your imagination ready to go?

(Allow student time to answer.)

Then let's get started! We've been learning about Jesus in these last few lessons. By this time, Jesus was all grown up. Let's read the start of today's story from the very best book, the Bible!

In those days John the Baptist came and preached in the Desert of Judea. He said, "Turn away from your sins! The kingdom of heaven has come near." John is the one Isaiah the prophet had spoken about. He had said,

"A messenger is calling out in the desert, 'Prepare the way for the Lord. Make straight paths for him.'"

John's clothes were made out of camel's hair. He had a leather belt around his waist. His food was locusts and wild honey. People went out to him from Jerusalem and all Judea. They also came from the whole area around the Jordan River. When they confessed their sins, John baptized them in the Jordan (Matthew 3:1–6).

Can you imagine wearing clothing made out of camel hair? Do you think it would be soft or scratchy?

(Allow student time to answer.)

Why?

(Allow student time to answer.)

Well, one day, Jesus went to see John the Baptist. What do you think happened?

(Allow student time to answer.)

Let's read from the Bible and find out what happened!

Jesus came from Galilee to the Jordan River. He wanted to be baptized by John. But John tried to stop him. So he told Jesus, "I need to be baptized by you. So why do you come to me?"

Jesus replied, "Let it be this way for now. It is right for us to do this. It carries out God's holy plan." Then John agreed.

As soon as Jesus was baptized, he came up out of the water. At that moment heaven was opened. Jesus saw the Spirit of God coming down on him like a dove. A voice from heaven said, "This is my Son, and I love him. I am very pleased with him" (Matthew 3:13–17).

Wow! What do you think it would have been like if you had been there?

(Allow student time to answer.)

A voice came from heaven when Jesus was baptized. Ooh, I heard a special new sound, did you hear it too? Voice. Our letter sounds like the S, but it is the C! The C is not a vowel, but it can make two different sounds. Usually, the C says c as in cat. But when the C sits next to an i, e, or y, it makes the same sound as the S! Let's look at some different C words; read this one with me:

This letter C isn't sitting next to an i, e, or y, so it says c! But what about this one?

cĕnt

Hmm, this letter C is sitting next to an E, so it makes the same sound as the letter S! Wow, reading sure is fun! Let's practice some more with the letter C! Remember the rule — if it sits next to i, e, or y, the C sounds like an S!

(Now begin the reading section below. If your child needs to take a break from the lesson, let him or her begin the first page of the Little Learner Activity Sheet. Be sure to go back to the reading section of this lesson to complete it.)

READING

Let's read some C words!

cĕnt

fāce

cōrn

īce

cŭp

cook

Great job!

(Have the student complete the Little Learner Activity Sheet.)

BONUS ACTIVITIES:

(Student has learned N, D, Ă, T, S, P, Ĭ, F, Ŏ, B, Ā, Ī, Å, J, Ē, M, L, Ŭ, Ō, R, C, W, H, G, K, TH, SP, CK, Ĕ, WH, OU, CH, Y, and soft C so far.)

- Read a story together. Have student point to familiar words or letters.
- Gather assorted toys and objects; ask student to sort the objects into piles based on their starting sounds.

Little Learner Activity Sheet

C c

Color the picture below!

C is for Voice. A voice came from Heaven when Jesus was baptized.

Writing: Let's practice writing the letters we know!

Nn   Dd   Aa

Tt   Ss   Pp

Ff   Oo   Bb

Sh is for **Sh**own. Jesus was **sh**own the temptations of the world, but He withstood the test.

Detach and hand the student the Little Learner Activity Sheet on page 231.

LESSON NARRATIVE

💡 *This lesson covers the Sh blend. The Sh blend can be heard in the words sheep, show, and ship. As you read through this lesson, place emphasis on the sound of this blend where it is found in* **bold** *throughout the text.*

Wow! We sure have been learning a lot! It is time for another adventure! Are you excited to begin?

(Allow student time to answer.)

Then here we go! After Jesus was baptized, He was led by the Holy Spirit to the wilderness. There, Jesus fasted for 40 days and 40 nights — that is a really long time! "Fasting" meant Jesus had given up food. He'd had nothing to eat for all that time. How do you think Jesus felt by the end of 40 days?

(Allow student time to answer.)

Jesus must have been very, very hungry! Then, the devil came to tempt Jesus, just as he had to Adam and Eve. Let's read what he said from the Bible!

> The tempter came to him. He said, "If you are the Son of God, tell these stones to become bread" (Matthew 4:3).

Oh, no! What do you think Jesus did?

(Allow student time to answer.)

Well, Jesus fought the temptation with God's words. Let's read what He said!

> Jesus answered, "It is written, 'Man must not live only on bread. He must also live on every word that comes from the mouth of God' " (Matthew 4:4).

Jesus didn't give in to temptation! Then the devil tried tempting Jesus another way. This time, the devil twisted God's words — let's read what happened!

> Then the devil took Jesus to the holy city. He had him stand on the highest point of the temple. "If you are the Son of God," he said, "throw yourself down. It is written, " 'The Lord will command his angels to take good care of you. They will lift you up in their hands. Then you won't trip over a stone' " (Matthew 4:5–6).

Uh-oh, do you think he tricked Jesus?

(Allow student time to answer.)

Let's read what Jesus said!

> Jesus answered him, "It is also written, 'Do not test the Lord your God' " (Matthew 4:7).

Wow! Jesus withstood the devil's temptations again! But then the devil tempted Jesus yet another time. Let's read from the Bible!

> Finally, the devil took Jesus to a very high mountain. He showed him all the kingdoms of the world and their glory. "If you bow down and worship me," he said, "I will give you all this" (Matthew 4:8–9).

That doesn't sound good! What do you think Jesus did?

(Allow student time to answer.)

Well, let's read what Jesus said:

> Jesus said to him, "Get away from me, Satan! It is written, 'Worship the Lord your God. He is the only one you should serve.' " Then the devil left Jesus. Angels came and took care of him (Matthew 4:10–11).

Wow! Jesus was tempted just like Adam and Eve, and just like we are, but Jesus did not give in to temptation. Jesus was **sh**own the temptations of the world, but He withstood the test. Oh my! Did you hear our new sound? Our sound for today is another blend. It is the sound the S and the H make when they sit right next to each other. The S H says **sh**.

The S H blend looks like this:

Sh

(Ask student to trace the letters with finger on the Little Learner Activity Sheet.)

Or like this:

sh

(Point to the blend and say the sound with student.)

Jesus was **sh**own the temptations of the world, but He withstood the test. The S H says sh. I can't wait to learn more about Jesus in our next lesson, but for now we've learned a new sound and we have more learning to do!

(Now begin the reading section. If your child needs to take a break from the lesson, let him or her begin the first page of the Little Learner Activity Sheet. Be sure to go back to the reading section of this lesson to complete it.)

When we see the letters S and H right next to each other, the sound they make is **sh**! Let's practice reading words with the S H blends!

shōw

sheēp

dăsh

căsh

shāpe

wåsh

dĭsh

shĭp

rŭsh

(Have the student complete the Little Learner Activity Sheet.)

BONUS ACTIVITIES:

(Student has learned N, D, Ă, T, S, P, Ĭ, F, Ŏ, B, Ā, Ī, Å, J, Ē, M, L, Ŭ, Ō, R, C, W, H, G, K, TH, SP, CK, Ĕ, WH, OU, CH, Y, soft C, and SH so far.)

- Have student practice writing the sh blend on a separate sheet of paper.
- Read student a story, and have student tell it back to you in his or her own words.

- Ask student to think of words that have the sh blend in them; write them for the student and ask student to copy the words onto lined paper or paper designed for early writers.
- Read verse on page 230 on an "off" day.

When we face temptation, we can pray and turn to the Bible to guide us. Let's read this verse together. Remember, letters that are grey play silly games—they stay silent! I'll read the first word, you can read the rest.

 Help student sound out words as necessary. Be sure to congratulate him or her after reading the verse!

Your word is līke a lămp thăt shōws mē the wāy. It is līke a līght thăt guīdes mē. (Psalm 119:105)

Little Learner Activity Sheet

Sh

Sh is for **Sh**own. Jesus was **sh**own the temptations of the world, but He withstood the test.

Reading the Bible, God's words to us helps us fight temptation. Color the picture of the Bible below.

Activity: Match each word to the picture!

shēēp

dĭsh

shĭp

cǎsh

Letter Recognition: Color the circles with lower case letters inside.

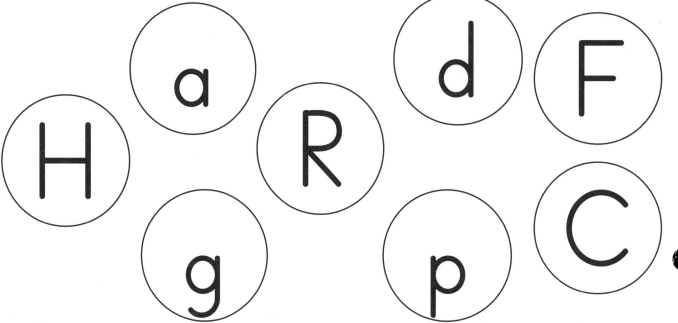

Review

N D Ă T S P Ĭ F

Ŏ B Ā Ī Å J Ē M

L Ŭ Ō R C W H

G K TH SP CK Ě

WH CH Y C SH

Detach and hand the student the Little Learner Activity Sheet on page 235.

LESSON NARRATIVE

Well, I think I'm pretty tired; we've done a lot of traveling on our great big adventure! We've learned about the prophecies, and how they would be fulfilled. We learned that the child was born — just as God said! We've learned about Jesus, and how He grew up just like we do. Then we traveled quite far and learned about Jesus' baptism and temptation!

Phew! What was your favorite story and letter?

(Allow student time to answer.)

After the temptation, Jesus chose 12 men to follow Him. We call these men the "disciples." The disciples followed Jesus, and Jesus taught them about God's ways and laws. These men listened and watched as Jesus taught the people and healed the sick. They witnessed many, many miracles!

All through the land, Jesus traveled and taught. Large crowds followed Him to see and hear Him. They were amazed by the things He said and the miracles they saw! We will learn about a couple of amazing miracles in our next lesson, but for now, we've worked quite hard and it's time for some fun!

(Have the student complete the Little Learner Activity Sheet.)

BONUS ACTIVITIES:

(Student has learned N, D, Ă, T, S, P, Ĭ, F, Ŏ, B, Ā, Ī, Å, J, Ē, M, L, Ŭ, Ō, R, C, W, H, G, K, TH, SP, CK, Ě, WH, CH, Y, soft C, and SH so far.)

- Read a story with your student. Look for words he or she has read!

- Visit your local library and allow your student to choose a book.

A library is a place where there are a lot of books! Color the picture below.

Foundations Phonics

Review

Writing: Let's write some of the letters we've learned so far!

Ss   Ll   Uu

Cc   Jj   Hh

Kk   Ii   Yy

Activity: Color the page.

Use a red crayon for "WH."

Use a blue crayon for "TH."

Use an orange crayon for "CH."

Use a green crayon for "SH."

Color the "S" yellow.

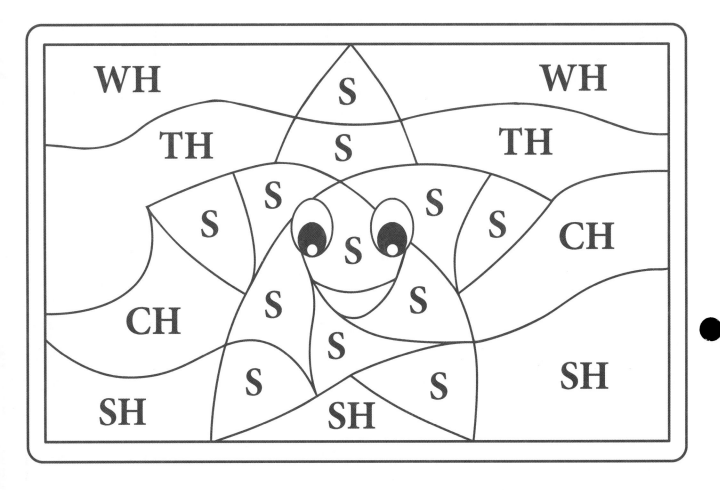

Foundations Phonics

Q is for **Quiet.**
Jesus said "**Quiet!**" and the storm obeyed!

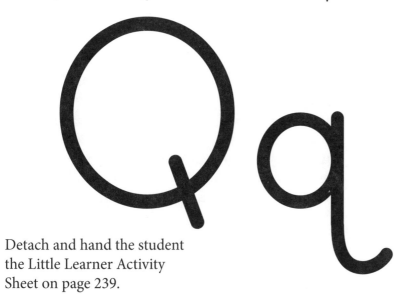

Detach and hand the student
the Little Learner Activity
Sheet on page 239.

LESSON NARRATIVE

💡 *Letter Q can be heard in the words queen, quiet, and quill. As you read through this lesson, place emphasis on the sound of this letter where it is found in* **bold** *throughout the text.*

Here we are again, ready for another learning adventure! We've been learning about Jesus and how He came to save us from sin. Jesus traveled along the country with the 12 disciples and He taught the people about God and God's ways. He healed the sick, and even brought the dead back to life! Jesus performed many miracles, and big crowds of people followed Him everywhere so they could hear Him teach. Sometimes, after days of teaching, Jesus and the disciples would go away **qu**ietly. That is how our adventure opens today.

Put on your imagination and get it started! Let's start this adventure reading from the Bible!

When evening came, Jesus said to his disciples, "Let's go over to the other side of the lake." They left the crowd behind. And they took him along in a boat, just as he was. There were also other boats with him (Mark 4:35–36).

Imagine the scene. The lake was **qu**iet. Maybe the sun was setting, painting a beautiful picture in the sky. The boats slowly drifted from the shore. A perfect ending to a perfect day, huh?

But then, something happened that terrified the disciples! What do you think happened?

(Allow student time to answer.)

Hmm, let's read the rest of the story from the Bible!

A wild storm came up. Waves crashed over the boat. It was about to sink. Jesus was in the back, sleeping on a cushion. The disciples woke him up. They said, "Teacher! Don't you care if we drown?"

He got up and ordered the wind to stop. He said to the waves, "**Qu**iet! Be still!" Then the wind died down. And it was completely calm.

He said to his disciples, "Why are you so afraid? Don't you have any faith at all yet?"

They were terrified. They asked each other, "Who is this? Even the wind and the waves obey him!" (Mark 4:37–41)

Can you imagine that scene? The clouds rolled in, and the wind started howling. Then the waves started splashing on the side of the boat. Higher and higher they splashed until they started coming over the boat! The boat began to fill with water as it rocked back and forth, back and forth. The disciples were shouting to each other above the storm — afraid for their lives!

But then they call to Jesus. Jesus quiets the storm — and it all stops. Again, there is peace on the water. Sometimes our lives can get a bit stormy, just like it did for the boat. But when we are afraid, we can call to Jesus. Jesus doesn't always calm the storms around us, but He does bring our hearts peace even when things are scary. Jesus said, "**Quiet!**" and the storm obeyed!

Our letter for today is the letter Q! The Q says q. The letter Q looks like this:

Qq

The uppercase Q looks like this:

Q

(Ask student to trace uppercase and lowercase Q with finger on the Little Learner Activity Sheet. Make sure the student points to the correct one.)

The lowercase q looks like this:

q

Jesus said "**Quiet!**" and the storm obeyed! Say it with me — the **Q** says **q**. Usually, the Q isn't alone; it likes to be with the letter U. When you see the Q and the U together, they make the sound "**qu**" as in **qu**ake! The Q U blend looks like this:

Qu qu

Jesus said "Quiet!" and the storm obeyed! The Q says q. Now it's time for some fun!

(Now begin the reading section below. If your child needs to take a break from the lesson, let him or her begin the first page of the Little Learner Activity Sheet. Be sure to go back to the reading section of this lesson to complete it.)

READING

Now we've learned a new letter, let's read some new words!

quĭt

queēn

quĭlt

quĭll

(Have the student complete the Little Learner Activity Sheet.)

BONUS ACTIVITIES:

(Student has learned N, D, Ă, T, S, P, Ĭ, F, Ŏ, B, Ā, Ī, Å, J, Ē, M, L, Ŭ, Ō, R, C, W, H, G, K, TH, SP, CK, Ĕ, WH, OU, CH, Y, soft C, SH, and Q so far.)

• Finger paint the student's favorite letter or story.

• Have student draw a picture of the scene from today's story. Once completed, write "Quiet" on a separate sheet of paper and ask student to copy the word onto the picture.

Q q

Q is for **Quiet**. Jesus said "Quiet!" and the storm obeyed!

Color the letter Q below!

Reading: Let's read these words.

When who åre

Whåt how I

Writing: Let's write the letter Q!

Q

q

Activity: Match the uppercase letter to the lower case.

B

D

P

p

d

b

G is for Hu**g**e. There was enough food to feed all the people. It was a hu**g**e miracle!

Detach and hand the student the Little Learner Activity Sheet on page 243.

LESSON NARRATIVE

> *This lesson covers the soft sound of the letter G. This sound can be heard in the words huge, wage, and cage. As you read through this lesson, place emphasis on the sound of this letter where it is found in **bold** throughout the text.*

Today, we have another amazing adventure! Put on your imagination, get it started, and let's get ready to go!

Jesus traveled all over the country with the 12 disciples teaching the people about God's ways. Jesus healed the sick and He raised the dead back to life! Sometimes, Jesus went away to be by Himself to pray, but as soon as the people heard where He was they followed Him. Large crowds followed Jesus everywhere He went!

At the start of our adventure today, Jesus had gone away to be by Himself. When He returned, a large crowd had gathered. When Jesus saw all the people, He had compassion on them and He began to teach them and heal the sick.

But soon the day was coming to an end, and the people had had nothing to eat. What do you think would happen?

(Allow student time to answer.)

Well, get your imagination started. Close your eyes and imagine as I read the story from the Bible!

When Jesus came ashore, he saw a large crowd. He felt deep concern for them. He healed their sick people.

When it was almost evening, the disciples came to him. "There is nothing here," they said. "It's already getting late. Send the crowds away. They can go and buy some food in the villages."

Jesus replied, "They don't need to go away. You give them something to eat."

"We have only five loaves of bread and two fish," they answered,

"Bring them here to me," he said. Then Jesus directed the people to sit down on the grass. He took the five loaves and the two fish. He looked up to heaven and gave thanks. He broke the loaves into pieces. Then he gave them to the disciples. And the disciples gave them to the people. All of them ate and were satisfied. The disciples picked up 12 baskets of leftover pieces. The number of men who ate was about 5,000. Women and children also ate (Matthew 14:14–21).

Wow, what an amazing miracle! There were only 5 loaves of bread and 2 fish, but Jesus multiplied it to feed the 5,000 men and all of their families! There was enough food to feed all the people — it was a huge miracle! Can you imagine what it would have been like to have been there?

(Allow student time to answer.)

There was enough food to feed all the people — it was a huge miracle! Our letter for today is the letter G again! The letter G isn't a vowel, but it makes different sounds depending on which vowel it is next to. If the G is next to e, i, or y, it makes a sound like the J!

(Now begin the reading section below. If your child needs to take a break from the lesson, let him or her begin the first page of the Little Learner Activity Sheet. Be sure to go back to the reading section of this lesson to complete it.)

READING

Let's try reading some words like this!

gĕl

āngĕl

gĕm

cāge

Great job reading! Now, look to see if the G is beside e, i, or y and read these words!

gōat

āge

wāge

găs

Good job! Let's go have some more letter fun!

(Have the student complete the Little Learner Activity Sheet.)

BONUS ACTIVITIES:

(Student has learned N, D, Ă, T, S, P, Ĭ, F, Ŏ, B, Ā, Ī, Å, J, Ē, M, L, Ŭ, Ō, R, C, W, H, G, K, TH, SP, CK, Ĕ, WH, OU, CH, Y, soft C, SH, Q, and soft G so far.)

- Practice sight words.
- Spread shaving cream on a baking sheet. Say a

word and see if student can write the letters.

Gg

G is for Huge. There was enough food to feed all the people. It was a hu**g**e miracle!

Writing: Let's practice writing some words!!

goat

gas

wage

age

Activity: Goat and pig both have the letter "G." Color the goat brown and the pig pink.

Ou is for W**ou**ld.
Jesus w**ou**ld die on the cross for you and me.

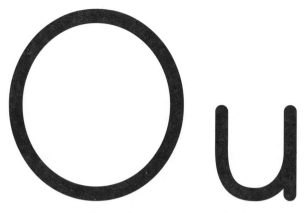

Detach and hand the student the
Little Learner Activity Sheet on page 247.

LESSON NARRATIVE

> 💡 *This lesson covers the Ou blend. This Ou blend sound like "oo" and can be heard in the words would, should, and could. As you read through this lesson, place emphasis on the sound of this blend where it is found in* **bold** *throughout the text.*

Are you ready for our new reading adventure today? In today's adventure, we begin to see how God's plan to save us from our sin was completed!

For over three years, Jesus traveled to different cities and towns teaching the people and healing the sick. At times, Jesus made the religious leaders, called Pharisees and Sadducees, very angry because Jesus did things God's way, rather than the way the religious leaders thought things should be done. They began to plot against Jesus, but this was all a part of God's plan.

Jesus and His disciples came to Jerusalem and celebrated the Passover feast. This was a feast God had set up for His people way back when they were slaves in Egypt right before Pharaoh let them go free. This feast was a picture of God's plan to save us.

After Jesus and the disciples had eaten, they traveled to the Mount of Olives to pray. Jesus knew that the time had come for God's plan to be worked out — and it required that Jesus give His life for us. Jesus knew the cost to pay the price of sin was very, very high. Jesus w**ou**ld die on the cross for you and me. I heard our new sound for today. Today, our sound is another blend. When the O and the U get together, they can say "ow" as in house, or "oo" as in w**ou**ld. Jesus w**ou**ld die on the Cross for you and me. After Jesus and the disciples finished eating, they went to pray in the Garden of Gethsemane. Let's read what Jesus prayed from the Bible!

> When they reached the place, Jesus spoke. "Pray that you won't fall into sin when you are tempted," he said to them. Then he went a short distance away from them. There he got down on his knees and prayed. He said, "Father, if you are willing, take this cup of suffering away from me. But do what you want, not what I want." An angel from heaven appeared to Jesus and gave him strength. Because he was very sad and troubled, he prayed even harder. His sweat was like drops of blood falling to the ground.
>
> After that, he got up from prayer and went back to the disciples. He found them sleeping. They were worn out because they were very sad. "Why are you sleeping?" he asked them. "Get up! Pray that you won't fall into sin when you are tempted" (Luke 22:40–46).

At that time, a large crowd came to them. Leading them was one of Jesus' disciples, Judas. Judas had betrayed Jesus and had come to hand Him over to the leaders who had plotted against Jesus.

Over the next several hours, Jesus was subjected to unfair trials in which they said He was guilty and deserved to die. He was beaten very badly and teased by the people. Pilate was the ruler over the people, and the people demanded that Pilate sentence Jesus to die. The people would not listen to anything else, and so Pilate sentenced Jesus to death.

Now, we learned way back at the beginning of our adventure that death is the consequence of sin. Before Adam and Eve sinned, there was no death. Because of sin, the world became imperfect and pain and death entered. But Jesus had faced temptation and never sinned. Jesus lived a sinless life and didn't deserve to die!

Jesus was led through the streets to a place called "Golgotha." There, the soldiers nailed Him to a wooden Cross. Jesus hung on the Cross for several hours as the people and soldiers mocked and teased Him. And then Jesus died. When Jesus died, the Bible says that the veil in the temple that covered the Holy of Holies was torn in two, the earth shook, rocks split apart, and some people who had died came back to life!

Because Jesus had never sinned, His death became the payment for our sins. Jesus became our sacrificial lamb, and His blood that was shed paid the price of sin forever!

Jesus' followers were very, very sad. After He died, they took him from the Cross and placed His body in a tomb. The tomb was sealed and guarded, then the people went home to mourn Jesus' death. Jesus died on the Cross for you and for me. But this wasn't the end of the story. Jesus would also win the victory over sin and death! We'll learn about that in our next lesson. Let's go have some more letter fun!

(Now begin the reading section below. If your child needs to take a break from the lesson, let him or her begin the first page of the Little Learner Activity Sheet. Be sure to go back to the reading section of this lesson to complete it.)

READING

Let's practice reading some words with the "oo" ou sound!

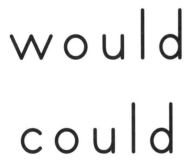

would

should

could

wound

The ou sometimes sounds like oo as in would and sometimes oo as wound. There is a slight difference. Those silly words! Good job!

(Have the student complete the Little Learner Activity Sheet.)

BONUS ACTIVITIES:

(Student has learned N, D, Ă, T, S, P, Ĭ, F, Ŏ, B, Ā, Ī, Å, J, Ē, M, L, Ŭ, Ō, R, C, W, H, G, K, TH, SP, CK, Ě, WH, CH, Y, soft C, SH, Q, soft G, and OU so far.)

- Say a word. Ask student to sound it out and write the letters in the word.

- Practice sight words.
- Use small round candies, like M&Ms®, to spell out sight words. Enjoy a sweet treat after the student has read the word!

O u

Ou is for W**ou**ld. Jesus w**ou**ld die on the cross for you and me.

Color the picture below.

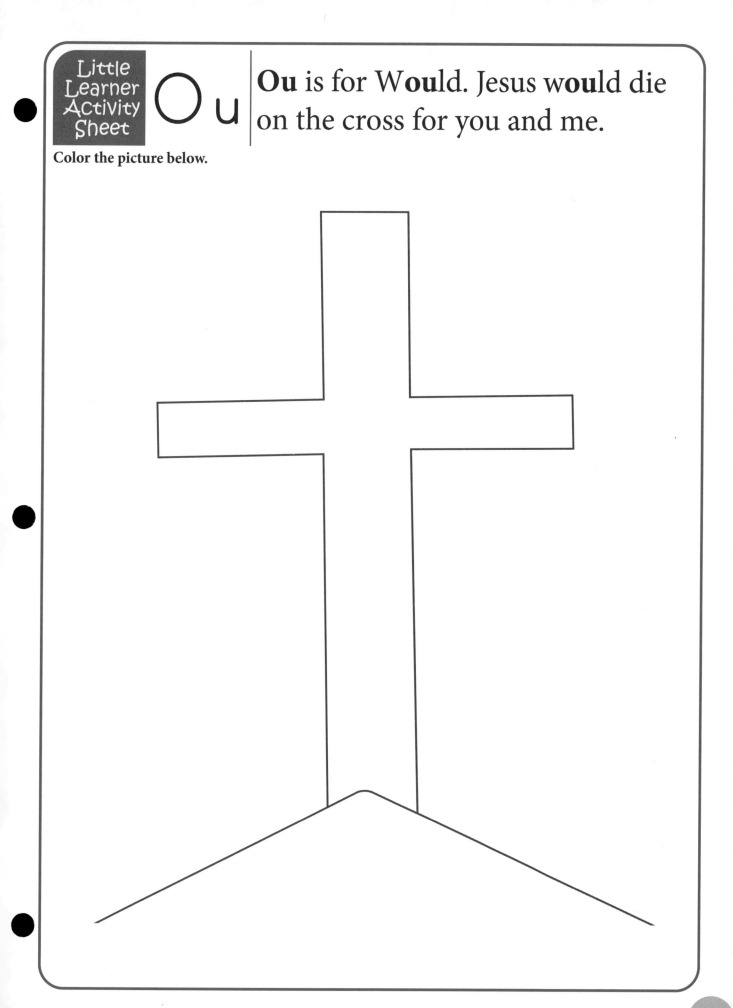

Let's sing the alphabet song and fill in the blanks of the missing letters!

Aa Bb Cc Dd __ __

Ff Gg Hh Ii __ __

Kk Ll Mm __ __ Oo

Pp __ __ Rr Ss Tt Uu

Vv Ww Xx __ __ Zz

Now, see if you can find the correct letter on the page when I say it. (If your student is having trouble with a particular letter, spend a little more time on it – saying the sound, writing it, finding it on the page, or having him or her trace the letter with his or her finger.)

V is for **V**ictory.
Jesus won the **v**ictory over sin and death.

Detach and hand the student the
Little Learner Activity Sheet on page 253.

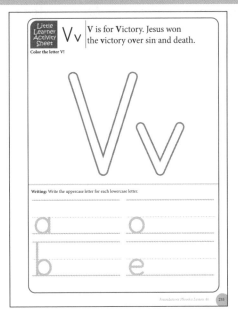

LESSON NARRATIVE

This lesson covers the soft sound of the letter V. This sound can be heard in the words victory, vet, and veto. As you read through this lesson, place emphasis on the sound of this letter where it is found in **bold** *throughout the text.*

On our last adventure, we learned about Jesus' death on the Cross. It was a sad adventure, but I have really good news for you today! You see, God's plan didn't end with Jesus' death on the Cross, and the story doesn't end there either! Are you ready to get started today? Well then, let's go!

It had been three days now since Jesus died on the Cross. Start your imagination, close your eyes, and imagine the scene as I read from the Bible!

It was dawn on the first day of the week. Mary Magdalene and the other Mary went to look at the tomb.

There was a powerful earthquake. An angel of the Lord came down from heaven. The angel went to the tomb. He rolled back the stone and sat on it. His body shone like lightning. His clothes were as white as snow. The guards were so afraid of him that they shook and became like dead men.

The angel said to the women, "Don't be afraid. I know that you are looking for Jesus, who was crucified. He is not here! He has risen, just as he said he would! Come and see the place where he was lying. Go quickly! Tell his disciples, 'He has risen from the dead. He is going ahead of you into Galilee. There you will see him.' Now I have told you."

So the women hurried away from the tomb. They were afraid, but they were filled with joy. They ran to tell the disciples. Suddenly Jesus met them. "Greetings!" he said. They came to him, took hold of his feet and worshiped him. Then Jesus said to them, "Don't be afraid. Go and tell my brothers to go to Galilee. There they will see me" (Matthew 28:1–10).

Wow! Death didn't defeat Jesus — Jesus rose back to life on the third day. Not only did Jesus pay the price of sin, He also conquered death. Jesus won the **v**ictory over sin and death. Our letter today is the letter **V**. The **V** says **v**. The letter V looks like this:

(Ask student to trace uppercase and lowercase V with finger on the Little Learner Activity Sheet. Make sure the student points to the correct one.)

The uppercase V looks like this:

V

The lowercase v looks like this:

v

The upper and lowercase letters look the same, don't they? The lowercase is just smaller than the uppercase! Jesus won the victory over sin and death. Say it with me: the **V** says v. We'll be learning more about what that victory means for us, but for now, let's go have some fun with the letter **V**!

(Now begin the reading section below. If your child needs to take a break from the lesson, let him or her begin the first page of the Little Learner Activity Sheet. Be sure to go back to the reading section of this lesson to complete it.)

READING

Let's practice reading!

văn

vīne

vĕt

lŏve

vŏw

Awesome! Now let's read a sentence!

Jēsŭs lŏves mē thĭs I knōw.

You probably recognize those words. They are from the song "Jesus Loves Me"! In a few more lessons, you will have read the whole song!

Since this song is so familiar to students, they may recite the song rather than read each word. Don't worry! This builds confidence and helps the student relate reading to their real world experiences.

(Have the student complete the Little Learner Activity Sheet.)

BONUS ACTIVITIES:

(Student has learned N, D, Ă, T, S, P, Ĭ, F, Ŏ, B, Ā, Ī, Å, J, Ē, M, L, Ŭ, Ō, R, C, W, H, G, K, TH, SP, CK, Ĕ, WH, OU, CH, Y, soft C, SH, Q, soft G, OU, and V so far.)

- Sing "Jesus Loves Me" with student, then help student write out the first line of the song, onto lined paper or paper design for students.

- Use paper letters from a previous lesson and have student find household objects with each sound in them. Place object on top of letter sheet.

- Review sight words on page 252 on an "off" day.

We know these words! Let's read them!

they

out

when

what

who

the

that

this

then

them

than

V v | **V is for Victory. Jesus won the victory over sin and death.**

Color the letter V!

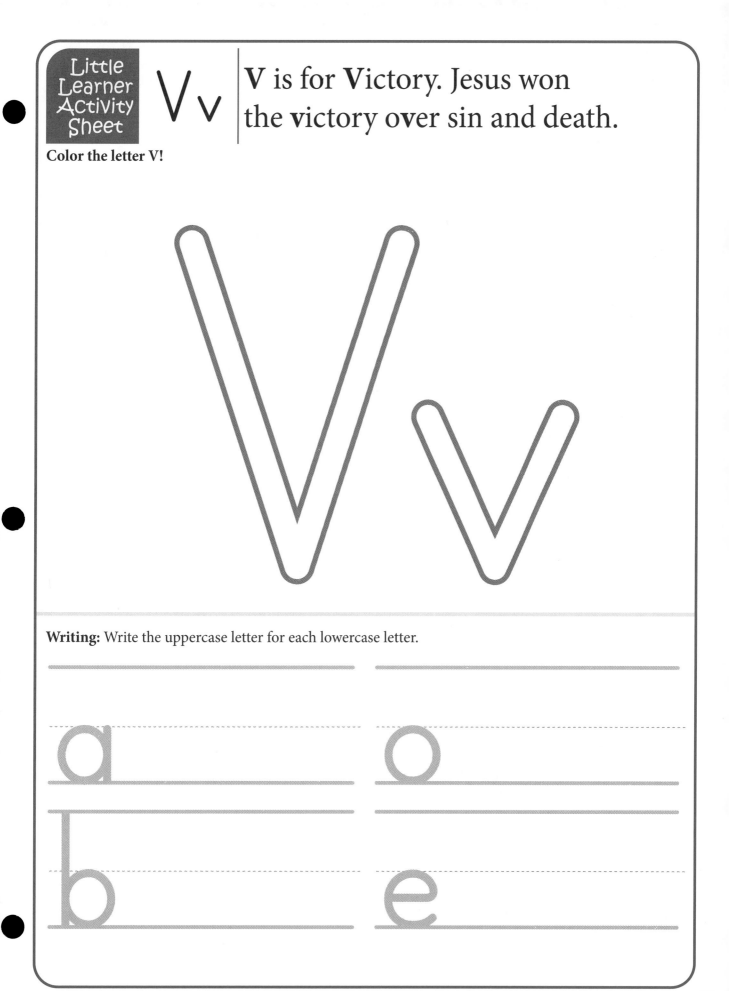

Writing: Write the uppercase letter for each lowercase letter.

a

o

b

e

Writing: Let's practice writing the letter V.

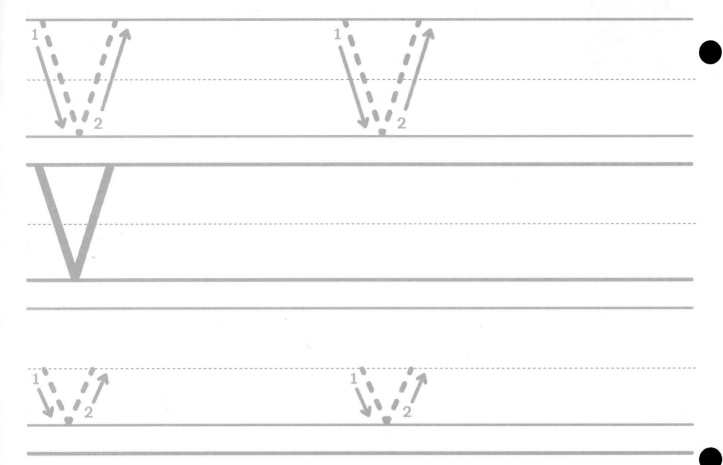

Letter Recognition: Circle the letter v.

q

E

d

A

c

O

v

W

Ea is for H**ea**ven.
We have the promise of H**ea**ven.

Detach and hand the student the
Little Learner Activity Sheet on page 257.

LESSON NARRATIVE

*This lesson covers the Ea blend. This Ea blend sound like "ĕ" and can be heard in the words Heaven and bread. As you read through this lesson, place emphasis on the sound of this blend where it is found in **bold** throughout the text.*

We are nearing the end of our reading adventure! You've learned so much and you're reading so well! I'm very proud of all the hard work you've done! We've learned so many letters and all of their sounds. Just a few more lessons and you will have learned them all!

Way back at the beginning we learned about the Fall of man and sin. Sin separates us from God. It's a very sad thing. Sin makes our hearts dirty, and keeps us from being able to be close to God. But Jesus paid the price of sin, and when we ask Him to forgive us for our sins and we put our trust in Him, He forgives us and washes our hearts clean. When our hearts are washed clean from sin, we can have a relationship with God again. He leads us and teaches us how to walk in His ways. But that is not

the end of God's promises to us! God also promises that when our hearts are clean through Jesus, we will spend forever with Him in heaven after we die. Because Jesus paid the price for sin, death is not the end of the story when we've trusted in Him. We have the promise of heaven!

Our sound today is another blend. It's the sound the E and the A can make when they sit next to each other. The E A blend looks like this:

Ea   ea

(Point to the blend and say ĕ with student.)

We have the promise of heaven through Jesus. Now it's time for some letter fun!

(Now begin the reading section. If your child needs to take a break from the lesson, let him or her begin the first page of the Little Learner Activity Sheet. Be sure to go back to the reading section of this lesson to complete it.)

Let's practice reading with our new **ea** sound!

brĕad   lĕad

dĕaf   hĕad

Let's read another line from "Jesus Loves Me"!

Jēsŭs lŏves mē
thĭs I knōw.
Fōr the Bīble
tĕlls mē sō.

(Have the student complete the Little Learner Activity Sheet.)

(Student has learned N, D, Ă, T, S, P, Ĭ, F, Ŏ, B, Ā, Ī, Å, J, Ē, M, L, Ŭ, Ō, R, C, W, H, G, K, TH, SP, CK, Ĕ, WH, OU, CH, Y, soft C, SH, Q, soft G, OU, V, and EA so far.)

- Lay out loose letters. Ask student to say the sounds as quickly as he/she can.
- Spread colored sand into a baking sheet. Have student practice writing sight words in the sand.
- Stack pool noodle letters from previous lesson into words.

Little Learner Activity Sheet

E a | **Ea** is for **H**e**a**ven.
We have the promise of H**ea**ven.

Color the picture.

Writing: Great job! Now can you write the first line from the song below? Remember to use your finger between writing words so you can leave enough space!

Jesus

loves

me this

I know.

Review

N D Ă T S P Ĭ F

Ŏ B̥ Ā Ī Å J Ē M

L Ŭ Ō R C W H̥

G K TH SP CK Ě

WH CH Y C SH

Q G OU V EA

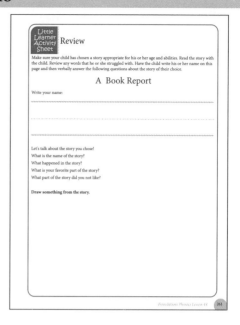

Detach and hand the student the Little Learner Activity Sheet on page 261.

LESSON NARRATIVE

Today's adventure is a celebration! Are you ready to begin?

God created a perfect world at the beginning, but mankind disobeyed and the world became imperfect. But, God loves us so much that He made a plan to save us! Though our sin separated us from God and the price was too high for us to pay, Jesus came and paid the price for us! Through Jesus' death and Resurrection, God won the victory over sin and death.

Now, our world is still imperfect, and sometimes bad things happen to us and to the people we love. But we have hope because while we still live in an imperfect world because of sin, Jesus saved us from the punishment of sin and death. Because of Jesus, our sin no longer separates us from God! In the Bible, Jesus tells us that we will face troubles in the world, but He also tells us something else. Can you guess what it is?

(Allow student time to answer.)

Let's read from the Bible!

"I have told you these things, so that you can have peace because of me. In this world you will have trouble. But be encouraged! I have won the battle over the world" (John 16:33).

Jesus won the battle, He overcame, and God has the victory! When we face trouble and hard things in our lives, we can know that Jesus won the battle over the world. While we will face hard things, we know that God's promises are always true. Though the world is still imperfect because of sin, Jesus paid the price for our sin and we have His promise!

The Bible also tells us in the Book of Revelation that one day Jesus is coming back to the earth. He will punish those who have not trusted in Him, and He will make a new heaven and a new earth — one that is perfect again! The new heaven and earth won't have any sin or death. It will be perfect again, just like God made it to be at the beginning. Though sometimes our lives are hard because of sin and the consequences of sin, we know that God won the victory over sin and death! Hurray!

Now, go pick out a story, and we will read it together.

(Have the student complete the Little Learner Activity Sheet.)

BONUS ACTIVITIES:

- Celebrate how Jesus won the victory over sin and death with your student!

Review

Make sure your child has chosen a story appropriate for his or her age and abilities. Read the story with the child. Review any words that he or she struggled with. Have the child write his or her name on this page and then verbally answer the following questions about the story of their choice.

A Book Report

Write your name:

Let's talk about the story you chose!

What is the name of the story?

What happened in the story?

What is your favorite part of the story?

What part of the story did you not like?

Draw something from the story.

Letter Recognition: Draw a line from lowercase to uppercase letters.

Y is for B**y**.
We are saved b**y** grace.

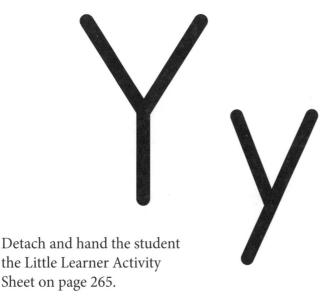

Detach and hand the student the Little Learner Activity Sheet on page 265.

LESSON NARRATIVE

> *This lesson covers the long sound of the letter y. This sound can be heard in the words by, fly, and dry. As you read through this lesson, place emphasis on the sound of this letter where it is found in **bold** throughout the text.*

Are you ready to continue learning about God's plan today? Well, let's dive right in!

Have you ever tried to work for something, to earn it?

(Allow student time to answer.)

Often in life, we have to work to earn things. We work for money and food, to earn the things we want or need. Sometimes, we begin to think that we even have to work to earn people's love, or even work to earn God's love. Have you ever felt like you needed to earn God's love or forgiveness?

(Allow student time to answer.)

When we feel that way, we must remember that there is nothing we can do to earn God's love and forgiveness — He has already given it to us! God loves us so much that He gives us grace that we can't earn from Him. It is His gift to us. Grace means His mercy; it is showing us favor that we do not deserve. The Bible talks about God's gift of grace in the Book of Ephesians. Let's read about it!

But God loves us deeply. He is full of mercy. So he gave us new life because of what Christ has done. He gave us life even when we were dead in sin. God's grace has saved you. God raised us up with Christ. He has seated us with him in his heavenly kingdom. That's because we belong to Christ Jesus. He has done it to show the riches of his grace for all time to come. His grace can't be compared with anything else. He has shown it by being kind to us. He was kind to us because of what Christ Jesus has done. God's grace has saved you because of your faith in Christ. Your salvation doesn't come from anything you do. It is God's gift (Ephesians 2:4–8).

We cannot earn God's grace. He has already given it to us if we put our faith in Him. We are saved b**y** grace. Today's letter is the letter Y again! Sometimes when a word ends in Y, the Y makes a sound like the letter I!

(Now begin the reading section. If your child needs to take a break from the lesson, let him or her begin the first page of the Little Learner Activity Sheet. Be sure to go back to the reading section of this lesson to complete it.)

Let's read some of these words — in each word the Y says ī:

> This lesson introduces the line "Little ones to Him belong." The word "belong" may be pronounced as bĭh-lŏng, bĕlŏng, or bēlŏng, depending on your accent. You may add a symbol to the "e" in this and the future lessons if you pronounce it as bĕlŏng or bēlŏng to help your student sound out the word.
>
> If you pronounce it as bĭh-lŏng, when your student comes to the word in the passage below, you may introduce this as a silly word in which the first two letters say the sound "bih" together. Then, add "belong" to the list of sight words the student is practicing.

Let's read! Read each line from the song below:

Jēsŭs lŏves mē thĭs I knōw. Fōr the Bīble tĕlls mē sō. Lĭttle ones to Hĭm belŏng.

(Have the student complete the Little Learner Activity Sheet.)

BONUS ACTIVITIES:

(Student has learned N, D, Ă, T, S, P, Ĭ, F, Ŏ, B, Ā, Ī, Å, J, Ē, M, L, Ŭ, Ō, R, C, W, H, G, K, TH, SP, CK, Ĕ, WH, OU, CH, Y, soft C, SH, Q, soft G, OU, V, EA, and Y so far)

- Use pipe cleaners to construct letters, then make words to read.
- Give student alphabet stamps and help him/her stamp sight words.

Y y

Y is for B**y**.
We are saved by grace.

Color the picture.

Writing: Now, let's trace the second line from the song.

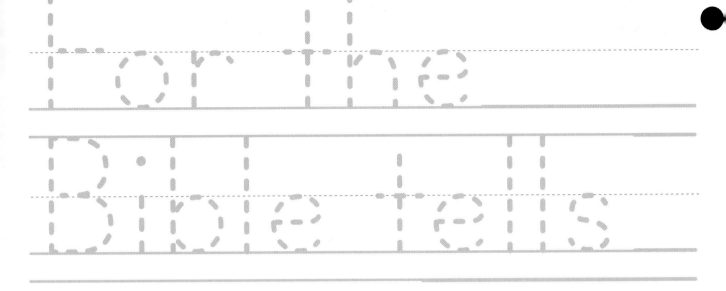

For the
Bible tells
me so.

Letter Recognition: Color in the circles with the following letters: **B i b l e.**

Ū is for You.
Have yo**u** put your faith in Jesus?

Detach and hand the student the
Little Learner Activity Sheet on page 271.

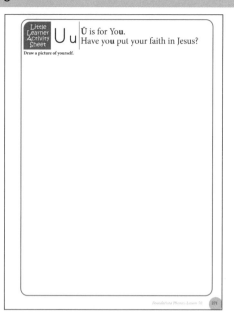

LESSON NARRATIVE

*This lesson covers the long sound of the letter U. It is designated within the lesson with the following symbol above the letters: Ūū. This sound can be heard in the words yoū, cūbe, and tūbe. As you read through this lesson, place emphasis on the sound of this letter where it is found in **bold** throughout the text.*

In our lesson today, we have something important to learn. We've learned about the creation, and how God told Adam and Eve to obey. We've learned about sin, and how the world became imperfect. We talked about how sin separates us from God — but God had a plan to bring us back to Him.

We've traveled all through history and learned about the people God used in amazing ways, like Noah, Ruth, and David. And we learned about how God sent His Son Jesus to earth to conquer sin and death. Can you see how God worked His plan out all through history?

(Allow student time to answer; guide as necessary.)

You and I have sinned against God. We've broken God's commandments, and our sin separates us from Him. But Jesus paid the price for our sin, and when we put our faith and our trust in Him, He covers our sins and makes us right before God again. When we put our faith in Jesus, He gives us

His grace and sin doesn't separate us from God anymore. Jesus saves us from our sins. When we die, He also promises that we will spend eternity — that is forever and ever — with Him in heaven. Today's letter is the letter **U**, as in yo**u**. But more important than our letter today is the question that goes with it: have you put your faith in Jesus?

(Allow student time to answer; guide conversation as necessary.)

In the Bible, the Book of Romans tells us how we can be saved from our sin through Jesus. Let's read it from the Bible:

> Say with your mouth, "Jesus is Lord." Believe in your heart that God raised him from the dead. Then you will be saved. With your heart you believe and are made right with God. With your mouth you say what you believe. And so you are saved (Romans 10:9–10).

If you have not put your faith in Jesus yet, we can pray together now. If you have already put your trust in Jesus, then we can trust that He has fulfilled His promises and cleansed us from our sins! We can have a relationship with God because we are saved. Have yo**u** put your faith in Jesus?

(Allow student time to answer; guide conversation or prayer as necessary.)

Our letter today is the letter U. The U is a vowel, and it can make different sounds! Today's U says its name, we call this the long sound. When you see a U with this symbol on top:

you can be sure it says its name, U, as in the word you! "You" is a word we use quite often. It looks like this:

you

The O is silent in this word, and the U says its name. Can you read it with me?

you

(Point to word and read with student.)

Another word we use a lot is the word your. This word looks like the word "you" but has an r at the end and it sounds different than "you" when we read it. Let's read it together:

your

(Point to word and read with student.)

Great! Are you ready for some more letter fun? Let's go!

(Now begin the reading section below. If your child needs to take a break from the lesson, let him or her begin the first page of the Little Learner Activity Sheet. Be sure to go back to the reading section of this lesson to complete it.)

READING

Let's read some new words!

cūbe

hūge

ūse

mūte

Now, are you ready to read the next line of the song? Let's read the first two lines, and then the new one!

Jēsŭs lŏves mē this Ĭ knōw. Fōr the Bīble tĕlls mē sō. Lĭttle ones to Hĭm belŏng, they are wēak bŭt Hē is strŏng.

Great job!

(Have the student complete the Little Learner Activity Sheet.)

BONUS ACTIVITIES:

(Student has learned N, D, Ă, T, S, P, Ĭ, F, Ŏ, B, Ā, Ī, Å, J, Ē, M, L, Ŭ, Ō, R, C, W, H, G, K, TH, SP, CK, Ĕ, WH, OU, CH, Y, soft C, SH, Q, soft G, OU, V, EA, Y, and Ū so far.)

- Write a few sight words on paper using a pen or pencil. Have student paint over letters using a q-tip and finger paint.

- Place pool noodle letters from previous lesson into a bin. Have student pull out a letter, say its sound, then toss the letter into a laundry basket.

- Read the verse on page 270 with your child on an "off" day. Have the child read the large words.

Isn't God's plan to save us from sin amazing? Let's read the verse below. I'll point to each word as I read, and when we get to the large words, you can read those. Remember, the grey letters play silly games—they don't say anything at all!

Some of the sight words below do not have symbols. If your student does not recognize the words yet and forgets a sound, simply remind him or her.

Gŏd's grāce has sāved you because of your fāith in Chrīst. Your salvation doesn't cŏme frŏm anything you do. It is Gŏd's gĭft.

(Ephesians 2:8)

Little Learner Activity Sheet

U u

Ū is for You.
Have you put your faith in Jesus?

Draw a picture of yourself.

and	of	but
an	on	to
as	not	for
at	a	from
is	I	or
it	be	so
if	see	no
did	all	are

X is for Example.
Jesus is our **example**.

Detach and hand the student the
Little Learner Activity Sheet on page 275.

LESSON NARRATIVE

This lesson covers the letter X. The sound of the letter X can be heard in the words example, x-ray, and box. As you read through this lesson, place emphasis on the sound of this letter where it is found in **bold** *throughout the text.*

We are almost through with our reading adventure, and we've almost learned all of the letters! Today, we will learn the letter X! The letter X says x as in example. As we live our lives and learn to follow Jesus, He is our example. Jesus teaches us how to follow God's ways, how to obey God, how to love other people, and how to become more and more like Him. Jesus is our example. The letter X looks like this:

(Ask student to trace uppercase and lowercase X with finger on the Little Learner Activity Sheet. Make sure the student points to the correct one.)

The uppercase X looks like this:

The lowercase X looks like this:

We can learn more about Jesus by reading the Bible. We can pray and ask Him to help us when we are tempted. As we live our lives, we can look to Jesus as our **ex**ample for how to follow God. The **X** says x. Can you say it with me? The **X** says **x**. Jesus is our **ex**ample. Are you ready for some letter X fun?

(Now begin the reading section. If your child needs to take a break from the lesson, let him or her begin the first page of the Little Learner Activity Sheet. Be sure to go back to the reading section of this lesson to complete it.)

Let's read some letter X words!

ăx   tăx

ŏx   bŏx

We are getting so close to reading the whole song. Let's read another line together!

Jēsŭs lŏves mē thĭs I knōw. Fōr the Bīble tĕlls mē sō. Lĭttle ones to Hĭm belŏng, they are wēak bŭt Hē is strŏng. Yĕs, Jēsŭs lŏves mē.

(Have the student complete the Little Learner Activity Sheet.)

BONUS ACTIVITIES:

(Student has learned N, D, Ă, T, S, P, Ĭ, F, Ŏ, B, Ā, Ī, Å, J, Ē, M, L, Ŭ, Ō, R, C, W, H, G, K, TH, SP, CK, Ĕ, WH, OU, CH, Y, soft C, SH, Q, soft G, OU, V, EA, Y, Ū, and X so far.)

- Use q-tips to form letters or words for student to read.

- Tear up pieces of tissue paper, trace letters on construction paper, and glue pieces into letter shapes!

- Read a story together. Help student read words he/she knows.

X x

X is for Example.
Jesus is our example.

Color the letter X below!

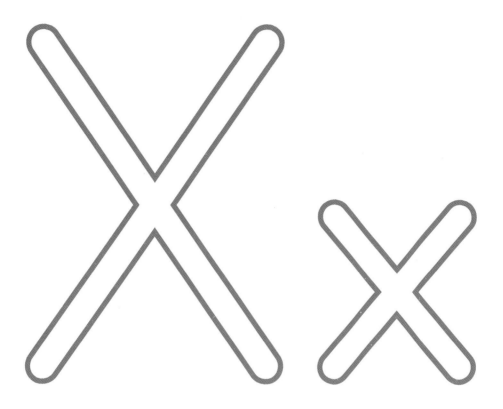

Color the box brown.

Writing: Now let's practice writing the letter X!

Activity: Trace the line below.

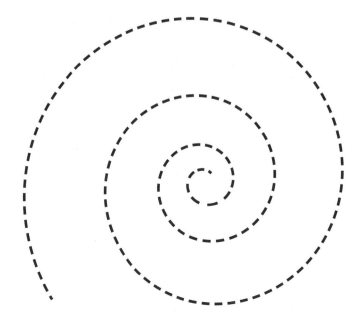

Ng is for Ki**ng**.
Jesus is the Ki**ng** of Ki**ng**s.

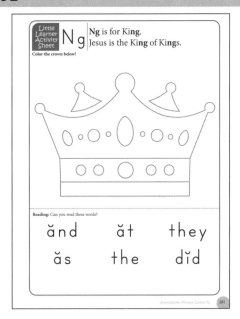

Detach and hand the
student the Little Learner
Activity Sheet on page 281

LESSON NARRATIVE

> *This lesson covers the Ng blend. This Ng blend can be heard in the words king, ring, and sing. As you read through this lesson, place emphasis on the sound of this blend where it is found in* **bold** *throughout the text.*

Don't you just love reading? I sure do! Are you ready to learn a new sound today?

(Allow student time to answer.)

Well, let's get started! Jesus won the victory over sin and death. Jesus also holds the rest of history — He is in control over everything. In the last book of the Bible, Revelation, Jesus is called the King of kings and the Lord of lords. Let's read the verse!

> And He has on His robe and on His thigh a name written: KING OF KINGS AND LORD OF LORDS (Revelation 19:16; NKJV).

Jesus is the King of kings. He rules over the past, the present, and the future. He conquered sin and death. He paid the price for our sin. Jesus is the Ki**ng** of ki**ng**s. Did you hear our sound for today? Today we are learning another blend, the N G blend! When the N and the G sit side by side, they make the "**ng**" sound, as in king. The N G blend looks like this:

ng

(Point to the example and say the sound with student.)

Jesus is the Ki**ng** of ki**ng**s, and He will rule forever! Wow! Let's go read some new ng words!

(Now begin the reading section. If your child needs to take a break from the lesson, let him or her begin the first page of the Little Learner Activity Sheet. Be sure to go back to the reading section of this lesson to complete it.)

Let's read some Ng words!

rĭng   sŏng

thĭng   lŏng

kĭng   wĭng

Now, let's read another line of "Jesus Loves Me" together! We'll start with the lines we've read and then add the new one.

- Jēsŭs lŏves mē
this I knōw.
Fōr the Bīble
tĕlls mē sō.
Lĭttle ones
- to Hĭm belŏng,
they are wēak
bŭt Hē is strŏng.
Yĕs, Jēsŭs lŏves mē.
Yĕs, Jēsŭs lŏves mē.

(Have the student complete the Little Learner Activity Sheet.)

BONUS ACTIVITIES:

- (Student has learned N, D, Ă, T, S, P, Ĭ, F, Ŏ, B, Ā, Ī, Å, J, Ē, M, L, Ŭ, Ō, R, C, W, H, G, K, TH, SP, CK, Ĕ, WH, OU, CH, Y, soft C, SH, Q, soft G, OU, V, EA, Y, Ū, X, and NG so far.)

- Read verse together on page 280.
- Write a line or two from the song on a sheet of paper. Have student trace each letter with a marker.

We've learned a lot on our adventure! We can trust that God's word to us—the Bible—is true. His promises to us are always true. Jesus is the same everyday and His promises to us never change. Let's read a verse from the Bible!

Jēsŭs Chrīst is the sāme yĕsterdāy and todāy and fōrĕver.

(Hebrews 13:8 NKJV)

N g

Ng is for Ki**ng**.
Jesus is the Ki**ng** of Ki**ng**s.

Color the crown below!

Reading: Can you read these words?

ănd   ăt   they

ăs   the   dĭd

Writing: Write the letters below:

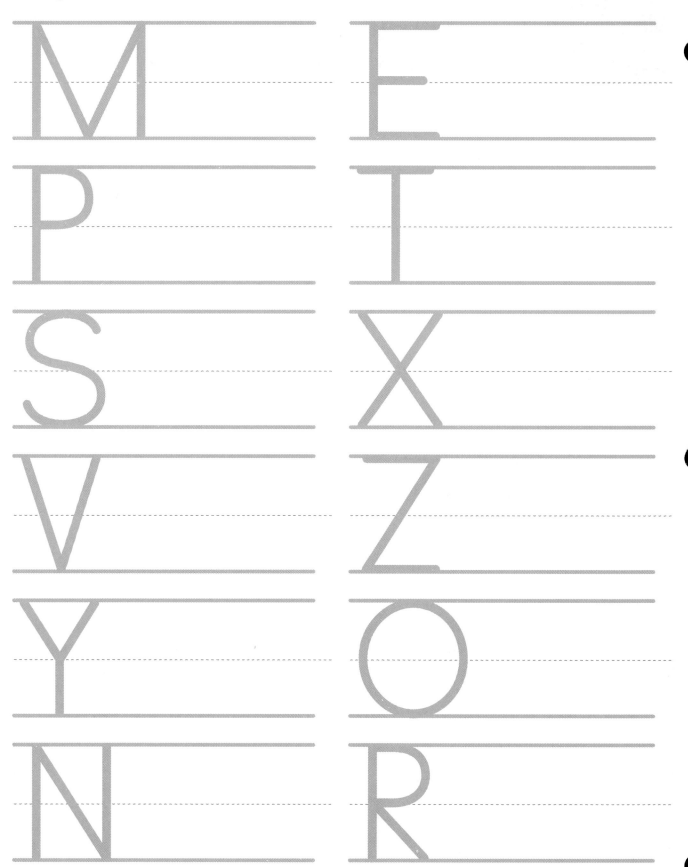

M   E

P   I

S   X

V   Z

Y   O

N   R

Z — God is the Alpha and Omega, the beginning and the end, the A to **Z**.

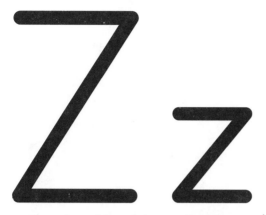

Detach and hand the student the Little Learner Activity Sheet on page 287.

LESSON NARRATIVE

*This lesson covers the letter Z. The sound of the letter Z can be heard in the words zebra, zero, and fizz. As you read through this lesson, place emphasis on the sound of this letter where it is found in **bold** throughout the text.*

(Sing the "Alphabet Song" with student.)

Today, we will learn the last letter of the alphabet! Do you know what letter that is?

(Allow student time to answer.)

The letter Z! The **Z** says **z**. Can you say it with me? The **Z** says **z**. The alphabet begins with A and ends with Z. A is the beginning, and Z is the end. These letters are special because they remind us of something Jesus said in the Book of Revelation. Let's read it from the Bible!

> "I am the Alpha and the Omega, the Beginning and the End," says the Lord, "who is and who was and who is to come, the Almighty" (Revelation 1:8; NKJV).

Jesus is the Alpha and the Omega, He is the beginning and the end. He is the Almighty! Our language, our words, and our voices remind us that God is the Almighty One, that He is the Beginning and the End. When we read, write, or speak, we

are reminded that God is the a to z, the Alpha to Omega, the Beginning and the End. We are reminded that He loves us, that He paid the price for our sin so that we can have a relationship again with Him. We are reminded that we can spend all of eternity with Him in heaven if we trust in Jesus. Isn't God amazing?

(Allow student time to answer.)

The letter Z looks like this:

Z z

(Ask student to trace uppercase and lowercase Z with finger on the Little Learner Activity Sheet. Make sure the student points to the correct one.)

The uppercase Z looks like this:

Z

The lowercase Z looks like this:

z

They are both the same shape, aren't they? One is just bigger than the other! God is the Alpha and Omega, the Beginning and the End, the a to **z**. Say it with me, the **Z** says **z**. Are you ready for some fun with the letter Z? Well then, let's go!

(Now begin the reading section below. If your child needs to take a break from the lesson, let him or her begin the first page of the Little Learner Activity Sheet. Be sure to go back to the reading section of this lesson to complete it.)

READING

Let's read some Z words!

zoom

zērō

sīze

fŭzz

We are so close to reading all of "Jesus Loves Me"! Let's add another line!

• Jēsŭs lŏves mē thĭs I knōw. Fōr the Bīble tĕlls mē sō. Lĭttle ones to Hĭm belŏng, they are wēak

• bŭt Hē is strŏng. Yĕs, Jēsŭs lŏves mē. Yĕs, Jēsŭs lŏves mē. Yĕs, Jēsŭs lŏves mē.

• *(Have the student complete the Little Learner Activity Sheet.)*

BONUS ACTIVITIES:

(Student has learned N, D, Ă, T, S, P, Ĭ, F, Ŏ, B, Ā, Ī, Å, J, Ē, M, L, Ŭ, Ō, R, C, W, H, G, K, TH, SP, CK, Ĕ, WH, OU, CH, Y, soft C, SH, Q, soft G, OU, V, EA, Y, Ū, X, NG, and Z so far.)

- Use play-dough to form sight words.

- Help student think of ways Jesus cares for him or her. Write these on a sheet of paper and have student trace over each word with a marker.

Z z | **Z** — God is the Alpha and Omega, the Beginning and the End, the A to **Z**.

Color the letter Z below!

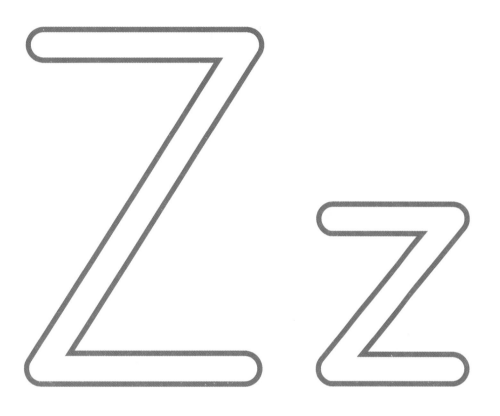

Activity: Zebra starts with the letter Z. Color the zebra's stripes black.

Writing: Now let's practice writing the letter Z!

1 →   2   3 →

Z

1 →   2   3 →

Z

Writing: Write the words below.

and it on

Review

N D Ă T S P Ĭ F

Ŏ B̦ Ā Ī Å J Ē M

L Ŭ Ō R C W H̦

G K TH SP CK Ĕ

WH CH Y C SH

Q G̲ OU V EA Y

Ū X NG Z

Detach and hand the student the Little Learner Activity Sheet on page 291.

> **Little Learner Activity Sheet** Review | Jesus Loves Me
>
> **Reading:** Let's read "Jesus Loves Me"!
>
> Jēsŭs lŏves mē
> thĭs I knōw.
> Fōr the Bīble
> tĕlls mē sō. Lĭttle
> ones to Hĭm belŏng,
> they are wēak
> bŭt Hē is strŏng.
> Yĕs, Jēsŭs lŏves mē.
> Yĕs, Jēsŭs lŏves mē.
> Yĕs, Jēsŭs lŏves mē.
> the Bīble tĕlls mē sō.
>
> *Foundations Phonics Lesson 54* 291

LESSON NARRATIVE

Conclusion.

Well, here we are on our very last adventure. We've learned all of the letters, and all of their sounds. You have learned to read! I'm so very proud. But more important than learning words is that you have learned the Word — the Bible! We've traveled all through history from the start of creation to man's sin, and we learned how sin separates us from God. We learned about Noah and the Flood, as well as Abraham, Isaac, and Jacob. We've read about Joseph, and Moses, and Joshua and how they trusted the Lord. We learned how God led His people, always.

We learned about King David and what happened when the nations did wrong. Then we learned about Jesus, and how He came to earth as fully God and fully man. We learned how He died for us, and paid the price for our sins. We've learned how Jesus conquered sin and death, and that we can spend forever with Him in heaven when we believe and trust in Him.

Now you've learned to read, and it is so exciting. You will read many, many things throughout your life. But the most important book you will ever read is the Bible. The Bible is the very best book because it is the Word of God. We can trust the Bible, and we know that it's true. God loves me, and God loves you — and when Jesus died on the Cross, He knew you by name. He paid the price for your sin because you are important to Him. More than anything else, I hope you remember that Jesus loves you more than I ever can and His free gift to you is called salvation. As you learn, grow, and experience things in this life, may you learn more about Jesus, may you grow to be more like Him, and may you experience His grace in your life.

(Have the student complete the Little Learner Activity Sheet.)

- Write lines from the song, or the entire song. Cut out each word and ask student to put the words back in order.

- Review the list of sight words below.

Let's review more sight words! Read each one out loud.

he	get	them
was	the	they
his	that	out
how	this	she
can	than	have
we	when	you
had	what	by
will	who	belong
has	then	my

Give your student a great big hug! You've completed the learning to read adventure. Congratulations!

Reading: Let's read "Jesus Loves Me"!

Jēsŭs lŏves mē
thĭs I knōw.
Fōr the Bīble
tĕlls mē sō. Lĭttle
ones to Hĭm belŏng,
they are wēak
bŭt Hē is strŏng.
Yĕs, Jēsŭs lŏves mē.
Yĕs, Jēsŭs lŏves mē.
Yĕs, Jēsŭs lŏves mē.
the Bīble tĕlls mē sō.

Wow! You have learned a lot of letters, sounds, and words. Let's review the alphabet one last time!

Aa Bb Cc Dd Ee

Ff Gg Hh Ii Jj

Kk Ll Mm Nn Oo

Pp Qq Rr Ss Tt Uu

Vv Ww Xx Yy Zz

Certificate of Completion

for

Foundations Phonics

presented to

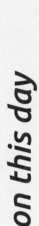

on this day

Teacher Aids

How to use this section

These pages are included for the teacher to provide to the student. The teacher may make copies of the practice pages, or they can be laminated (or put in page protectors) and used with dry erase markers.

Phonics Charts are for reference and for further study as needed.

The activities and games are fun ideas to use with lessons or for extra practice.

Table of contents

How to Hold Your Pencil

How you hold your pencil can make it easier or harder for you to write letters correctly. Here is one of the best ways to hold your pencil:

- Curl your hand into a loose fist.
- Pick up your pencil and position it between your index finger and your thumb. The back end of the pencil should rest on your hand between the thumb and index finger.
- The weight of the pencil should be resting on your other fingers that are partially curled.
- Press your index finger and thumb against the pencil so it is held securely.
- Start writing!

Assessment

We have included a Course Assessment Chart that covers each week. It may be used for grading purposes.

Grading Options for This Course

It is always the option of an educator to assess student grades however he or she might deem best. For *Language Lessons* the teacher may evaluate whether a student has mastered a particular skill or whether the student needs additional experience. A teacher may rank these on a five-point scale as follows:

Skill Mastered				Needs Experience
5 (equals an A)	4 (B)	3 (C)	2 (D)	1 (equals an F)

A — Student shows complete mastery of concepts with no errors.

B — Student shows mastery of concepts with minimal errors.

C — Student shows partial mastery of concepts. Review of some concepts is needed.

D — Student shows minimal understanding of concepts. Review is needed.

F — Student does not show understanding of concepts. Review is needed.

Course Assessment Chart

		Skill Mastered	Needs Experience
Lesson 1	Letter N, Sound recognition		
	Uppercase recognition, Lowercase recognition		
	Letter writing		
Lesson 2	Letter D, Sound recognition		
	Uppercase recognition, Lowercase recognition		
	Letter writing		
Lesson 3	Letter A, Ă sound recognition		
	Uppercase recognition, Lowercase recognition		
	Letter writing		
Lesson 4	Blending		
	Letter recognition		
	Writing words		
Lesson 5	Letter T, Sound recognition, Alphabet review		
	Beginning letter sounds		
	Letter writing		
Lesson 6	Letter S, Sound recognition		
	Reading words, Big and little pictures		
	Letter writing		
Lesson 7	Letter P, Sound recognition		
	Reading words, Uppercase recognition, Lowercase recognition		
	Letter writing		
Lesson 8	Letter I, Ĭ sound recognition		
	Reading words, Sight word reading		
	Letter writing		
Lesson 9	Letter F, Sound recognition		
	Reading words, Reading passage		
	Letter writing		
Lesson 10	Letter O, Ŏ sound recognition		
	Reading words, Scripture reading		
	Letter writing, Uppercase and lower case recognition		
Lesson 11	Letter B, Sound recognition		
	Reading word families, Letter recognition, Beginning letter		
	Letter writing		

		Skill Mastered	Needs Experience
Lesson 12	Review, Sound recognition		
	Reading words, Word families		
	Uppercase and lowercase letter recognition		
Lesson 13	Letter A, Ā sound recognition		
	Reading ā		
	Alphabet practice		
Lesson 14	Letter I, Ī sound recognition		
	I reading		
	Letter and sound recognition		
Lesson 15	Letter A, Å sound recognition		
	Review "A" sounds: Ă, Ā, Å		
	Letter recognition		
Lesson 16	Letter J, Sound recognition		
	Word family, Letter and sound recognition		
	Letter writing		
Lesson 17	Letter E, Ē sound recognition		
	Double-e and silent-e sound, Reading words without phonetic markings		
	Letter writing		
Lesson 18	Review: N, D, Ă, T, S, P, Ĭ, F, Ŏ, B, Ā, Ī, Å, J, Ē		
	Three letter "A" sounds: Ă, Ā, and Å.		
	Letter recognition: e, a, j, b, f, o; Uppercase and lowercase		
Lesson 19	Letter M, Sound recognition		
	Reading M sounds, Reading sight words		
	Letter writing		
Lesson 20	Letter L, Sound recognition		
	Reading word families, Letter recognition		
	Letter writing		
Lesson 21	Letter U, Ŭ sound recognition		
	Reading Ŭ words,		
	Letter writing		
Lesson 22	Letter O, Ō sound recognition		
	Reading Ō words, oo words		
	Writing words		
Lesson 23	Letter R, Sound recognition		
	Reading ar words, Reading sight words		
	Letter writing		

		Skill Mastered	Needs Experience
Lesson 24	Review		
	Reading word families		
	Line tracing		
Lesson 25	Letter C, Sound recognition		
	Reading word families, Reading a story		
	Letter writing		
Lesson 26	Letter W, Sound recognition		
	Reading beginning and ending w sounds, Plural w words		
	Reading sight words, Letter writing		
Lesson 27	Letter H, Sound recognition		
	Reading, Story comprehension		
	Letter writing, Letter recognition		
Lesson 28	Letter G, Sound recognition		
	Reading G words, Reading a verse		
	Letter writing		
Lesson 29	Letter K, Sound recognition		
	Reading K words		
	Letter writing, Beginning sounds		
Lesson 30	Review		
	Reading words, Reading sentences		
	Tracing shapes		
Lesson 31	Letters TH, Sound recognition		
	Reading TH words, Story reading and comprehension		
	Writing words		
Lesson 32	Letters SP, Sound recognition		
	Reading words, Reading a story		
	Coloring comprehension		
Lesson 33	Letters CK, Sound recognition		
	Reading words,		
	Writing words		
Lesson 34	Letter E, Ĕ sound recognition		
	Reading Ĕ words		
	Writing words		
Lesson 35	Letters WH, Sound recognition		
	Reading words		
	Sentence writing		

		Skill Mastered	Needs Experience
Lesson 36	Review		
	Story reading		
	Story comprehension		
Lesson 37	Letters OU, OU sound recognition		
	Reading ou words		
	Alphabet review, Writing words		
Lesson 38	Letters CH, Sound recognition		
	Reading sentences		
	Writing sentences		
Lesson 39	Letter Y, Sound recognition		
	Reading words		
	Letter writing, Review A sounds		
Lesson 40	Letter C, C sound recognition		
	Reading C words		
	Letter writing		
Lesson 41	Letters SH, Sound recognition		
	Reading SH words		
	Word matching, Letter recognition		
Lesson 42	Review		
	Letter writing		
	Letter recognition review		
Lesson 43	Letter Q, Sound recognition		
	Reading Q words		
	Letter writing		
Lesson 44	Letter G, Sound recognition		
	Reading G words		
	Writing words		
Lesson 45	Letters OU, Sound recognition		
	Reading ou words		
	Review alphabet		
Lesson 46	Letter V, Sound recognition		
	Reading sight words		
	Letter writing		
Lesson 47	Letters EA, Sound recognition		
	Reading		
	Sentence writing		

		Skill Mastered	Needs Experience
Lesson 48	Review		
	Book Report		
	Review letter recognition		
Lesson 49	Letter Y, Y sound recognition		
	Reading words, Reading passage		
	Sentence writing, Letter recognition		
Lesson 50	Letter U, Ū sound recognition		
	Reading Ū words		
	Reading sight words		
Lesson 51	Letter X, Sound recognition		
	Reading		
	Letter writing		
Lesson 52	Letters NG, Sound recognition		
	Reading NG words		
	Writing letters		
Lesson 53	Letter Z, Sound recognition		
	Reading		
	Letter writing		
Lesson 54	Review		
	Reading sight words		
	Review alphabet		

Book Reading List

Be sure to keep a record of the books your student is reading. There are spaces below for title, author, and the date of completion. It can be a positive experience as the student sees this list being filled in and knows that he or she is mastering the important skill of reading. It can be helpful to know the authors and/or specific topics your student expresses interest in by allowing him or her to help make choices in selecting books. These selections should be fun for the student!

Book Title	Author	Date Completed

Book Title	Author	Date Completed

Recommended Book List for Reading Practice

All books listed are published by Master Books or New Leaf Publishing Group.

Please select books that match your student's reading level. The books in each group are listed alphabetically, not according to the reading level.

Early Learner Board Books

A is for Adam

All God's Children

D is for Dinosaur

Inside Noah's Ark 4 Kids

It's Designed to Do What It Does Do

My Creation Bible

N is for Noah

Remarkable Rescue

The Very Best Plan

When You See a Rainbow

When You See a Star

Early Learner Books Grades K–3

44 Animals of the Bible

Big Thoughts for Little Thinkers — Gospel

Big Thoughts for Little Thinkers — Missions

Big Thoughts for Little Thinkers — Scripture

Big Thoughts for Little Thinkers — Trinity

Charlie & Trike

Cool Creatures of the Ice Age

The Creation Story for Children

Dinosaurs: Stars of the Show

The Door of Salvation

God is Really, Really Real

Not Too Small at All

Tower of Babel

The True Account of Adam & Eve

The True Story of Noah's Ark

Whale of a Story

What Really Happened to the Dinosaurs?

When Dragons' Hearts Were Good

The Work of Your Hand

Grades 4–6 Books

Answers Book for Kids, Vol. 1–8

Dinosaurs by Design

Dinosaurs for Kids

Dinosaurs of Eden

Dry Bones and Other Fossils

God's Amazing Creatures and Me

How Many Animals Were on the Ark?

Inside Noah's Ark — Why it Worked

Life in the Great Ice Age

Marvels of Creation — Birds

Marvels of Creation — Mammals

Marvels of Creation — Sea Creatures

Men of Science, Men of God

Noah's Ark and the Ararat Adventure

Noah's Ark: Thinking Outside the Box

Operation Rawhide

The Story of In God We Trust

The Story of The Pledge of Allegiance

What's so Hot about the Sun?

Why Is Keiko Sick?

Grades 7–8 Books

The 10 Minute Bible Journey

The Building of the ARK Encounter

Champions of Invention

Champions of Mathematics

Champions of Science

Dragons of the Deep

Footprints in the Ash

The Great Alaskan Dinosaur Adventure

Great for God

If Animals Could Talk

Life Before Birth

Quick Answers to Tough Questions

Uncovering the Mysterious Woolly Mammoth

and	of	to
an	on	for
as	not	from
at	a	or
in	I	so
is	be	no
it	see	are
if	all	he
did	but	was

his	that	out
how	this	she
can	than	have
we	when	you
had	what	by
will	who	my
has	then	belong
get	them	your
the	they	

Vowels can make different sounds. We sometimes use symbols to help us remember what sound the vowel is making in a word.

A vowel can make the short sound. Example: ă as in dăd.

A vowel can make the long sound. The long vowel sound says its name. Example: ā as in cāpe.

Study the chart to review different sounds vowels can make.

Vowel	As In	Vowel	As In	Vowel	As In
ă	dad	ĕ	men	ŏ	not
ā	cape	ē	be	ō	bone
å	far	ĭ	sit	ŭ	sun
		ī	like	ū	use

Some teachers may want to introduce the schwa sound to their students. *Foundations Phonics* and the *Language Lessons for a Living Education* series do not cover this sound until dictionary pronunciations are covered in Level 5. Instead, schwa sound words are listed among sight words.

All vowels can make the schwa sound. The schwa sound makes a sound like the short-u sound. It sounds like /uh/. The symbol for the schwa sound is an upside-down e: ə

Those who wish to introduce the schwa sound may use this chart:

Vowel	As In	Example
a	was	wəs
e	the	thə
i	family	faməly
o	gallon	gallən

Letters	Sounds Like	As In	Read
sp	/sp/	spout	spĭn
wh	/w/	whale	whĭp
ck	/ck/	sick	dŭck
ng	/ng/	wing	sŏng
sh	/sh/	ship	shŏp
ch	/ch/	child	chĭp
qu	/qu/	quilt	quĭz
ou	/oo/	could	would
ou	/ü/	through	croup

Additional Reading Practice

These words may be read at the end of each week for additional practice. You may also create your own practice word lists each week. Letters the student has learned to that point are included in the Bonus Activities section after each lesson.

WEEK 1:

Review letters

N   D   Ă

WEEK 2:

Dăn   săt   tăd

tăn   săd   dăd

WEEK 3:

fĭn   sĭp   făn

dĭd   tĭn   făt

WEEK 4:

ădd   pŏt   nŏt

păss   bĭn   tŏt

WEEK 5:

săp   băt   tĭn

păt   fĭb   fĭn

WEEK 6:

dīne   āte   jăb

pīne   jŏt   fīne

WEEK 7:		
måll	mīne	fāte
Jĭm	lāte	māne

WEEK 8:		
rĭp	tōne	jår
rĭm	lāne	tår

WEEK 9:		
cŏt	cår	bålls
căn	fĭns	cålls

gāte   gōes   kīte

fāte   kĭds   sēēk

dŭck   bŭck   spăt

săck   spĭn   păck

tĕn   rĕnt   bĕnt

sĕnt   cŏb   dĕnt

chĭll   yĕs   săck

yăck   răck   sound

rāce   shĭn   băsh

pāce   răsh   dăsh

rāge   bōat   sāge

wāge   cāge   fĭsh

trĕad   mŭch   rŭsh

drĕad   sŭch   mŭsh

try   ĕnvy   nāvy

fry   cārry   dårt

sĭng   hŭng   rŭng

zĭng   lŭng   thānk

N n	**N** is for **n**othing, **n**one, **n**ot eve**n** a bit!
D d	**D** is for **D**esign. Throughout all of creation, **Go**d place**d** gran**d** **d**esign!
A a	**A** is for **A**dam!
T t	**T** is for **T**old. God **t**old Adam **t**o obey.
S s	**S** is for **S**in. **S**in **s**eparate**s** u**s** from God, it's a very **s**ad thing.
P p	**P** is for **P**lan. God had a **p**lan to **p**ay the **p**rice for our sin.
I i	**I** is for **I**mperfect. Because of s**i**n, the world is now **i**mperfect.
F f	**F** is for **F**lood. During the **F**lood, the earth was **f**illed with water.

O o	**O** is for **O**ffered. After the waters went down, Noah **o**ffered G**o**d a sacrifice.
B b	**B** is for **Bab**el. Men **b**uilt a tower at **Bab**el with **b**ricks.
A a	**A** is for **A**braham. God changed **A**bram's name to **A**braham.
I i	**I** is for **I**saac. **I**saac was Abraham's son.
A a	**A** is for **A**ltar. A lamb was provided for the **a**ltar.
J j	**J** is for **J**acob. God changed **J**acob's name to Israel.
E e	**E** is for **E**gypt. Joseph was sent to **E**gypt.
M m	**M** is for **M**oses. God saved **M**oses for a special **m**ission.

L l	**L** is for **Led**. God **l**ed His people as they **l**eft Egypt.
U u	**U** is for **Under**. Men were **u**nder the law in the Old Testament.
O o	**O** is for **Obeyed**. Joshua served and **o**beyed God.
R r	**R** is for **Ruth**. **R**uth was blessed by the Lord.
C c	**C** is for **Cry**. God heard Hannah's **c**ry.
W w	**W** is for **Would**. God **w**ould choose a new king.
H h	**H** is for **Had**. David **h**ad been a shepherd boy before God chose him to be the new king.
G g	**G** is for **Greater**. **G**od is **g**reater than fear!

K k	**K** is for **K**ing. **K**ing David followed God.
T h	**Th** is for **Th**e. Solomon built **th**e temple.
S p	**Sp** is for **Sp**lit. The kingdom of Israel was **sp**lit apart.
C k	**Ck** is for Ba**ck**. Israel was sent ba**ck** into captivity and exile.
E e	**E** is for **E**sther. God had a very special plan for **E**sther.
W h	**Wh** is for **Wh**en. **Wh**en Jonah disobeyed, things went wrong!
O u	**Ou** is for Ab**ou**t. The prophecies ab**ou**t God's plan would be fulfilled.
C h	**Ch** is for **Ch**ild. A **ch**ild was born, just as God said.

Y y	**Y** is for **Y**oung. Jesus was **y**oung, just like **y**ou!
C c	**C** is for Voi**c**e. A voi**c**e came from Heaven when Jesus was baptized.
S h	**Sh** is for **Sh**own. Jesus was **sh**own the temptations of the world, but He withstood the test.
Q q	**Q** is for **Q**uiet. Jesus said "**Q**uiet!" and the storm obeyed!
G g	**G** is for Hu**g**e. There was enough food to feed all the people. It was a hu**g**e miracle!
O u	**Ou** is for W**ou**ld. Jesus w**ou**ld die on the cross for you and me.
V v	**V** is for **V**ictory. Jesus won the **v**ictory o**v**er sin and death.
E a	**Ea** is for H**ea**ven. We have the promise of H**ea**ven.

Y y	**Y** is for B**y**. We are saved b**y** grace.
U u	**U** is for Yo**u**. Have yo**u** put your faith in Jesus?
X x	**X** is for E**x**ample. Jesus is our e**x**ample.
N g	**Ng** is for Ki**ng**. Jesus is the Ki**ng** of Ki**ng**s.
Z z	**Z** — God is the Alpha and Omega, the Beginning and the End, the A to **Z**.

Bonus Activities

These activities may be used at any time to enhance your student's learning. Letters the student has learned to that point are included in the Bonus Activities section after each lesson. We also encourage co-reading simple books with your student, allowing the student to read more and more of the words as their reading ability progresses.

- Gather fridge magnets, blocks, or loose letters and practice letters, sounds, and reading words.

- Use washi or painter's tape to tape letters on the floor (spot test first to make sure the tape will not damage the floor). Ask the student jump to the letters you call out.

- If the student has siblings, have everyone work together to create letters with their bodies.

- Get a book or a magazine and go on a letter scavenger hunt for a specific letter or word. How many times can you find that letter or word?

- Using a cake pan, bury fridge magnet letters (or similar letters) in flour, uncooked rice, or sugar. Give student a brush and ask him/her to find and "excavate" the letter you call out.

- Call out a letter and see if your student can think of an object or animal name that begins with that letter.

- Call out a letter and see how many objects you can find at home or out and about that begin with that letter.

- Write letters the student has learned on pieces of paper or sticky tabs. Spread the papers out on the floor and give the student a beanbag (or similar object). Instruct the student to toss the beanbag onto a letter sheet and say the sound as you call out the letter's name.

- Spread playdough out flat and have student use a plastic butter knife to carve letters into the play-dough. Alternatively, carve words into the play-dough® and ask student to read the word, then roll up the playdough and start again!

- Form simple words on the fridge using letter magnets for the student to read.

- Build a tower with letter blocks using letters the student has learned. Ask student to say the name and sound on each block as you build the tower. You can also build word towers for the student to read.

- Use letter fridge magnets or similar loose letters to practice word families with student.

- Point out words the student has read when he/she uses them in conversation to reinforce the connection between speech and reading, and have the student point out when he/she hears or sees one of the words discussed in daily life.

- Make sugar cookie dough and use letter cookie cutters or shape the dough into letters the student has learned. Bake cookies and enjoy after putting together some words to read!

- Finger paint letters or words the student has learned.

- Cut a pool noodle into 26 pieces. Use a permanent marker to write the letters of the alphabet on them (set aside letters the student hasn't learned for now). Use the pieces to put together words for the student to read, or practice letters and sounds by having the student toss the letter into a bin while saying its name and sound.

- Write sight words on popsicle sticks. Place sticks upside down in a container, then have student pick up a stick and read the word.

- Quiz students on letters and sounds as you go about your day.

- Spread shaving cream onto a cookie sheet. Write letters or words.

- Say a simple word to the student (e.g., sun, man, etc.). Ask student if he/she can figure out which letters make up the word. Write the word.

- Use pillows, blankets, or other objects to make upper and lowercase letters.

- Write letters the student has learned on sticky tabs. Place tabs on the floor. Give student a straw and mini pom-pom/ball fringe. Call out a letter or sound and ask student to blow the pom-pom onto the correct sheet.

- Use small, round candies like M&Ms® to construct letters or words. Enjoy a sweet treat after!

- Make words for student to read using alphabet stamps.

- Use toothpicks and marshmallows to construct letters. Turn letters into words.

- With your finger, "draw" a letter on the student's back. See if he/she can figure out which letter it was and write it on paper.

- Read student a story, and have student tell it back to you in his or her own words.

- Lay out loose letters. Ask student to say the sounds as quickly as he/she can.

- Use pipe cleaners to construct letters, then make words to read.

- Write a few sight words on paper using a pen or pencil. Have student paint over letters using a q-tip® and finger paint.

a

b

c

d

e

f

g

h

i

j

k

l

m

n

o

p

q

r

s

t

u

v

w

x

y

z

A

B

C

D

E

F

G

H

I

J

K

L

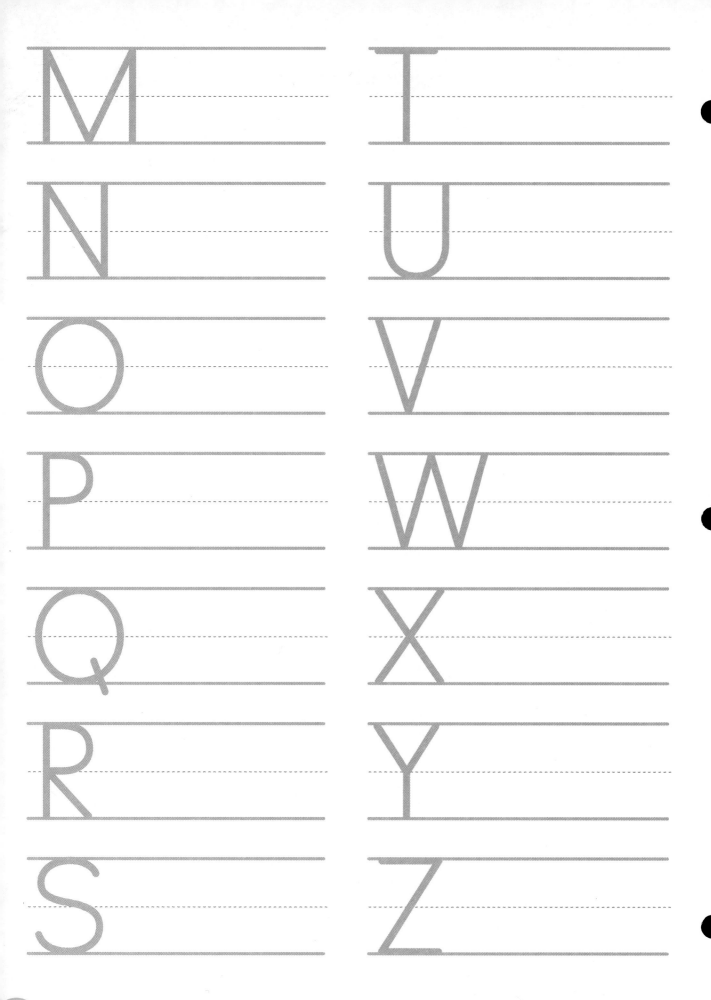

Copywork Practice

For extra practice, student may practice their name, copy Scripture verses, or words from books. Assign according to the needs and abilities of the student.

Language Lessons for a Living Education

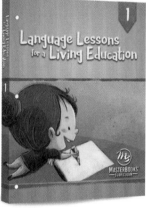

GRADE 1
LANGUAGE LESSONS FOR A LIVING EDUCATION 1

978-1-68344-211-0

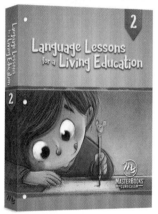

GRADE 2
LANGUAGE LESSONS FOR A LIVING EDUCATION 2

978-1-68344-122-9

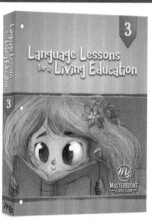

GRADE 3
LANGUAGE LESSONS FOR A LIVING EDUCATION 3

978-1-68344-137-3

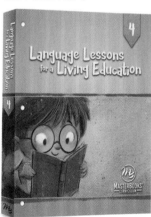

GRADE 4
LANGUAGE LESSONS FOR A LIVING EDUCATION 4

978-1-68344-138-0

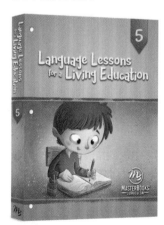

GRADE 5
LANGUAGE LESSONS FOR A LIVING EDUCATION 5

978-1-68344-178-6

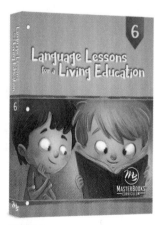

GRADE 6
LANGUAGE LESSONS FOR A LIVING EDUCATION 6

978-1-68344-209-7

LEVELS K-6
MATH LESSONS FOR A LIVING EDUCATION
A CHARLOTTE MASON FLAVOR TO MATH FOR TODAY'S STUDENT

Level K, Kindergarten
978-1-68344-176-2

Level 1, Grade 1
978-0-89051-923-3

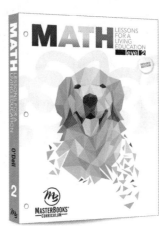

Level 2, Grade 2
978-0-89051-924-0

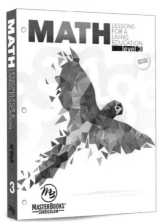

Level 3, Grade 3
978-0-89051-925-7

Level 4, Grade 4
978-0-89051-926-4

Level 5, Grade 5
978-0-89051-927-1

ATTRACTIVE FULL-COLOR LESSONS

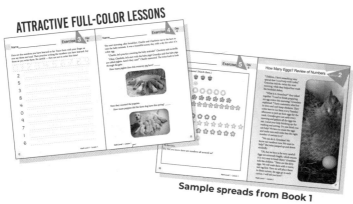

Sample spreads from Book 1

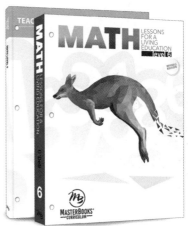

Level 6, Grade 6
978-1-68344-024-6

MASTERBOOKS® CURRICULUM

AVAILABLE AT **MASTERBOOKS.COM** & OTHER PLACES WHERE FINE BOOKS ARE SOLD.

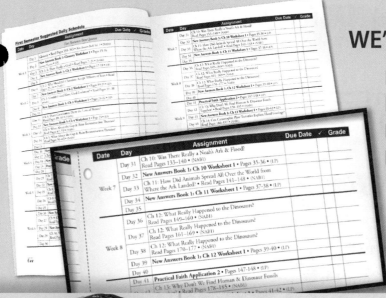